Wild Men in the
Middle Ages

Wild Men in the Middle Ages

A STUDY IN ART, SENTIMENT, AND DEMONOLOGY

RICHARD BERNHEIMER

1970

OCTAGON BOOKS

New York

Reprinted 1970

by special arrangement with Harvard University Press

OCTAGON BOOKS

A DIVISION OF FARRAR, STRAUS & GIROUX, INC.

19 Union Square West

New York, N. Y. 10003

LIBRARY OF CONGRESS CATALOG CARD NUMBER: 70-120229

Preface

It has been found expedient to tell the case of the imaginary figure to which this book is devoted in a manner different from the usual historical exposition. A purely chronological presentation seemed neither advisable nor even possible, since the extreme brevity of many medieval references to the wild man called for elucidation through source material from more recent times. In European folklore and postclassical mythology it has always been necessary to fill gaps in their scant historical documentation by reference to material more recently observed. Taking the risk involved with due caution, this method could show how persistently the content of popular consciousness is maintained and how successfully it often defends itself against modification through contact with higher levels of culture. In the case of the wild man the testimony from the thirteenth century is often identical with that from the nineteenth.

It was decided, therefore, to divide the book not according to periods, but to groups of motives and to follow them, whenever possible, through the centuries, giving full play thereby to the human possibilities of the theme. Within this scheme the character of the material involved was allowed to determine the method of presentation, so that developments of a literary or artistic kind, which took place in the plain light of history, were given the chronological treatment they demand. It is hoped that this synthetic approach, which combines the methods of folklore, mythology, and the history of literature and of art, will result in a picture of our subject which will be comprehensive as well as sharply focused.

No attempt was made to present all the pertinent material, which in the case of works of art would have amounted to many thousands of usually repetitious items. I shall be satisfied if I have succeeded in presenting and explaining the main trends of thought connected with the figure of the wild man. In stating that a belief or practice is "modern" or "contemporary" I mean to imply only that it could still have been observed within the last century. It would be impossible to discover in each individual case whether an ancient tradition has or has not survived the revolutionary changes of our own day.

Among those who contributed to this book by giving of their erudition are Rhys Carpenter and Berthe Marti of Bryn Mawr College, Erwin Panofsky of the Institute of Advanced Study, Richard Ettinghausen of the Freer Gallery, and M. F. Ashley Montagu of Rutgers University. Fritz Metzger of Bryn Mawr College helped through his translation of a medieval Dutch text. Dorothy Leadbeater aided through translations from old Spanish and by allowing the reproduction of one of her photographs. Special thanks are due to Samuel Chew of Bryn Mawr College for undertaking the onerous task of correcting unidiomatic passages in the manuscript. Miss Priscilla Metcalf of the Harvard University Press, whose task was rendered difficult by the author's absence in Europe, has been an unfailingly sympathetic and courteous editor.

All translations except where otherwise noted are by the author. Permission for the reproduction of Fig. 9 has been granted by Bernard Quaritch, London; for Fig. 46, by Grafton & Co., London; for Figs. 42, 44, and 45, by A. Schroll, Vienna.

Erratum: The legend under Fig. 50 should read "engraving," not "etching."

Contents

Illustrations

Wild Men in the Middle Ages

1

The Natural History
of the Wild Man

Since the title of this book is startling, implying a concern
with madness, passion, and violence, it may be well to assure the
reader from the start that wild men are imaginary creatures and
that their name is a technical term. It would be difficult, in fact, to
find another less shocking name for them, since the one employed
here has been in common usage ever since the Middle Ages and
is one of the few which denote the subject unambiguously. This
book does not deal with actual outlaws, lechers, and bad men,
then, or at least not primarily.

Instead, it deals with a literary and artistic figure whose imaginary character is proved by its appearance: it is a hairy man
curiously compounded of human and animal traits, without, however, sinking to the level of an ape. It exhibits upon its naked
human anatomy a growth of fur, leaving bare only its face, feet,
and hands, at times its knees and elbows, or the breasts of the
female of the species. Frequently the creature is shown wielding a
heavy club or mace, or the trunk of a tree; and, since its body is
usually naked except for a shaggy covering, it may hide its nudity
under a strand of twisted foliage worn around the loins. Where
any characteristics other than these appear, there is a possibility

that instead of a wild man we may be beholding another imaginary figure such as a devil, faun, or satyr. The creature itself may appear without its fur, its club, or its loin ornament. Any one of its characteristics may be said to designate the species.

This strange relative of Homo sapiens, a lively and sometimes pungent commentary on the bestial side of his nature, plays an astoundingly persistent, although on the whole subordinate, part in the art and literature of the Middle Ages. But even though the frequency of the wild man's appearance in art and letters is not quite matched by the importance accorded to him in medieval thinking, his ubiquity must be regarded as a sign that he represented a major, if unacknowledged, trend of thought. His presence is like the running commentary with which a man's half-conscious imagery accompanies his conscious ideals and aspirations: a reminder that there are basic and primitive impulses clamoring for satisfaction.

Medieval literature and art are shot through with the mythology of the wild man: we find him in the clipped verses of French Arthurian romance, in the epics by German minstrel singers, and in the writings of Cervantes and Spenser. The whole vast field of late medieval secular art is his playground, from prints and paintings by Albrecht Dürer and Pieter Brueghel to the love caskets and tapestries which medieval swains presented to their ladies, or the tools of chivalry, such as saddles and ornamented weapons. His place in medieval daily life was assured by the appearance of his image on stove tiles, candlesticks, and drinking cups, and, on a larger scale, on house signs, chimneys, and the projecting beams of frame houses.[1] His figure even invaded religious buildings and liturgical books, being found on the borders of illuminated manuscripts, on capitals, choir stalls, baptismal fonts, tomb plates, and as a gargoyle on the eaves of churches. Once, on the façade of a Spanish church, it usurped the place which should have been given to the saints, standing full size on the jambs of its main portal.

So great, then, was the ubiquity of the wild man in medieval life and so wide his acceptance in art, that the question arises what function, individual and social, a figure such as this could have exerted and what needs it could have satisfied within the framework of medieval civilization. This book will be devoted to an attempt to answer this question historically. In order to put the problem into its proper setting, we shall begin with a few general remarks, which may serve as a preface to the rest of the chapter.

Figures such as the medieval wild man occur almost throughout the long history of Western civilization. The earliest one on record is the hairy beast-man Enkidu in the Babylonian epic of Gilgamesh, who spends all his early years with the animals in the fields, ignorant of the existence of other human beings. Among the most recent specimens is the movie hero Tarzan. How powerful is the fascination exerted by the notion of primordial life, unencumbered by civilized facilities, is shown by the rousing welcome which Boston accorded in 1913 to a self-styled nature man.[2] He claimed to have spent three months in the Maine wilderness, running down his prey and defending himself against all perils by his unaided strength and ingenuity. It is an ironical sidelight upon the imaginary character of such achievements that the widely acclaimed hero proved to be a fraud, who had found it impossible, in practice, to make good his promise to shun all outside help. Between this recent story, a comment on the gullibility of modern city dwellers, and the story of Enkidu lies the whole range of recorded history, containing in its span such figures of wild men as the satyrs and fauns, the legendary inhabitants of the Golden Age, and the noble savages of the period of Enlightenment.

It appears that the notion of the wild man must respond and be due to a persistent psychological urge. We may define this urge as the need to give external expression and symbolically valid form to the impulses of reckless physical self-assertion which are hidden in all of us, but are normally kept under control.[3] These impulses, which are strongest and most aggressive in the very young, are restricted slowly, as the child learns to come to terms with a civilized environment which will not tolerate senseless noise, wanton destruction, and uncalled-for interference with its activities. But the repressed desire for such unhampered self-assertion persists and may finally be projected outward as the image of a man who is as free as the beasts, able and ready to try his strength without regard for the consequences to others, and therefore able to call up forces which his civilized brother has repressed in his effort at self-control. In contrast to civilized man, the wild man is a child of nature, upon whose hidden resources he can depend, since he has not removed himself from its guidance and tutelage.

Individual and social factors thus contribute toward the genesis of the wild man: individual insofar as the awareness of disturbing, untried, elementary forces in each of us is the prime factor in his formation; social, since the restraints which prohibit direct and destructive utterance are always exerted by the human group, for the sake of goals and concerns which the child cannot fully comprehend when they begin to interfere with his activities. The wild man's existence is therefore a life of bestial self-fulfillment, directed by instinct rather than volition, and devoid of all those acquired tastes and patterns of behavior which are part of our adjustment to civilization. He embodies a negative ideal in all its harshness and one-sidedness.

Toward this figure of his own imagining man was free to take his stand and to evaluate it in the light of his traditions, raising it thereby from a mere product of compulsive inner processes to the rank of a historic theme. A number of distinct attitudes could be taken, depending upon the degree of emotional detachment which the observer was able to achieve. The most primitive of these, and hardly more than a mere reaction, was the feeling of fear and terror with which the spiritually unprepared confronted a creature compounded of intransigence, lust, and violence. As man learned to increase his inner distance and to look upon the wild man from the vantage point of his own superiority, this fear turned into laughter and mockery, as it always does when a demon loses the terror which previously surrounded him. What had been formidable, now became grotesque and, being grotesque, it appeared pathetic. The wild man's life, originally regarded as the utterance of nature's impetuous disdain for man, revealed itself now as a state of unrelieved degradation. As the observer moved further toward an attitude of complete emotional neutrality, he came to look upon the wild man as a mere curiosity, interesting for his outlandish appearance and for his strange habits of life. Finally, when the pendulum of emotional reaction had gone full swing, man was prompted to endorse the superiority of primitive force over any more advanced form of behavior by passing from fear or contempt of the wild man to outright admiration. To take this attitude meant of course to reject all of man's civilized accomplishments and to declare oneself in favor of their abolition. It is noteworthy, however, as will be explained in the pages which follow, that it was impossible to take this stand without modifying the figure of the wild man. So strong is the natural connection between man's inner longings and the notions of kindness and peace on earth, that the idealization of the savage creature involved its automatic endowment with shining human virtues.

A difficulty arises at this point. To be effective as the common possession of a human group, an imaginary figure must be endowed with the character of reality which alone assures it of an existence beyond the psychological. Since in the Middle Ages the Divine and the diabolical were both monopolized by figures from the Christian pantheon, the wild man's mode of existence had to be construed as that of a creature not unlike man himself. What, then, was his status? Was he a human being, as his anatomy suggested? Or was he to be classified as an animal, as seemed fitting when one considered his coat of hair and his bestial behavior pattern? The Middle Ages were singularly ill prepared to answer a question of this kind, since the gradations and transitions involved were inconsistent with the universally assumed hieratic order of beings and with the position which man was believed to occupy in it. We find, therefore, that medieval authors and artists, incapable of thinking in any but rigid categories and without reliable intellectual guidance in matters pertaining to the wild man, contradicted each other freely in defining him.

There were those who believed that he was a man. Among them was, for instance, Chrétien de Troyes, who, in his "Yvain," created a singularly revolting and at the same time funny figure of a wild man. "I am a man," says this creature when asked to explain his hideous presence.[4] Similarly Heinrich von Hesler, in the fourteenth century, explains in his "Apocalypse" that wild men are "Adam's children in form, face, and human intelligence, and are God's own handiwork."[5]

But the opposite opinion was maintained just as often and with the same degree of assurance. Richard de Fournival, for instance, included the wild man in his moralized zoology, the "Bestiaire d'amour," implying thereby that the creature had no other connection with human life than that which might be conferred upon it through the erotic interpretation of its animal practices.[6] Or, to take an example from the field of art: the German engraver known as the "Master of the Playing Cards," to whom we owe the earliest European card game now extant, used the pictures distinguishing the various suits to record his conviction regarding the nature of the wild man. This set, like many others which came after it, is an abbreviated image of the universe and thus is planned to offer information as well as entertainment, the scheme being to provide a display of subhuman creation on the suit cards and a survey of secular society on the face cards. The face cards show the townsman, the knight, the king, and the queen, representatives of a graded hierarchy. The suit cards, which alone interest us here, are divided into wild flowers, game animals, animals of prey, and finally wild men in a variety of guises and attitudes.* The fact that the latter are bracketed with the plants and the beasts is a clear sign that the artist thought of them as more closely akin to the other wild inhabitants of the forest than they were to representatives of human society. But other artists shared Heinrich von Hesler's conviction about the human status of the wild man. Jean Bourdichon, in the fifteenth century, included him in a set of miniatures showing the stages of human society, as a creature beneath but akin to the poor man, the artisan, and the nobleman who are also represented.[7]

The wild man holds thus a curiously ambiguous and ill-defined position in God's creation, being neither quite man enough to command universal agreement as to his human identity, nor animal enough to be unanimously classified as such. It was only natural that writers and artists should have vied with each other to give to the wild man animal traits not contained in the minimum definition of his anatomy, and thus to render him more comical and ridiculous. It seemed legitimate to tack a tail on him, as if he were an ape, or to endow him with boar's tusks rising out of the corners of his mouth, as a sign of his ferocity, or to give him greatly elongated ears.[8] The outcome of such tendencies toward playful multiplicity had often more in common with the fleeting creatures of drollery than it had with the standard figure of the wild man.

* Fig. 2.

We shall not attempt to enumerate the various appendages which appear here and there in miniature depictions of the wild man, since there is nothing to be learned from them but that the public for which they were designed had lost its fear and awe before the creature portrayed.

But there is another convention to which we should make reference, since it is uniquely revealing of the opinions held about the animality of the wild man. Authors and artists alike were inclined sometimes to describe or delineate the wild man as a creature incapable of maintaining human posture and thus reduced to crawling on all fours. It is clear that this device, which emphasized the wild man's bestiality, served also to underline his funny and pathetic quality. An English miniaturist,* for instance, was consciously appealing to the rough sense of humor of his contemporaries when, on one of the pages of his book, he showed an uncouth and hirsute wild man and woman trying to endear themselves to each other, although too limited to a prone posture to rise to any but awkward and ineffectual gestures. It is interesting to note, however, that not even this definition of the wild man's subhuman habits of life was in itself sufficient to range him with the beasts. In the thirteenth-century German epic of "Wolfdietrich" the Raue Else, a wild woman crawling on all fours, is, as her name suggests, a human being, not an animal; and the same is true of the wild man in Spenser's *Faërie Queene*, whose noble ancestry stamps him as a man.[9]

How, then, could a creature on the border line between beast and man be fitted into the medieval system of thought, which insisted upon the unique metaphysical dignity of man and the purity of all created species? It stands to reason that it was impossible to think of the wild man, as one would today, as a missing link, even though this consequence of the theory of evolution had been approached by Arabic philosophers.[10] Even if we assume that speculations of this kind were available to the most enlightened Western minds — which is beyond proof — such ideas could not have appreciably influenced that stratum of popular and poetic thought within which the figure of the wild man was most at home.

No more could the creature be explained in terms of gradualism, on the assumption that, to correspond to God's fullness and suf-

* Fig. 1.

ficiency, there must be a transition from one created species to the
next, so that nothing capable of existence would be omitted from
the divine plan.[11] Ideas of this kind had been indeed expounded
by some of the most eminent scholastic philosophers in the West,
and Albertus Magnus had even applied them to the interrelation
of the various species of animals. But such ideas had proved too
one sided to be enunciated without a tempering by other strains
of thought, since their cosmic determinism was irreconcilable with
the complete freedom of God's will. To make it valid, such philosophy had to be combined with the usual and opposite one of the
creation of distinct species predetermined by the ideas in God's
mind. At no time, so far as I know, was gradualism applied to the
relation of man and beast, presumably because to do so would have
been to deny those premises upon which the Christian system of
salvation was built.

We find therefore that instead of explaining the existence of
the wild man on theological grounds, medieval writers preferred
to think of him psychologically and sociologically. God had not
created the wild man in his present lowly estate. Instead, the creature had been brought to its condition by loss of mind, by upbringing among beasts, or by outrageous hardships, all conditions
which tended to depress man to something less than human. The
status of the wild man was thus reached not by a gradual ascent
from the brute, but by a descent. And that this was so is apparent
from the fact, to be commented on later, that the state of wildness
was usually not regarded as irrevocable, but as amenable to change
through acculturation. With removal of the conditions that had
caused the lapse from human status, the wild man was thought
capable of resuming his place among men; and all that then remained of his former plight was the occasional application to him of
a name such as "Sir Dodinel le Sauvage" or "the knight of the salvage man," to commemorate the fact that in the past he had been
forced to remain in or revert to the bestial state.[12] No stigma was
attached to such appellations.

Since wildness in human beings was thus due to degeneration
caused by extraneous circumstances and therefore was morally
irrelevant and without theological implications, most medieval
scholars found it unnecessary and unrewarding to devote to the

phenomenon any part of their systematic thought. I know of only one medieval author, Heinrich von Hesler in the fourteenth century, who was at all concerned about the fate of the bestial man. Even he found an extenuating circumstance for the wild people's behavior pattern in the fact that they were *also verwildet*, grown so wild, that it seemed hard to apply to them the usual standards and demands. He ends his exposition of wild-man lore by stating, with obvious embarrassment, that it will depend on God's grace whether they will recover their health (*genesen*) or whether they will be hurled into hell.[13]

The picture drawn by medieval authors of the appearance and life of the wild man is thus very largely a negative one, dominated by the loss or absence of faculties which make of human beings what they are. The wild man may be without the faculty of human speech, the power to recognize or conceive of the Divinity, or the usual meaningful processes of mind. What remains, after losses of this kind and magnitude, is a creature human only in overall physical appearance, but so degenerate that to call him a beast were more than an empty metaphor. For these deficiencies the wild man is compensated by the growth in him of powers which fully conscious and responsible human beings cannot boast, since such powers arise only when all the usual controls have lapsed. In presenting the natural history of the wild man we shall deal only shortly with these supernatural endowments which belong in the chapter on mythology. Here we shall concentrate on the deficiencies, trying to give a composite picture of traits gathered from the scattered descriptions of various authors.

About the wild man's habitat and manner of life medieval authorities are articulate and communicative. It was agreed that he shunned human contact, settling, if possible, in the most remote and inaccessible parts of the forest, and making his bed in crevices, caves, or the deep shadow of overhanging branches. In this remote and lonely sylvan home he eked out a living without benefit of metallurgy or even the simplest agricultural lore, reduced to the plain fare of berries and acorns or the raw flesh of animals. At all times he had to be ready to defend his life, for the inner forests teemed with savage beasts, real and imaginary, which were wont to attack him. If he was to survive, he had to be the physical equal, if not the superior, of creatures such as dragons, boars, or primeval bulls. In many ways his life resembled that which we now attribute to the raw beginnings of human cultural existence in the Stone Age.

Heinrich von Hesler, for instance, relates of them that their dwelling is *in bruchen und in walden, in wazzeren und in bergen, in holn und in kruten* — in quarries and in forests, in water and in mountains, in holes and in shrubbery — that is, in places remote and savage enough to exclude usual human habitation.[14] His testimony is supplemented by Edmund Spenser's poetic description of a wild man's retreat:

> Farre in the forrest, by a hollow glade
> Covered with mossie shrubs, which spredding brode
> Did undeneath them make a gloomy shade,
> Where foot of living creature never trode
> Ne scarse wyld beasts durst come, there was this wights abode.[15]

The fourteenth-century author of "Gawain and the Green Knight" speaks of the stone crags which are the wild man's dwelling, and relates how his company consists of serpents, wolves, and primeval bulls.[16] So persistent are the accounts of the wild man's life that, until recently, natural landmarks preserved such names as "the wild man's hole" or "the wild man's den." There are such mythologically tagged holes in the Tyrolean and Swiss mountains from Sölden in the Ortler region to the Val d'Altro near Alagna in the Italian Alps. Others were shown, until recently, in the Eifel and in certain parts of Baden.[17] That the habit of naming places in this way is not of recent date, is suggested by the occurrence in a Hessian document of the eleventh century of the designation *wildero wibu hus* — house of the wild woman.[18]

The conditions of the wild man's life thus required much more than the usual human strength, if he were to maintain himself without tools and almost without weapons in a raw and hostile environment. His survival was assured only by his possession of that all-enveloping pelt which was the outward sign of his bestial strength and, at the same time, its magical cause. We know from the story of Samson and Delilah as well as from other early myths how intimately hairiness is connected with physical power, and how quickly the strongest man is reduced to the usual frailty once he is deprived of his bristly covering.

Like Samson's, so the wild man's strength is the mainspring of
his actions, driving him in a continuous effort to release the explosive force which is in him by trying it out in combat. No beast,
no matter how mighty or savage, is ever secure against the wild
man's perpetual aggressiveness.[19] * Nor is this vehemence a natural
propensity only, for, when still young, the wild man may be carefully trained to fight all comers without flinching. Spenser's wild
man, Sir Satyrane, is taught by his father to put his hand "upon
the Lyon and the rugged Beare; and from the she Beare's teats
her whelps to teare." [20] His native tendencies respond so favorably
to this savage upbringing that his mentor has to warn him against
excess and himself learns to tremble before his ward. The wild
man's combativeness does not even shrink before his own kind,
and when several wild men meet, the result is usually a battle of
all against all, fought fiercely, without regard for those rules which
medieval custom imposed upon the knight. This trait entered even
into poetic imagery; Malory found it natural to refer to the wild
man's fierceness by calling a bitterly contested passage of arms between knights one in which the participants fight "like woodmen"
or strike "as wild men." [21]

Because of his irrationality the wild man suffers from failings
which serve to distinguish his behavior from that of his civilized
counterpart. Several authors inform us that the wild man did not
enjoy the benefit of human speech, apparently because a creature
limited to the expression of his impulses neither needs nor is able
to communicate. Orson, the wild man, and Shakespeare's Caliban
are both originally afflicted with aphasia.[22] And Spenser relates of
his wild man that

> . . . other language had he none, nor speech,
> But a soft murmure and confused sound
> Of senselesse words, which nature did him teach
> T'expresse his passions, which his reason did impeach.

His wild man is thus reduced to showing "faire semblance . . . by
signes, by lookes, and all his other gests." [23]

This intellectual deficiency is paralleled and aggravated by a
spiritual one. For the wild man is devoid — perhaps incapable — of

* Fig. 45.

any knowledge of God, and thus suffers from a defect which a religious age could not but regard as a decisive obstacle against brotherhood with civilized man.[24] He could not even be looked upon as an infidel who, while too stubborn to accept the Christian revelation, was at least capable of some distorted misconception of God. The wild man did not worship idolatrously because he did not worship at all. One can realize the seriousness of his plight by considering that, according to the widely accepted Augustinian doctrine, knowledge of God, however dim, was the prerequisite and basis for any further mental activity. So long as his spiritual blindness prevailed, the wild man had to be portrayed as either out of his mind or without one. His status was no better than that of the godless man in the psalter, whom medieval miniaturists depicted as insane, half naked, and senselessly trying to bite a stone.

We are thus led to a consideration of the wild man's third deficiency, which gave rise to more elaboration and commentary during the Middle Ages than the others: many of the wild men with whom medieval writers concerned themselves were insane, and thus effectively debarred from communication with other human beings. We may suspect that the category of wildness had its corollary in contemporary reality, even though the writers may have forced the facts into a pattern of their own. It was a habit in the Middle Ages to let many lunatics go free unless they were believed to be obsessed and subject to the exorcism appropriate to their case.[25] Such insane persons were thus at liberty to follow their irrational urges and desires. If we are to believe the romances, they commonly chose to retire into the woods, thus laying a barrier of distance between themselves and their fellow men. We find in consequence that to the Middle Ages wildness and insanity were almost interchangeable terms; and that, for Malory for instance, "wylde" is synonymous with what we call mad or frenzied.[26] To the present day, in certain country districts of Bavaria, a mentally deranged person is actually called a wild man.[27]

In describing the phenomenon of wildness induced by loss of mind, writers and artists could rely upon the description of the insanity of Nebuchadnezzar, who, to quote Daniel 4:33, "was driven from men and did eat grass as oxen, and his body was wet with the dew of heaven, till his hairs were grown like eagles'

feathers, and his nails like birds' claws." In medieval miniatures he
is therefore almost regularly depicted as a crouching wild man
with long beard and hair.[28] * There was also the man possessed with
devils in Luke 8, who was "driven . . . into the wilderness."

It was in the high Middle Ages and in Celtic territory that this
idea of the insane man of the woods was first applied, on a literary
scale, to persons other than the fallen king of Babylon. The lunatic
was now also a prophet, whom his mental waywardness had endowed with oracular faculties, while it compelled him also to forsake human company and to seek shelter in the woods. Among the
creatures thus enhanced and degraded by their insanity was the
Welsh prophet Lailoken of whose stay in the Caledonian forest and
of whose prophetic utterances we are informed in the so-called
Lailoken fragments.[29] The prophet Merlin is of the same literary
family, at least as long as he persists in choosing the Caledonian
forest as his home and in drawing his inspiration from his abnormality. A whole epic, the twelfth-century "Vita Merlini" by
Geoffrey of Monmouth,[30] was devoted to his insanity and cure,
drawing a picture of his life as a wild man which has competed
successfully for centuries with that other view of Merlin as King
Arthur's counselor. It is curious, and has never been successfully
explained, that the same Geoffrey of Monmouth who, in his *Historia regum Britanniae*, established the Arthurian image of the bard
should have been prompted to draw this widely divergent picture
of him, leading later medieval writers to the erroneous distinction
between two Merlins, Merlinus Ambrosius of Arthurian fame and
Merlinus Caledonicus or Silvester, the wild man.[31]

As depicted by Geoffrey of Monmouth, the madness that drives
people into the woods is an intermittent phenomenon, punctuated
by periods of lucidity, during which Merlin allows himself to be
brought back to his native haunts. Accordingly, the state of insanity
is not impervious to treatment and can be alleviated temporarily by
the application of music as a palliative. Only when his insanity
has full sway over him does Merlin act under the compulsion to
be a wild man. Then "fury seizes him," "he enters the woods," there
becomes a "sylvan man," and finds his only pleasure in watching
the wild animals while himself "hidden like a beast." Forgetful of

* Fig. 3.

all that he had been, Merlin lives the miserable life of the outcast, feeding on roots and herbs, and complaining bitterly when winter takes his livelihood away from him, as well as his garment of leaves. Later, when his awareness returns to him, he wonders at his madness and hates it, "groening at the names of his wife and sister" whom he has heedlessly abandoned.[32] But his distress is renewed by every human contact, and the story tells us of Merlin's repeated and successful efforts to evade the watchfulness of his captors and return to the woods.

The cause of Merlin's insanity, appropriate in a heroic age, is the loss of his brothers in battle. It fell to a somewhat later and more polished generation to introduce the motive of love madness, which from then on was to be the fashionable reason for becoming a wild man. In courtly society, which exalted the lady far above her worshiper and taught him the merits which lie in suffering for love's sake, such motivation was no more than an exaggeration of a knight's normally agitated emotional state. It was, therefore, a flattery for the great lady whose favor was sought, if grief over her inattention or fickleness carried a man to the point of melancholy or irrational violence. The greater the warrior thus brought to grief, the greater the implied prestige of the lady who had caused his fall. Indeed, some of the most renowned knights of romance, Yvain, Lancelot, and Tristan, fell victim to this strange occupational disease of knight-errantry. When they believe that they have been slighted in love, these warriors have a way of breaking all bonds, sometimes stripping themselves naked, and invariably repairing to the woods, expressing their sadness and degradation by leading the life of the wild man.[33] Having lost the tie that bound them most strongly to courtly society, they find the wilderness the only environment congenial to their sense of disorientation. There they wander aimlessly through the glades, subsisting on the raw flesh of wild animals or on the alms handed to them by pious hermits, until a miracle or the soothing touch of femininity restores them to reason.

For Yvain and Tristan such insanity is a passing state caused by grief or jealousy, and they recover from it quickly, once the appropriate remedy is applied to them. Lancelot, whose emotional balance is more precarious, suffers four separate shocks of insanity, only the last of which is caused by the usual misunderstanding between lovers. He spends years as a forlorn wild man in the woods, and, just like Merlin, though at much longer intervals, he winds his way in and out of courtly society, whose mental hazards for a person of his passionate temperament he is not always able to weather successfully. It must be added in parenthesis, that the writers of the romances do not regard hairiness as a necessary symptom of wildness induced by insanity; they are satisfied with describing the victim's total disarray, or with letting him turn all black as a sign of his demoniac state.[34]

It is in the short German epic, "Der Busant," a version of the French romance of "Peter of Provence," that the story of the lovelorn wild man, which in other works of literature had been a mere episode, comes into its own as the main theme of an entire romance.[35] The story enjoyed some popularity in the late Middle Ages, as attested by a Rhenish fifteenth-century tapestry, now cut in several parts, giving the entire sequence in visual terms.* The epic recounts how a king's son met a princess who enthralled him and who also returned his love, and how the two succeeded in eloping together on the very day the princess was to be married to another king. They ride through the forest in sweet unison on the prince's horse, until they decide to dismount and rest. The princess, tired from the day's events, falls asleep with her head on the prince's lap, while he looks at her ring which he has pulled from her finger. Suddenly a buzzard swoops down from the heavens and snatches the trinket away. As he pursues the bird, trying in vain to hit it with sticks and stones, the prince penetrates deeper and deeper into the forest and loses his way. It dawns upon him after a frantic search that he cannot find his beloved, whom he has left behind. He becomes violent and demented, tears off his fine clothes, the tokens of his humanity, and proceeds to roam the woods, beastlike, on all fours, as a wild man. The princess, meanwhile, much less perturbed than he, finds refuge in a mill, and later is received incognita into the castle of a local nobleman. A year passes. Then chance wills it that the hunters should venture upon a hairy wild man whom they bring to the castle as a curiosity. The kindly duke, aware that the creature may not always have been wild, sees

* Fig. 8.

to it that he is treated with consideration and taught to walk upright. Recognition of the wild man's former identity and the reunion of the lovers is effected when the prince, upon being taken to the hunt, engages in the eccentricity of biting off the head of a buzzard. Asked what had brought on such strange behavior, he explains that he hates buzzards because, years ago, a buzzard had caused him to lose his ladylove. A gorgeous wedding feast for the prince and princess terminates the attractive and romantic sequence.

If we are to believe the romances, the vast stretches of forest between medieval settlements were thus alive with unfortunates whom loss of rational powers had driven into a life of wanton isolation in the woods. We may imagine that there the lunatics were joined by other forlorn souls: eccentric recluses, criminals attempting to escape the arm of justice, organized *maquis* who had made the woods headquarters for raids upon their better-favored neighbors, and, presumably, persons threatened with religious persecution. The acute misery in which such outcasts lived is movingly described in the epic of "Renaud de Montaubon," whose universal popularity throughout Europe brought the subject close to the heart of many. In medieval opinion such outcasts were regarded as a kind of wild man, and, if we are to believe the author of "Renaud de Montaubon," these unfortunates themselves were ready to agree with the general verdict. After a long period in the woods under conditions of harrowing privation, Renaud finds no better word to describe their plight to his little band of robbers, and thus to urge their return to civilization, than to call them *noir et velu com ours enchainé*, "black and hairy like a bear on a chain." [36]

Usually, however, the wild man's return to civilization, if it took place at all, was not a spontaneous act of free will, unlikely in a creature which lacked rational control over its impulses. If the wild man was to see the mansions of human beings after a prolonged stay in the woods, it was usually as a captive and in chains. Medieval writers are fond of the story which tells how hunters, venturing farther than usual into unknown parts of the forest, would chance upon the wild man's den and stir him up; and how, astounded at the human semblance of the beast, they would exert themselves to capture it, and would drag it to the local castle as a curiosity. We have met an example of this motive in the story of "Der Busant"; others occur in the Lailoken fragments, in the "Vita Merlini," in the epic of Orson the wild man and his civilized brother Valentine, and in one of Grimm's fairy tales.[37] Even the hallowed precincts of the saints' legends were not immune against the introduction of this kind of tale, which appears quaintly incongruous in its ecclesiastical environment. According to the late-medieval legend of St. John Chrysostom, the hermit was caught alive by hunters, after having spent years in the forest under conditions of self-inflicted penance, walking on all fours and observing a vow of absolute silence. In the course of the years his weather-beaten body had grown a protective coat of long hair, giving him so much the appearance of a beast that, when the king's hunters stumbled upon him, they were at first deceived into thinking that they had caught a queer and unheard-of animal, crawling on the ground.* [38]

The wild man's own reaction to the sudden encounter with his civilized counterpart varies according to type and temperament. While some wild men, like one humorously depicted in the fourteenth-century Psalter of Queen Mary,† are seized with panic and attempt to escape in headlong flight, others, like Orson, offer dogged resistance and are overcome only after a struggle in which they may defend themselves literally tooth and nail. But whether they be elusive or combative, the result of the encounter is the same: the wild man is dragged out of his habitat and brought to the castle, there confined, and immediately exposed to the efforts of his captors to return him to fullfledged human status. Only if all endeavor fails, and the hairy man remains morose and speechless in spite of blandishments or torture, can he hope to be released again.[39] Usually, however, the captors find their patience well rewarded by the wild man's quick response to his new environment and its combination of physical ease with cultural suggestion. Good food, baths, and ointments, administered by experienced feminine hands, bring the prince in "Der Busant" quickly to his senses. The reaction of Orson to the courtly scene is even more immediate, since he is in full possession of his powers at the time when he is overcome by his brother Valentine. He gains amazingly rapid

*Fig. 4. †Fig. 5.

insight into the nature of courtly intrigue and handles it deftly even before he learns to talk. Subsequently he is shorn, arrayed in courtly dress, and taught the niceties of civilized behavior, a process which culminates in the power of speech being bestowed upon him by the simple surgical procedure of cutting a vein under his tongue. The rehabilitation of Orson is completed by teaching him the doctrines of the Christian religion, the possession of which will put him on an equal footing with other knights and will endow him with that active idealism which will make him use his strength for worthy causes. It is a touching element in the tale that his career, which began in the forest, also ends there, for, after years devoted to knightly pursuits, Orson becomes a hermit, vowed to the praise of the God whom he had not known in his early days. As the cycle of his life closes, the forests which sheltered him before his reception into human society behold his rejection of it for a higher good.[40]

It is thus clear that having been a wild man is no impediment to the pursuit of a knightly career, once the defects appurtenant to the wild estate have been removed. Indeed, if we are to believe some authors of the fifteenth and sixteenth centuries, the limits between wildness and knighthood were fluid, and to become a gentleman the wild man did not have to shed much of his savagery. Anthony Munday's "knight of the salvage man" in "Palmerin" *is* a wild man, and the same applies to the *caballero* in Diego di San Pedro's "Carcel de Amor" (1492), who belies his name and title by his hairy nudity.[41]

Clearly the wild man's prowess and physical power make of him a potentially successful candidate for a career as a knight at court, where strength and courage are in high demand, even though the knight's love of strife, unlike the contentiousness of the wild man, is justified on highly ethical grounds. We find, in consequence, that stories about the transformation of the wild man into a knight carried considerable favor in the Middle Ages. The story of Orson, the wild man, and of his exploits after his defeat by his brother, Valentine, is reiterated in the similar romance of a wild man, "Tristan de Nanteuil," who goes out into the world after having received instruction in the meaning of chivalry. Related to both of these in turn is the story of the wild man Sir Satyrane,

whose deeds form one of the many strands in the allegorical weave
of Spenser's *Faërie Queene*.[42]

It would indeed appear as if a wild upbringing in the woods
could at times be regarded as an advantage for persons aspiring to
the highest honors of chivalry. To have been raised by a beast as
was Orson, the bear's son, and Tristan de Nanteuil, a siren's foster
child, was regarded as a special favor of fate which entitled the
hero endowed with it to high accomplishments.[43] Even where no
such nurture by wild beasts is involved, the very fact that a man
was brought up in the woods may confer upon him a certain in-
corruptible quality which alone enables him to resist temptations
to which others succumb, and thus to attain aims inaccessible to
them. Among the human inhabitants of the woods there are those
children who know of no better life, because they were born in
the forests, brought up there by their human mothers, and thus
spent their early years in sylvan solitude. They are the innocents
of the pure life, whose early ignorance and lack of social grace
gives them an inner strength, enabling them later to outbid the
knights at court by their own shining virtue and attainments in
chivalry. As they enter into the world, eager and untarnished by
its wiles, these forest fools have all the appearance of wild men.
Chrétien de Troyes' Perceval is appropriately called by him *le valet
sauvage*.[44] And another similar figure is Hélias in the thirteenth-
century "Chevalier au Cygne," who, when ready to go out into the
world, appears all dressed in large leaves, unkempt and hairy, giving the impression of a fool or madman, an appearance seemingly
borne out, at this stage, by his total ignorance of all that pertains
to ordinary human life.[45] The existence in literature of figures
such as these, whose wildness in their formative years is the cause
or condition of their later eminence, affords us a first glimpse of an
evaluation of wild-man life, not in terms of its imperfections as
compared with civilized practice, but of superiority. We shall be
able to observe in a later chapter how profoundly wild-man lore
was affected by this thought.

The wild man's wildness is therefore not a simple concept; it
has sociological, biological, psychological, and even metaphysical
connotations. Wildness meant more in the Middle Ages than the
shrunken significance of the term would indicate today.[46] The

word implied everything that eluded Christian norms and the established framework of Christian society, referring to what was uncanny, unruly, raw, unpredictable, foreign, uncultured, and uncultivated. It included the unfamiliar as well as the unintelligible. Just as the wilderness is the background against which medieval society is delineated, so wildness in the widest sense is the background of God's lucid order of creation. Man in his unreconstructed state,[47] faraway nations, and savage creatures at home thus came to share the same essential quality. This quality was one which held considerable fascination for many men in the Middle Ages, as a counterpoise against traditional limitations of thought and behavior. It is true that to venture into the woods and there to prove one's mettle by slaying the dragon, the giant, or the Saracen meant to combat the ever present threat of natural and moral anarchy, and thus to strengthen the beneficent rule of Christianity. But wildness embodied not only a task but a temptation, to which one exposed oneself by plunging into the great wild unknown. No wonder that, before the Middle Ages were out, it became fashionable to identify oneself with savage things, to slip into the wild man's garb, and thus to repudiate that very principle of hieratic order upon which medieval society was founded.

What holds of the English word *wild* and its German equivalent is true also, with minor modifications, of other European languages. French *salvage* and *sauvage*, Anglo-Norman *salvage*, and English *savage*, Italian *selvatico* or *selvaggio*, Rhaeto-Romanic *salvadegh*, and Spanish *salvaje* have the same extension and overtones as their Germanic synonym. In addition these Romance words have a closer connection with the forest, the scene and matrix of all untamed life, than the Germanic ones.[48] Their derivation is, of course, from the Latin *silva*. The names given to the wild man — *homme sauvage*, *salvage man*, *huomo selvatico* — indicate, therefore, not only his inner character, but also the nature of his habitat.

2

His Mythological Personality

Up to this point we have retained the medieval fiction that the wild man is no more than a man living by choice or by fate beyond the limits of established society. But even though we may grant that in a society as loosely organized as that of the Middle Ages the woods were allowed to harbor many wanton lunatics and outcasts, this overflow would not suffice to explain the extraordinary hold that the wild men had on the imagination of the Middle Ages. Primarily, the wild man is a mythological creature; if he is attired in the colors of contemporary reality, this serves only to lend vividness to his uncanny appearance. He belongs to the pre-Christian world and thus to that large group of figments of native religion to which the church learned to extend limited toleration after having failed to exterminate them. This creature, which so often appears in medieval literature and art as less than human, may very well at a time beyond the reach of written sources have commanded the stature and honor of divinity.

The wild man's appearance in the art and literature of the Middle Ages is thus in the nature of a survival. We may gauge the kind and quantity of information that has been lost when it is considered that most of the literary material dealing with the wild man dates from the twelfth century and after; that the first indubitable

*art
B th
Century*

representations in art appear in about the middle of the thirteenth century; and that the period of his great popularity does not begin before the second part of the fourteenth century, when a general broadening of the basis of Christian society brought the citizens of the towns into the orbit of cultural activities. It would appear that at least some of the pagan ideas current toward the end of the Middle Ages must have circulated among the inarticulate masses long before they were written down. We may assume, on the other hand, that the great increase in the wild man's ostensible popularity was compensated for by at least a partial lowering or loss of his religious status. Whatever aura of awe may have surrounded him in pagan times, or among peoples and in areas still devoted to pagan cults and beliefs, was very largely dissipated once his uncouth figure began to appear in drolleries and pageants and to be subjected to allegorical interpretation.

Yet the wild man did not lose his mythological personality when he was deprived of the respect and allegiance that may have bound his former votaries to him. His habits and idiosyncrasies and even his hairy appearance, while they may have seemed quaint and laughable to a skeptical public, remained those of a pagan demon. So did his other supernatural endowments, notably his exorbitant strength and his power over the animals. It would seem likely, therefore, that inhabitants· of rural regions, uninfluenced by the ironic mood prevalent in the cultural centers, could have retained much of the former attitude toward the wild man.

*peasant
belief*

In fact, in some of the remoter parts of Europe the wild man did survive as the subject of credulous peasant belief. The nineteenth-century collectors of popular tales and superstitions found him still vital and gathered a full harvest of stories about him, just in time to preserve a record of his activities before he finally succumbed, along with fairies and gnomes, to modern advances in education and technology. These stories present to us the mythology of the wild man as conceived by villagers uninfluenced by the medieval preoccupation with moral allegory or by the medieval contempt for the lowborn; thus, in spite of their late date, these modern legends may be closer in some ways to the sources of wild-man mythology than much that is preserved in the more sophisticated literature and art of the Middle Ages. Instead of being used for allegorical purposes or modified by being embedded in long trains of epical thought, the wild man is here presented for his own sake. Since, furthermore, in the case of a figure looked upon askance by the church as the wild man was, the medieval records may be incomplete, the evidence of modern folklore should be accepted gratefully as a means of supplementing them.

The modern geography of the wild man centers in the mountains of central Europe; it omits large parts of France, where he was absorbed early into theology, poetic fiction, and pageantry. And it includes England only insofar as the national flair for ritual and mummery kept him precariously alive until recently. In Italy there is a sprinkling of wild-man tradition which is densest near the rim of the Alps and in Lombardy, but extends as far south at least as the neighborhood of Florence. It is in the mountainous regions and particularly in the Alps that the wild man has survived most vigorously, partly because such areas offer an excellent defense for archaic modes of thinking against modern depredations, partly because there is a kinship between the raw grandeur of the mountains and the indomitable strength of the wild man. Ideas which had long since died out in the culturally more advanced milieu of the plains could retain their hold over men's minds in isolated and retarded mountain valleys. This retreat of the wild man into the remotest and least accessible parts of Europe is part of the shrinking of his popularity from that point in the high Middle Ages when stories about him were told at the courts and miniaturists were called upon to adorn the margins of manuscripts with scenes from his life. Town and wilderness, which almost bordered upon each other in the Middle Ages, have grown far apart.

As described by modern folklorists, the Alpine wild man is a formidable creature. Huge and hairy and mute, according to some, he may be so large that his legs alone have the size of trees. His temper when aroused is terrible and his first impulse that of tearing trespassers to pieces. When moved to revenge, he may make lakes disappear and towns sink into the ground. He abducts women and devours human beings, preferring unbaptized children, and — according to a belief held in the Italian Tyrol and in the Grisons in Switzerland — makes a practice of exchanging his own worthless progeny for human offspring. Occasionally he may also take the

lead of those relentless hunters or marauders known as the Wild
Hunt or the Wild Horde — that spectral chase known also as the
Furious Host — which races in certain winter nights through the
valleys and deserted villages, destroying every living thing it meets
in its way.[1]

So far the wild man is a kind of ogre, a creature designed to
spread terror among the credulous. It is not surprising that old-
fashioned nurses should have used stories about him as pedagogical
fictions to frighten obstreperous children into obedience.[2]

Other traits come to the fore as the wild man's dwelling is localized and as men adjust themselves to the task of living with their
uncanny neighbor. The wild man becomes a creature of woods
and rocks, so bound up with the forest that his very life depends
upon that of certain chosen trees. According to a story told in
Vorarlberg, the wild man came expostulating as lumbermen prepared to cut down the large tree which apparently contained his
life substance. But even now his connection with man's elementary
fears is unbroken, for he is a demon of storm and fury who rejoices when the treetops are shaken by the gale and rain and hail
are lashing the ground. According to a belief held in the Tyrol and
in Vorarlberg the wild man sits wrapped up, shivering and morose,
when the sun is shining, while smilingly exposing his body to the
elements when the weather is bad. The same story is reported from
Hesse, with the significant addition that when the storm rages, the
wild man goes over the mountains and shakes the trees, as a true
demon of destruction.[3]

shepherd He feels his kinship with the animals and regards the creatures
of the forest as entrusted to his care, keeping a stable for mountain
goats in a mountaintop and severely reprimanding those who have
shot one of his wards. It may be in part this kinship with animals that
makes him enter into human service, for a creature capable of tending the wild animals, which heed no human call, must do as well or
better with the tame. Accordingly the wild man takes it upon
himself to tend the cattle, to feed and water them and to brush them
down, and especially to herd them during their summer stay in the
high Alpine pastures. When a head of cattle is lost, he may be
trusted to go out and find it.[4]

Further domestication is indicated by the wild man's readiness to talk to the peasants and to reveal some of his wisdom; as a demon he shares nature's secrets and thus is in a position to give advice about the weather, the harvest prospects, medical herbs, and even about processes in the dairy business. Accordingly he tells the peasants when to sow and to gather the rye, and thus is responsible for the ensuing abundance.[5]

There are finally the stories, coming mainly from the Italian and German parts of the Grisons, of how men tried to capture the wild man in order to force him to reveal some of his preternatural wisdom. The method is always that of making him drunk by pouring wine or, even better, brandy into holes or into the troughs of fountains. Caught and tied, the wild man buys his freedom by making disclosures. For us the interest of the story lies mainly in the fact that in it we behold a residue of an ancient Greco-Roman tradition that may have been carried into the Alps in early days. For the report that shepherds had caught a demon, in this case Silenus or Faunus, and induced him to reveal hidden truth, goes back to the days of Xenophon, is reiterated by Pausanias, Ovid, and Aelian, and plays a part even in the medieval wild-man lore of other countries. We shall encounter it as the discussion proceeds.[6]

What the Middle Ages and the Renaissance have to tell us about the mythology of the wild man agrees with the findings of modern folklorists in astonishing detail. There are, it is true, no medieval stories about services rendered by the wild man to peasants and country laborers, presumably because in the Middle Ages these social groups were held in such contempt that nothing affecting their welfare was apt to elicit much popular sympathy. But similar reports were known, even though it was not peasants who were thought of as the beneficiaries, as attested by Spenser, whose wild man uses herbs to tend the wounds of a knight strayed into his forest empire:

> A certaine herbe from thence unto him brought,
> Whose vertue he by use well understood;
> The juyce whereof into his wound he wrought,
> And stopt the bleeding straight . . .[7]

An interesting and revealing example of the continuity of motives through the centuries is a sculpture of a wild man, the oldest known to me, on the north portal of the mid-thirteenth-century church in Semur-en-Auxois in Provence,* which shows the hairy creature putting his hand through the arm of a man counting money into a sack. It would seem that this intimate and friendly association of the demon with a mortal is meant to show the profit that man can reap by wisely availing himself of the service and advice of his ghostly counterpart.

There is furthermore a great deal of testimony about the wild man's nonutilitarian activities, showing that beliefs restricted today to a few isolated mountain areas were once the common possession of all Europe. The tree torn out by its roots, token of the storm demon's preternatural strength, appears in artistic representations such as a wild-man tournament by the "Master of the Housebook" (called also "Master of the Amsterdam Cabinet") † and some of the tapestries of the fifteenth century from the area of the upper Rhine. In carnival disguises such as those of Nuremberg and Basel the mummers were often required to carry a little tree; and even where the artist made the wild man carry a club or mace, instead of the tree out of which it was fashioned, the weapon was given a buckled and twisted shape to make sure that its origin from wood uprooted and coarsely hewn be well understood.‡

Like the wild man's weapon, his habit of placing changelings in human families was known well beyond its present geographical limits, for it was the subject of a Florentine print of the fifteenth century showing a noble hunting party in pursuit of a family of wild men.§ As they run, the wild men carry a struggling human baby. The hairy changeling holds on to his unwilling foster mother's horse as best he can. The battle has begun and a young nobleman, member of the rescuing party, is wielding a large sword determined to make the thieves give up their prey.

By far the most striking of the traits attributed to the wild man as well as the one most frequently commented upon by pictorial and literary means is his mastery over the animals, a mastery due as much to his application of physical violence as it is to their instinctive acknowledgment of his kinship and superiority. His usual method of attack is the direct and frontal one either with the weight of the club added to his native strength or by muscular

*Fig. 7.   † Fig. 11.   ‡ Figs. 12, 15.   § Fig. 9.

force alone; and just as in ancient times there were no creatures which could withstand the concerted physical effort of Hercules or Gilgamesh, so we find that the wild man's victory over his opponent, although often hard won, is a foregone conclusion. Bears and lions, serpents and dragons, creatures native, foreign, and imaginative have to acknowledge the superiority of their overlord and, if so required, accommodate themselves to serving as the wild man's steeds.*

Other animals whom the wild man does not deign to fight, probably because their elusive nature renders them unfit as opponents, are willingly at his service as mounts: in Swiss and Rhenish works of art such as tapestries or the prints by the "Master E.S." and the "Master of the Housebook," wild men and women are shown astride speedy stags and unicorns.† And in "Der Ring" by Heinrich von Wittenweiler, a south German poet also of the fifteenth century, the wild man is introduced entering battle on a stag, whom he has trained to assist him by battering all comers with his antlers.[8]

Only rarely do we find that the wild man abandons his reliance upon his own strength for recourse to civilized weapons by introducing into the hunt the conventional human tools of the bow and arrow. It is certainly an artificial reversal of the usual, for the sake of enhancing the prestige of the human hero, when in the thirteenth-century romance of "Seifried de Ardemont" the wild man Paltinor invokes the help of Seifried in his failure to overcome a dragon, and actually even faints from exhaustion, so that he must be revived with water from a helmet.[9]

The most famous, however, of all the works of art and literature describing the wild man as lord over the beasts does not come from central Europe; it is an early Arthurian romance, and its scene is laid in Celtic territory. In Chrétien de Troyes' "Yvain," of the twelfth century, Calogrenant, an errant knight on the usual search for adventure, finds himself in the enchanted forest of Brocéliande in Brittany. As he advances along a shaded path, he encounters a group of primeval bulls charging each other with such savagery that the woods resound with the din of their battle. As he looks further, he sees in the position of a nursemaid watching her frisky wards a creature, seated with club in hand, whose fearsome and

* Figs. 6, 34.   † Figs. 24, 36.

preposterous aspect would be enough to arrest the most uninquisitive. It is a giant man, clad in the skin of bulls, his anatomy incongruously composed of a head as large as a battle horse's, a broad barrel chest passing without neck into the chin, and a twisted hunchback, with such superfluous features thrown in for good measure as owl's eyes, a boar's tusks, and the ears of an elephant. He is, in his own words, the forest guard charged with the safety of the animals therein, whom he keeps in submission by an occasional show of violence. It suffices for him to try his power upon some recalcitrant creature to make all the others accept his authority.[10]

To Calogrenant, however, the monster shows its friendliest side and, though unasked, accommodates its visitor by pointing out to him the one local feature that may satisfy a knight's desire for adventure. It appears that by proceeding to a neighboring spring and sounding the gong fastened to the overhanging branches of a tree, it will be possible for anybody to release a rainstorm so destructive of vegetation and fauna alike that it will be meritorious to have survived the result of his own foolhardiness. Calogrenant takes the hint, provokes a brief but destructive thunderstorm, is challenged by the defender of the spring, the knight Esclados, and duly defeated. Yvain, who later goes through the same sequence of experiences, succeeds in killing the defender of the spring and succeeding him in the affections of his wife, Laudine.

There are thus two guardians in the forest of Brocéliande, one charged with the safety of the animals, the other of the spring: a division which has long been recognized as due to Chrétien's eagerness to raise the first husband of Laudine to the rank of a knight worth defeating.[11] In the original Breton myth, which Chrétien transformed to suit the social assumptions of his hearers, the wild herdsman was probably the guardian also over the miraculous spring, and thus had the authority to release or restrain all the explosive forces in his magic empire.[12] Like any wild man's his affinities lay with all forms of inhuman violence, bestial or meteorological.

It is likely also that it is Chrétien himself who is responsible for the incongruous appearance of this wild man, which could hardly have come out of the popular myth but was apt to appeal to the rude sense of humor of his noble listeners. To make the lowbred villein seem ridiculous was accepted social and literary practice in the Middle Ages; so it is not astonishing to find that Chrétien's exaggerations and distortions should have been gladly revived in later medieval literature, wherever the task arose of describing a figure of a woodsman similar to this one. Of this kind is the ugly but utterly harmless creature whom Aucassin meets on the way to his reunion with Nicolette. Again derived from the same source is the creature that appears under the allegorical name of "Danger" in the "Roman de la Rose." And finally in the "Roman d'Artus," also of the thirteenth century, the situation depicted by Chrétien is reiterated in detail, only that the creature sitting on a stump supervising the play of his wards is no other than the volatile Merlin in one of his gratuitous disguises, his physical incongruity now enhanced by adding to his disharmonious features several taken from ancient teratology. From the description, he must have been a thing of truly extravagant ugliness.[13]

In most later romances, however, the ironic primitivism of Chrétien's "Yvain" was not retained, probably because the wild man later was conceived as attached to the court of a lady, from whom the poet of "Yvain" had divorced him so carefully, and thus acquired a veneer of gentility through her humanizing influence. Chrétien himself in his "Perceval" tells of a villein in the service of the enchanted "Castle of the Perilous Bed," who lets loose a lion against unwelcome visitors, pretty much as if the beast were a trained guardian dog. Similarly, in "La Mule sans Frain" by Païens de Maisières, an Arthurian romance of the thirteenth century, there is a villein, bushy-haired, black, and of frightful appearance, whose task it is to keep and feed two lions and two dragons. The transformation of the wild beasts into mere household pets is completed in the sixteenth-century English romance of the "Carl [churl, villein] of Carlile," in which the giant ogre keeps his wards in the main hall of his castle, beside the fireplace, and pacifies them by a single domineering word. Although they behave like dogs and creep under the table when told to do so, they are, in fact, a wild bull, a boar, a lion, and a huge bear.[14]

The civilizing influence of Arthurian romance thus touches even the churl in charge of the animals, unready as his savage nature is to adapt itself to the demands of polite society. It is mainly outside

French
+
English
Arthurian
Poetry
becomes
civilized

of the enchanted circle of French and English Arthurian poetry
that the wild lord of the beasts survives in literature retaining his
original frightfulness. We find him, undaunted, in the Danish song
of "Swend Vonwend," where instead of guarding the animals on
the ground before him he offers his huge body to them as a playground, carrying a bear in his arm and a boar on his back, while
deer and rabbits frisk along the length of his fingers. While no
other literary description reaches this one in emblematic concentration, the wild man appears again in German epic poetry such as
"Dietrichs Drachenkaempfe" where, as in "Yvain," he is the lord
over all the animals and comes to the rescue of one, a huge boar,
which had the ill luck of finding itself in the path of the pugnacious
hero. The result of the encounter, in this instance, is a fight between
the forest man and Dietrich, in which the hero wins and subsequently forces the giant to accompany him, carrying the boar.[15]

Finally, there is in the twelfth-century German epic of "Orendel" a description of a work of art, an embossed harness, devoted
to the celebration of the wild man as lord of animals, which would
have to be regarded as one of the earliest renditions of the theme
were it not known that the passage in question is a later interpola-
tion:

> Unter den linden gestrecket lak
> Ein lewe und ein trac
> Ein ber und ein eberswin
> Waz mohte kluoger dâ gesîn
> Daran stuond der wilde man
> Fuer wâr ich iuch daz sagen kan
> Von gold reht als er lebte.

"Stretched out under a linden tree lay a lion and a dragon, a bear
and a boar, as pretty to see as could be. There stood the wild man,
and I can tell you, that although made of gold, he looked as if he
were alive." [16]

As we review the literary material presented, it becomes clear
that the notion of the wild man as lord of animals was widespread
in Europe during the Middle Ages, difficult as it may be to decide
whether this diffusion is due to a common background of pagan
mythology or to the dispersion of Arthurian prototypes. It is likely
that one center of wild-man mythology was in or near the Alps,

where the scene for "Dietrichs Drachenkaempfe" is laid. Another center, much more influential, was located in Celtic territory, in Brittany and probably also in the ancient scene of Arthurian history, Wales and Cornwall. It is certain, at any rate, that in the Celtic regions of western England the stories about the man of the woods have survived almost as vigorously as in the Alps. There are the tales about the *bachlach* or herdsman, sometimes a creature with only one eye and foot who may surprise a stray visitor by his extraordinary ugliness and size.[17] And in the Welsh story of "Owein" or "The Lady of the Fountain," preserved in Lady Guest's *Mabinogion*, Chrétien's "Yvain" or some similar continental saga becomes the property of the tellers of popular tales: Chrétien's wild man of the woods is now a huge black man, one-eyed like Polyphemus and with only one foot, who boasts of being "the woodward of this wood." Asked what powers he has over the animals, he says disdainfully, "I will show thee, little man," and then, unlike the "wild herdsman" in "Yvain," he proceeds to give a demonstration of his prerogatives: he strikes a deer with his club; hearing its snorted warning the animals rush together from all sides, stay in hushed obedience until he bids them go feed, and bow their heads to him in parting, as vassals to their overlord.[18]

We return to the resemblance between modern folklore and medieval beliefs to take note of the curious use made by medieval poets of the wild man's habit of lamenting the good weather and rejoicing over the bad. It will be remembered that this paradoxical idiosyncrasy was commented upon by peasants in the central Alps and in Hesse. In the Middle Ages the story seems to have been told first in Provence, an indication perhaps that it may be of Mediterranean origin. Did not the wild man smile when it rained? And was this not a lesson for the knight unhappily in love and waiting desperately for a sign of favor from his mistress? The question was asked by such troubadours as Raymond Jordan and Rambautz de Bélioc in the thirteenth century; they were thus among the first to see a desirable moral implication in the wild man's mythology, and to find in his animalism something that man might emulate. The idea of the *conort del salvatge*, the wild man's solace, spread together with the Provençal doctrine of love and the values found in suffering for its sake. It was adopted by Richard de

Fournival in his "Bestiaire d'amour" (about 1250), in which the wild man was introduced among the animals in order to tell this story and to teach through it hope and courage in the periods of love's adversity. And one of the love poets of northern France asks:

> Ne rit li salvages hom
> Quant il pluet?

"Does not the wild man laugh when it rains?" — only to answer himself:

> Que bel atent
> Qui la taut sa soupecon
> Qui soffrir set
> Ne se voist ja doutant.

"What fine hope for him who can silence his apprehension. He who knows how to suffer, finds himself never doubting." [19]

From southern France the idea spread also to Italy, first to the Sicilian schools of poetry and then to those on the mainland, where it occurs in the works of Sordello, Guido Orlando, and Cecco Angiolieri. So persistent was it from the thirteenth to the fifteenth centuries that one might ask oneself whether we are dealing with a literary metaphor only, or whether the poetic image was fed from fresh springs of popular folklore. One of the last to use it was Boiardo, in his "Orlando Inamorato" in the fifteenth century; free from the constraint of allegory, he found it possible to tell the legend in full. He makes of the wild man a kind of Eulenspiegel who complains when descending from the mountains and smiles when ascending, because he lives not in actuality but in anticipation.

> E dicesi ch'egli ha cotal natura
> Che sempre piange quando è il ciel sereno
> Perch'egli ha del mal tempo allor paura
> E che l'caldo del sole gli venga meno
> Ma quando pioggia e vento el ciel saetta
> Allor sta lieto che l'buon tempo aspetta

"And it is said that his nature is thus that he cries when the skies are serene, because he is then afraid of the bad weather and of receiving less of the sun's heat, but when the sky shoots down rain and wind, then he is glad, because he thinks of the good weather to come." [20]

The wild woman holds an even larger place in modern folklore than the male of the species, for her presence is recorded in areas which either never possessed any wild-man mythology or have allowed it to fade out.[21] Since her habitat is considerably larger than that of the wild man, extending beyond the mountainous areas into the plains, we find that her nature has become more diversified than that of her spouse, varying according to local tastes and traditions. Where the environment has attributes of grandeur and strength, as in the Alps, the wild woman tends to grow to giant size. By far the most portentous of her subspecies is the so-called Faengge or Fankke, as she is called in the Tyrol and in the Bavarian Alps, a colossal ogre of great strength and appalling ugliness. Bristly all over, she has a mouth forming a grimace that reaches from ear to ear. Her black, untended hair is interspersed with lichen, and according to a report from Switzerland, she has breasts so long that she can throw them over her shoulders. She is prone to eat human children.[22]

Where the landscape is mild, as in the Oberpfalz region of Bavaria and in central and northern Germany, with few strong accents and contrasts, the wild woman shrinks in size and her character becomes more lenient. The wood and moss damsels of that area are described as merely hairy, clad in moss, and having creased and oldish faces oddly contrasted against heads of long and silken hair. Small and modest in behavior, these retiring creatures are associated not with the largest trees, as are the wild men and their spouses in the Alps, but with the underbrush.[23]

A third species of wild women lived not so long ago in the hearsay of Tyrolean peasants. Known as the "Selige Jungfern," the "Blessed Damsels," and plainly conceived as revenant ghosts, these creatures were said to appear wearing beautiful flowing white robes, thus lacking the chief criterion of wildness, the naked body covered with hair. We find it necessary, nevertheless, to include them here, since their habits of life are in some respects very similar to those of their mythical sisters in central Germany. They hire themselves out as maids, share with the peasants their knowledge of medical herbs, and occasionally advise them in vital matters of agricultural routine — friendly gestures, by creatures otherwise aloof, which popular hearsay ascribes also to the wood damsels and even to the fearful Faengge. In addition to this the Faenggen and wood damsels may keep a stable of animals in a subterranean cave and may regard themselves as responsible for their safety. The "Blessed Damsels," like the Faenggen, may be found to be stealing human children.[24]

The most persistent as well as the most revealing of the traits common to the various species of wild women is found in their erotic attitude, for all of them are obsessed with a craving for the love of mortal men and go out of their way to obtain it. Indeed, so universally are they charged with this instinctive immodesty, that this trait may well be the key to their origin psychologically. An imaginary creature capable of being overwhelmingly brutal and oppressive and yet prone to erotic passion could hardly have arisen out of any subjective experience but that of nightmares, which so often contain a sudden transition from the monstrous to the sexual. It would be natural for such a creature to be conceived as belonging to an order of existence other than the human, yet as capable of being admitted into the intimacy of the household, for it would be in the sleeper's bedchamber that the phantom would first take shape.[25] It must be added that the wild man of modern folklore would, in his turn, play more often than he does the part of the oppressive and lascivious incubus, were it not that the experience of several centuries taught storytellers to omit this aspect of his activities in order to avoid unpleasant contact with the Inquisition. We shall see that in the Middle Ages the wild man's inability to control his sexual passions was regarded as an essential part of his primitive personality.

It is true, at any rate, that the wild woman behaves, when she meets a man, as if she were a volatile transient figure out of a dream. She changes appearance with rapidity, transforming her monstrosity into the semblance of glamorous youth. And while she may retain this new appearance for a long time, leading her unsuspecting victim into the bond of marriage, she may also terminate the deception by revealing her identity through some vicious act. In Sweden, for instance, according to numerous stories, the wood damsel has a way of appearing to charcoal burners and hunters as a beautiful and tempting maiden, so that only the initiated may guess her true identity from the sudden whirlwind that accompanies her. If she is not recognized, she may destroy her victim by exposing him after initial advances to the rage and jealousy of the wild man. If she is and her offer is rejected, she may disappear lamenting, leaving behind her a narrow path of storm and destruction. Similarly in Franche Comté the *dames vertes* have a way of luring human lovers into the thickets, to haunt them or drive them to their death, once they have yielded to their enchantment. How great the deception is which such creatures practice will be realized when it is considered that, according to a widespread tradition, the real wild woman, when undisguised, is distinguished by shrunken flesh and long sagging breasts which are either slung over the shoulder or allowed to drag over the ground.[26]

The wild woman is thus a libidinous hag and it would seem entirely appropriate to apply to her the term used for centuries to designate creatures of her kind by calling her a witch. In the demonological vocabulary of the Middle Ages this identity is assumed from the very beginning. *Lamia, holzmoia vel wildaz wip* (wild woman), says a tenth-century glossary from Mondsee in Austria, in commenting on an appropriate quotation from Isaiah. The same equivalence is asserted in a glossary of the eleventh century from Tegernsee in Bavaria. And again, in two alphabetical glossaries of the twelfth century, one written in an undisclosed locality in southern Germany, the other from Schaeftlarn near Munich, *holzwib* (woman of the woods) or *vvildiz wip* (wild woman) are equated with *lamia*.[27]

To understand these identities, one will have to remember that *lamia*, the child-devouring ghoul from Greek antiquity, was regarded in the Middle Ages as a living reality whose existence was accepted without question by such popular writers as Gervasius of Tilbury, of the thirteenth century, or even by the Bishop of Paris in the early thirteenth century, William of Auvergne. These were the writers who established the identity between *lamia* and *strix*, the latter the precise technical term for what we call a witch, and imposed it upon authors of later centuries dealing with the unsavory subject of witchcraft.[28] If there is any difference between *lamia* and *strix*, it would be that *striges* had greater mobility and thus were able to keep on the heels of their human prey, while *lamiae* were tied to their abodes in the wilds, dangerous mainly to those who ventured into the range of their power. But by the time the first witch trials began, this distinction had long been obliterated. Originally both *lamiae* and *striges* were demons only. It was through the acceptance by ecclesiastic authorities of the popular notion that such demons could incarnate themselves in human beings, particularly old women who shared some of their physical defects, that the fear arose of their presence within human society itself, and with it the need of combating them.

At the time when the lexicographers established the place of the wild woman in demonology, the first protests were heard against the belief in these ghostly creatures. The superstition was referred to in the eleventh century by Burchard of Worms in his *Decretals*, describing the demons as *agrestes feminae quas silvaticas vocant*, "women of the field called wild," and decrying the belief that these demons could show themselves to their lovers bodily and in human form, in order to enjoy their embraces, and then dematerialize again.[29] That same superstition, according to a confessional of the twelfth century, is to be penalized by ten days of fasting with only water and bread.[30] After the fourteenth century, when the existence of witches had become an accepted ecclesiastic tenet, it was not the belief in female demons which was regarded as punishable, but active intercourse with them. The accusation figured prominently in most of the proceedings against so-called heretics, for instance in the trial of the Knights Templar in 1310;[31] and that the same idea survived throughout and beyond the period of the witches trials, which were dedicated to the same superstition in reverse, is shown by the fact that as late as 1691 a young man in Sweden was accused of having indulged in carnal relations with a Skogra, a wild woman, and condemned to death.[32] As late as 1701 another similar trial was held in Sweden, which, however, did not end with the death penalty. The victory of enlightenment in the decades following upon these dates removed the threat against human happiness and safety held in the acceptance of this ancient superstition.

It is a significant comment upon the limitations of ecclesiastical influence in the Middle Ages that the Church's disapproval of the belief in the wild woman did not keep secular writers from telling of their inroads upon human life. Giraldus Cambrensis of the twelfth to the thirteenth century, tells the story of one Meilerius of Caerleon, who linked his fate to a woman demon and lost his mind when he learned what he had done.[33] While this tale, like the related one of the "Ritter von Stauffenberg" (about 1300),[34] has the tragic ending which one would expect when man has been misled by a demon, it can actually happen that he is none the worse off for having complied with the demon's desires, as the following story reveals.

Wolfdietrich, in the thirteenth-century Bavarian epic of that name, gains his wife by overcoming his natural revulsion against a hairy monster which treads upon his heels. As he sits by the fire keeping guard for his sleeping comrades, Wolfdietrich is approached by the ungainly and hairy Raue Else, a creature which crawls on all fours and yet has the impudence to demand his love. He refuses twice, whereupon she takes revenge upon him by using her magic and first making him fall asleep and then bewitching him. He loses his reason and is forced to roam in the woods as a "forest fool," living on roots and herbs, a wild man in his own right. Finally she consents to disenchant him upon God's own demand and after he has led this blighted life for half a year. It is at this point that moral sensitivity would rebel against the sequel: in return for her disenchantment he promises to marry her, provided she be baptized; she agrees, takes him with her to her kingdom of Troy, there is transformed in a fountain of youth, and greets her betrothed as the beautiful princess Sigeminne.[35]

The denouement does not seem to have troubled medieval sensitivities, for, with some modifications, the story of the Raue Else was repeated in one version of another German epic, "Ortnit." The theme was altogether a popular one, for it appears in several English, Danish, and Norwegian ballads, with the modification, however, that the ugly "hill troll's" love is rejected altogether, with dire results for her unyielding favorite.[36]

The picture drawn by modern folklore of the wild woman's love habits is thus well borne out by medieval testimony. There is similar agreement in regard to her other idiosyncrasies, although, as in the case of the wild man, medieval literature and art are silent about anything pertaining to her relations with the peasantry. We do hear, however, that occasionally she makes humane use of her knowledge of the healing arts, as does the wild woman who imparts her lore to Wate in the "Kutrun" epic (thirteenth century); and that she may take care of wounded heroes, as does the *wilde frouwelin* in the "Eckenliet" (about 1200), who tends Dietrich's injuries and readies him for battle with her pursuer Fasolt.[37]

But more frequently, as in the following thirteenth-century romances, she is herself the pursuer and an opponent as strong as she is ugly. The wild woman in Wirnt von Gravensberg's "Wigalois" carries the hero to her hideout, disarms him, and would do away with him altogether, were it not that he manages to rally his last strength to make a comeback. Equally formidable is the wild woman in "Seifried de Ardemont" who is in league with a dragon, battles the hero with her club, and is overcome only with great difficulty; and the wild woman in "Diu Crône," by Heinrich von den Tuerlein, is again of the same kind. Since it is not love, but combat, that these creatures are after, they have no reason to hide their terrifying appearance; thus we are told of the wild woman in "Wigalois," for instance, that she is hairy as a bear, has the drooping breasts of the Alpine Faengge, and shows the huge black head, the flat nose, the big teeth, and twisted hunchback of the Arthurian wild man. Nor do the authors who introduce these demons make any secret of their opinion about them, for they refer to them as *diu tiuvelin*, the she-devil, *des tiuvels trut*, the devil's love, or *des tewffels brawt*, the devil's bride.[38]

It should be added that, like the wild man, these females of the species have their lair in the woods, from which they emerge when a prospective human victim appears upon the scene. The wild women in "Seifried de Ardemont" and in "Wigalois" live in caves; and even the *wildaz wip* in "Wigamur," who dwells in the sea and thus is more siren than conventional wild woman, has her home in a hollow stone near the coast.[39]

There remains the question of the artistic representation of the wild woman, which at first sight seems to contradict the testimony of literature. For the creature whose life and habits are portrayed on the manuscripts, love caskets, and tapestries * of the late Middle

* Figs. 30, 36, 42, 44, 45.

Ages seems to have almost none of the formidable traits recited with such relish by storytellers. Her appearance, if exception be made of her shagginess, is distinctly human and even moderately attractive, and her behavior is usually that of a faithful housewife operating efficiently under the primitive conditions of a camping trip. She is, in short, seen not from the vantage point of a civilized intruder, who may have reason to fear her, but of her wild spouse, who has equally good cause to appreciate her help. But this circumstance alone should make us realize that the figure of the wild woman as elaborated in late medieval art is a secondary one, brought into existence in order to provide the wild man with a feminine complement, so that he may not be alone in his trackless paradise. It would seem that we are here dealing not so much with a mythological as with a sentimental device. This is shown by the fact that in the epic poetry of the twelfth and thirteenth centuries, which antedates most such artistic representations, and again later, in modern folklore, the wild man and woman figure singly, as isolated apparitions. We shall, at any rate, defer all descriptions of the wild man's family life to a later chapter.

There is, however, one type of artistic representation, and a very ancient one, which does seem to be connected with the notion of the wild woman as decribed by literary sources of the high Middle Ages. This is the figure of Luxuria, or carnality, in Romanesque sculpture.[40] These renditions, of which that in Moissac in Aquitaine is the most famous,* show a revolting hag with hanging breasts and putrefying flesh, and would thus fully correspond to the literary image of Lamia, the woman of the woods, were it not that in addition to her other unendearing traits she is crawling with snakes and other vermin. But this detail, which the sculptors took from earlier artistic models, may itself serve to confirm our supposition.[41] The woman with the snakes, a type well known in art of the ninth and tenth centuries, is meant to be the personification of Terra, the earth. What could have been more fitting, then, than to use this established image for the depiction of an earth demon, who, at the same time, was the visual embodiment of carnal desire?

The last of the types of wild folk we have to introduce are the wild men and women who inhabit not the woods, but the water.

* Fig. 10.

The reader may well be familiar with them, if he remembers Grimm's fairy tale of the Eisen Hans, a wild man occupying a pond not far from the king's castle. The creature in question is an ogre who dispatches people by pulling them under the surface of the water. Significantly the pond is located in the midst of a wild wood, and the wild man is caught and imprisoned in a manner that reminds one of the capture of his sylvan brother. But aquatic wild men are not always limited to a habitat in stagnant ponds, and one, described as tailless and hairy but bald, is supposed to have been caught in 1161 in the sea near Orford on the English coast, and to have been dumped back again, when it turned out that nobody could make him talk.[42]

The wild woman, too, may be a maritime creature, and may then be referred to in the glossaries as *lamia vel Meerminne* (woman of the sea) just as the hairy man (*pilosus*) may occasionally be rendered in German as *alpe* (elf) *vel merewonder* (sea monster). In Denmark, where the presence of the sea on three sides may have suggested the mythological change, the wild woman very often takes up her abode in the water.[43]

In all these instances the change of habitat implies no change of habits, which are the same as those of corresponding demons above water level. Indeed the writers of medieval epics, when they consign their creatures to an aquatic life, make sure that their kinship to creatures on land is well understood. The wild woman and mermaid in "Wigamur" has two brothers living in the forest; and the *wilde wazzerman* in "Diu Crône," an ugly creature all crawling with snakes, like the Luxuria at Moissac, calls when wounded to his companions in the forest, whereupon they come to his rescue in crowds, shouting revenge and carrying tree branches.[44]

Even the story of the wild man's crying in good weather and singing when it rains has its maritime counterpart, for Philippe de Taun in his bestiary written early in the twelfth century attributes this to the siren;[45] and the Comte de Bretagne, in one of his songs, adds to this the Provençal comparison with the lover:

> Tot ausi com la serene
> Qui chante quant il fet torment
> Chante je quant plus aie painne.

"Like the siren who sings when it storms, so do I sing the more I feel the pain." [46] The reader will concede that, meaningful as it is on land, the legend here presupposed could hardly have arisen out of a marine creature's mythology, and that thus the two poems, although early, presuppose an antecedent story about the wild man. That story must have been in circulation by the beginning of the twelfth century.

A tapestry made in Tournai in the early sixteenth century (Germanic Museum, Nuremberg)* may serve to demonstrate the continuity of the tradition about the aquatic wild man. Eight pairs of wild men and women are shown as inhabitants and perhaps as tutelary demons of a spring which wells forth from a rocky structure in the middle of a forest. A round enclosure of poles and basketry isolates the central area of the spring from the surrounding landscape. The wild men and women show a lack of real intimacy with the element by the fact that they do not swim but only wade in the water up to their knees or loins. The only creature really wedded to the element is a sea monster, half knight and half fish, which has suddenly appeared in the midst of the unsuspecting wild folk and is carrying one of their women away, while her sisters engage in futile gestures and her male companions in attempts at disorganized counterattack. Representations like this prepared the way for such later allegorical use of the hairy creatures as on the main door of the Old Palace in Bamberg, where two wild folk, a man and a woman, recline in attitudes derived from Michelangelo's allegorical figures on the Medici tombs; according to a credible local tradition they are the rivers Main and Regnitz. Even Neptune is shown sometimes with the wild man's strand of twisted foliage around his loins, as on a fountain of the seventeenth century in Bamberg.

Having now surveyed the mythology of the wild man, we must embark reluctantly upon an undertaking that has proved the undoing of many a scholar, for we cannot leave the subject without at least attempting to shed additional light on the question of mythological origins from the testimony of philology. When the European languages were first recorded in medieval glossaries, the native demons were sufficiently established to be known by their own proper

* Fig. 30.

names in the vernacular. To the collective term *wild man* there corresponds in Anglo-Saxon *wudewasa, wudewasan,* which became *wodewose* or *woodehouse* in the Late Middle Ages. The etymology of the word suggests that the creature named was a being living in the woods. The corresponding term in Old High German is *Schrat* (*scrato, scrazo*), used in early glosses as a translation for Latin *fauni, silvestres, pilosi,* and thus surely meant to name a hairy apparition living in the woods.[47]

It is, however, not so much the Germanic names of the wild folk as the Latin ones and those derived from Latin roots which are the most revealing, since they disclose their connection with, or at least their resemblance to, well-known figures in the Roman pantheon. Even though we should hesitate before postulating a dependence where there may not have been more than an analogy, such identities of name give invaluable clues for unraveling the historic truth. Thus *salvan, salvang,* heard not so long ago in Lombardy and in the Italian-speaking parts of the Alps, is clearly derived from Latin *silvanus* and helps us to relate the wild man to the Roman god of gardens and the fertile countryside.[48]

Among the German-speaking populations of southern Switzerland and of the Tyrol this classical reminiscence gives another allusion to Latin mythology, for here the wild woman is called *Fangge, Fanke, Fänke,* a word clearly derived from *fauna,* the feminine faun. The term *Faengge* was created not so long ago, for the neologism was unknown in the Middle Ages. The medieval name for the creature was, as we saw, either *lamia,* a Greek derivation, or in German, *Holzmuoia, -moia, -mūa,* or *-mowa,* the latter clearly related to Latin *maia* and thus a link between the wild woman and Maia, a Roman goddess of the earth and of fertility.[49]

The most interesting, and to some perhaps the most surprising of the wild folk's affinities, is the very strong one of the wild man with Orcus, the Italic god of death and the underworld. It comes out in the Tyrolean habit, prevalent until recently, of calling wild men either *Orke, Lorke,* or *Noerglein.*[50] In France it has led to the creation of the *ogre,* who has so many things in common with the wild man, and in Italy to that of the *orco* or *huorco,* who cuts his capers in Basile's *Pentamerone* (seventeenth century).[51] It would perhaps be somewhat rash to call the latter a wild man outright, because in Basile's collection of fairy tales he appears in many guises, benign and malicious, and the descriptions of him vary accordingly. But it is certain that to Basile's seventeenth-century contemporaries *orco* and *wild man* tended to be the same: when the Florentine poet Lorenzo Lippi looked for a prototype upon which to model his description of the *hom selvatico Magorto*, a wild man born of a sprite and a fairy in the cavity of a wall near Fiesole, he found it entirely natural to borrow his appurtenances from Basile's *orco*.[52]

Most important of all, the name Orcus appears in one of the most ancient documents which we can connect with the wild man, a Spanish penitential of the ninth or tenth century copied presumably from a still older Frankish source. We are told that it was the practice for doubtful Christians to relapse into the pagan custom of dancing in the guise of Orcus and Maia, for which misdemeanor proper penitence was to be imposed upon them: *Qui in saltatione femineum habitum gestiunt et monstrose se fingunt et maiam et orcum et pelam et hic similius exercent, unum annum penitentiae —* "for those who wear feminine garb in their dances and carry on the monstrous fiction of being Maia and Orcus and Pela [an unidentified figure] or for those who engage in similar practices, one year of penitence." [53] It is perhaps rash to surmise at this point whether this dance might have been a *hieros gamos*, a wedding ceremony of pagan gods, as the combination of male and female figures would suggest. What seems almost certain, however, is that Maia is no other than the Holz-moia of later German glossaries, and that, accordingly, by a simple extension of interpretation, Orcus must be identified with the wild man. Back in pagan times Orcus had always been a somewhat shadowy figure, better known among simple peasants than in the cities, where no official cult was accorded him. Now, centuries later, he was rewarded for his former obscurity by remaining a live religious entity at a time when the more respectable gods of Olympus were no more than learned memories. He paid the price for such long survival by submitting to thoroughgoing mythological change.

Philological evidence thus endows the wild folk with a dual nature, depicting them as demons of the fertile earth and at the same time as ghosts from the underworld. To the wild man Silvanus, benefactor of fields and woods, there corresponds the wild man

Orcus, enemy of living things and of man himself; and similarly to the wild woman Maia, the munificent goddess of the earth, there corresponds Lamia, the child-devouring fiend, a rampant ghoul at large to beset the living. The antithesis of derivations and attributes seems fraught with meaning when it is considered that, in contrast to the secular attitude, which cannot but see in life and death irreconcilable opposites, religion, on all of its levels, has always insisted upon their being involved in each other. In the midst of life we are confronted with death, which in its turn has secret powers to benefit the living. We may assume that the wild folk attracted from the pantheon of antiquity traits taken both from the mythology of life and of death, because it was felt that the return of the deceased, although accompanied by terror and danger to all who witnessed the event, favored the continuity of life.

It was the synthesis of the two conflicting interpretations which made possible the mythology of the wild folk: on the side of life their care for the animals and their readiness to make their advice available to the human community; and on the side of death their appalling ugliness, cannibalism, frightful temper, and wilderness habitat, unfit for any but spectral occupants, and finally their predilection for hail and storm, the weather most suitable for the return of the dead.

Both interpretations meet in the idea of their overpowering strength, a requirement for mastering the living and an attribute of those who bring with them the uncanny powers bestowed in another world. But death prevails in the concept of the wild man and his spouse; their destructive aspect is stronger than their salutary one. It would even seem that whatever benefits their appearance may hold for the human community are ultimately derived from their macabre traits. To call them merely demons of vegetation and of fertility, as earlier scholars have often done, is therefore to misunderstand them completely.[54] A creature which rejoices in hail and storm and in the uprooting of great forest trees has little claim to friendship for quiet seasonal growth.

Now comes a question, minor in itself, yet important in determining the wild man's relation to other creatures of folklore: the matter of size. Since, obviously, a very large wild man would be a giant, a very small one a dwarf, it behooves us to inquire about the limits of their physical variability. It has been shown that the wild man can be very large, large enough, in fact, to associate with trees and lower mountains on something like equal terms. We have seen also that he will not always retain this impressive size, since friendly intercourse with human beings will cause him to adjust his stature to theirs. When tending the cattle in the stable, he will have to assume human stature in order to pass through the doorway. We find, furthermore, that in some regions and localities the wild man is conceived as permanently possessed of moderate physical proportions. The Faengge in the Grisons, in contrast to her sisters in the Tyrol, is, in the words of a local historian of the eighteenth century, "somewhat shorter and stouter than man." [55] And the Fankkenmanli, who live in the highest Alpine regions, as well as the Tyrolean Orgen or Noerglein, are usually conceived as dwarfs; [56] the latter may even occasionally wear dwarfs' costume instead of exposing their bodies to the elements. How variable the wild woman may be has already been commented upon.

Like many other demons the wild man is thus a size shifter, whose appearance may vary with the conditions under which he is beheld and with the doctrine in the mind of the beholder. It is not surprising to hear that, like the poodle in Goethe's Faust, he may actually grow from human size to giant stature while the beholder catches his breath in amazement. Caesarius of Heisterbach in the thirteenth century reports how a priest from the neighborhood of Cologne, to whom it befell to witness this phenomenon, perceived an ugly demon leaning against a tree, watched it outgrow the forest, and finally took to his heels as the whirlwind surrounding the apparition began to pursue him.[57]

Since the wild man may assume the guise both of dwarfs and of giants, the question arises whether there is any means of distinguishing between them. As far as the giants are concerned, the only line of demarcation, apart from nomenclature, is a historical one, for, at least according to traditions preserved in modern folklore, they have long since died out because of their incorrigible stupidity, which rendered them easy victims of people with smaller but better organized brains; whereas the wild man is usually conceived as very much alive. The distinction between wild men and dwarfs is a sociological one, for the wild man tends to live alone or, at the most, in family groups, while the dwarfs are gregarious and have managed to give themselves a political organization under a king. Consequently, when wild men occur in more than average numbers, they shrink and become dwarfs, while the lone individuals tend to retain their powerful physique.[58]

Confusion between wild men and their mythological cousins was almost inevitable and expresses itself in the licence assumed by medieval writers in distinguishing between them or identifying them at will. Giants may be given the wild man's attribute of hairiness, as they are in several French *chansons de geste* such as "Boeve de Haumtone" (thirteenth century?) or "Mort Aymeri de Narbonne" (late twelfth century?), with the intention of adding to the portentous character of what is usually a captain of the Saracen infidels.[59] Or, again, wild men and giants may be separate, as in that chapter in Cervantes' *Don Quixote* where two wild men are introduced as servants of a more colossal master.[60]

Between wild men and dwarfs there are many kinds of social relations, from the enmity between the dwarf king Laurin and the wild man whom he ousted from his realm, to friendly symbiosis in the same mountain cave, of which we are told in "Wolfdietrich." The two groups may even be organized into a community ruled by a dwarf king as in "Goldemar," by Albrecht of Kemenaten (thirteenth century), and, least likely of possibilities, a wild man may be set up as ruler over giants and dwarfs, one group his physical, the other his mental superiors. There is not very much to learn from these manipulations, which merely testify to the fact that it was hard for the minstrel poets to find new variants upon well-worn themes, and that they did exert themselves in order to provide them.[61]

In art the distinction between wild-man giants and wild-man dwarfs is obscured by the existence of representational conventions which may produce variations of size independent of the narrative conveyed. Wherever this is the case, one will have to let the context determine the issue. A wild man, for instance, like the one on a fifteenth-century misericord in Norwich, England,[62] holding two undersized but fully developed lions on leashes as if they were pet dogs, can only be a giant and thus belongs to the same breed as the colossal "Carl of Carlile" in the English epic of that name. The same may apply to the wild men of a German tapestry of about 1400,* one of whom has thrown a dead lion over his shoulder to bring it home as his prey. Among the dwarfs is the naked and bearded demon whom the "Master of the Berlin Passion" drew as rising out of a cluster of leaves holding on to a flower stem and pulling viciously at a bird's tail.63 He is like a *putto* aged without abandoning his playfulness. Also among the dwarfs are the wild men and women, the former fitted out with clubs, bows, and arrows, whom Israel von Meckenem portrays in one of his prints as finding their way upward through the twisting foliage of a plant to the winding petals of its flower.† The print has an inscription which refers to the creatures as "frivolous vermin" and compares them with honey-gathering bees, making it obvious that the artist wanted us to think of them as of elfin size.

Finally, there are the creatures in the card game by the "Master of the Playing Cards," of which we spoke before. It will be remembered that in designing the suits for his game the master had admitted different types of the species to mark the suit colors: not merely flowers, but columbine and cyclamen; not just game animals, but deer, fallow deer, and the unicorn. In the same way the wild men were divided into the hairy and the leafy type, the latter rather attractively designed so that the leaves seem to be issuing from the body and enveloping it without impairing movement.‡ We shall not attempt to determine the size of the hairy species, although it may be surmised to have been not less than human. The leafy demons, however, are sure to be no more than tiny sprites, for the greenery which covers their bodies seems so large in comparison that what it hides could not be anything but diminutive. It would seem likely that these creatures are meant to represent the wood damsels and their mates, whose kinship with moss and lichen is thus convincingly rendered.

What are we to think, however, of the leafy wild men in one of the rare prints by the "Master of the Housebook," § creatures which sport both fur and the trailing scrolls of leaves and are large enough to use tree stems as lances while jousting? 64 The intention here is jocular and the humorous artist combines all possible attributes of wood demons to ridicule them through redundance. It will be noted

* Fig. 45.　　　† Fig. 38.　　　‡ Fig. 2.　　　§ Fig. 11.

that the scrolls enveloping horses and men cover the faces like helmets, impeding mobility and vision alike, and that the tops of the helmets, which should be emblazoned with noble escutcheons, consist of bunches of onions and radishes. One can imagine how funny these creatures must have seemed to medieval beholders — self-appointed knights getting merely involved in the filament of their own bodies when trying to lower their visors for battle.

1. Page from Walter de Milemente's "De Nobilitatibus et Sapientiis Regum." English, fourteenth century. Christ Church, Oxford.

2. Engraved playing card by "Master of the Playing
Cards." German, fifteenth century. Cabinet d'Estampes,
Bibliothèque Nationale, Paris.

3. Nebuchadnezzar as a wild man, illustration for a world chronicle.
German, fifteenth century. Staatsbibliothek, Munich.

4. St. John Chrysostom captured as a wild man. Woodcut from Fyner's edition of "Lives of the Saints," 1481.

5. Drollery from Queen Mary's Psalter. English, fourteenth century. British Museum, London.

6. Misericord, choir stalls, Chester Cathedral. English, fifteenth century.

7. Wild man and peasant, north portal, Notre-Dame, Semur-en-Auxois, Provence, thirteenth century.

8. The mad prince and the princess, tapestry of "Der Busant." German, fifteenth century. Formerly Figdor Collection, Vienna.

9. Recapturing the stolen child, engraving. **Florentine,** *c.* 1460. Cabinet d'Estampes, Bibliothèque Nationale, Paris.

10. The devil and Luxuria, porch of St. Pierre, Moissac. French, twelfth century.

11. Wild-man tournament, dry point by "Master of the Housebook." German, fifteenth century. Rijksmuseum, Amsterdam.

12. "Signs of honor" of Klein Basel, carnival figures from colored etching. Daniel Burckhardt-Wildt, 1784. Historisches Museum, Basel.

13. Wild-man dance in Oberstdorf, Algäu, Bavaria. Twentieth century.

14. Play of the death of the wild man, detail of painting. Pieter Brueghel the Elder. Kunsthistorisches Museum, Vienna.

15. Carnival figure from a Schembart book. German, sixteenth century. Stadtbibliothek, Nuremberg.

16. Play of the death of the wild man, woodcut. Pieter Brueghel the Elder.

17. Mouthless wild men of India, from the "Livre des Merveilles."
French, fifteenth century. Bibliothèque Nationale, Paris.

18. A charivari, from the "Roman de Fauvel." French,
fourteenth century. Bibliothèque Nationale, Paris.

19. Wild-man dance at court, tapestry. French, fifteenth century. Notre-Dame de Nantilly, Saumur.

20. Cannibal wild man in India, from manuscript on
"Marvels of the East." English, eleventh century.
British Museum, London.

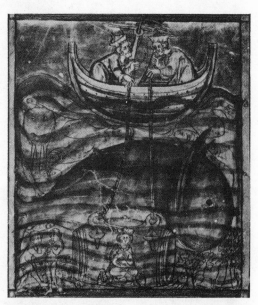

21. Alexander the Great in his diving bell, from a manuscript of the Alexander legend. French, fourteenth century.
Bibliothèque Royale, Brussels.

22. Wild man among the beasts, capital from Saint-Aignan, Orléans. French, *c.* 1000.

23. "Bal des Ardents," from Breslau Ms. of Froissart's "Chronique." Dated 1468. Formerly in Breslau.

24. Wild youth on a unicorn, engraving by "Master of the Housebook." German, fifteenth century. Rijksmuseum, Amsterdam.

25. The abduction of Proserpina, from manuscript of Guillaume de Machaut. French, fourteenth century. Bibliothèque Nationale, Paris.

26. Wild man abducting a damsel, drollery from the Taymouth Hours. English, fourteenth century. British Museum, London.

27. Hercules as a wild man, from manuscript of Robert de Blois. French, thirteenth century. Bibliothèque de l'Arsenal, Paris.

28. The abduction of Proserpina, etching. Albrecht Dürer. Dated 1516.

29. The Age of Silver, painting. Lucas Cranach. Schlossmuseum, Weimar.

30. Sea monster abducting a wild woman, tapestry. Tournai, sixteenth century. Germanisches Museum, Nuremberg.

31. Victory of a knight over a wild man, four sides of a casket. Rhenish, fourteenth century. Museum für Kunst und Gewerbe, Hamburg.

32. Victory of a wild man over a knight, four sides of a casket. Rhenish, fourteenth century. Kunstgewerbe Museum, Cologne.

33. Lady kidnapped by a wild man, and a wild-man banquet, from a tomb plate. Flemish(?), fourteenth century. Schwerin Cathedral.

34. Wild men battling for the castle of love, tapestry. Rhenish, fifteenth century. **Germanisches Museum, Nuremberg.**

35. Wild man in the bonds of love, tapestry. Swiss, fifteenth century. National Museum, Copenhagen.

36. The pleasures of wild-man life, lid of a love casket. South German, c. 1500. Osterreichisches Museum, Vienna.

37. Knight rescuing a damsel from a wild man, ivory casket. French, fourteenth century. Metropolitan Museum, New York.

38. Wild men climbing to the flower of love, engraving. Israel von Meckenem. German, fifteenth century.

39. Wild men and bathing beauties, page from the Golden Bull. Bohemian, *c.* 1400. Nationalbibliothek, Vienna.

40. Wild men as shield-supporters, from the Wenceslaus Bible. Bohemian, fourteenth century. Nationalbibliothek, Vienna.

41. Wild men as agriculturists, details of tapestry. Rhenish, fifteenth century. Osterreichisches Museum, Vienna.

42. The pleasures of wild-man life, details of tapestry. Rhenish, fourteenth century. Town Hall, Regensburg.

43. Tapestry with Feer escutcheon. Rhenish, fifteenth century. Historisches Museum, Basel.

44. The pleasures of wild-man life, two parts of tapestry. Rhenish, fifteenth century. Formerly privately owned, Germany.

45. Wild-man life, details from tapestry. Rhenish, *c.* 1400. Formerly in Museum, Sigmaringen.

46. Wild man with statue of Venus,
woodcut from "Carcel de Amor." Barcelona, 1492.

47. Wild man with coat of arms, engraving. Martin
Schongauer.   German, fifteenth century.

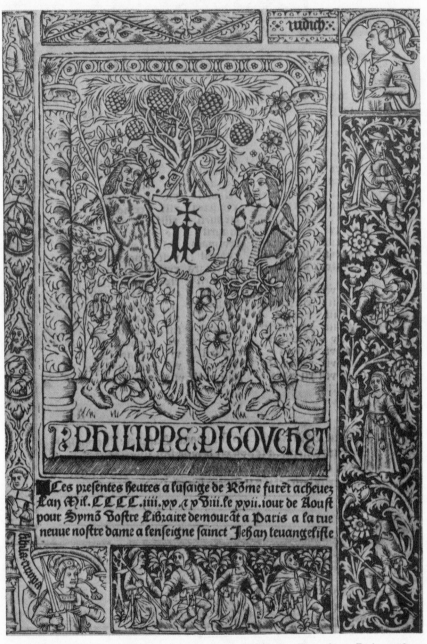

48. Printer's mark on a title page, book of hours. Philippe Pigouchet. Paris, 1498.

49. Wild men as jamb figures, façade, San Gregorio, Valladolid. Spanish, fifteenth century.

50. The coat of arms of death, etching. Albrecht Dürer. Dated 1503.

3

His Theatrical
Embodiment

It is a test for the social importance of any mythology, whether there is at its core a ritual or cult that is explained, strengthened, or embroidered upon by storytellers. Mythology without ritual may be no more than a learned pastime or a suitable but idle entertainment for ladies and gentlemen in the intervals between love and war; while the combination of tale and ritual is at best the very point of unity that holds a society together through common belief and action.

It is therefore important for us to realize that the wild-man stories have a corollary in the wild man's cult, which existed alongside them and provided a justification for them; and that this cult managed to survive not only after the Christianization of Europe, but also through the Middle Ages into modern time. We cannot expect that a cult which had to withstand the strictures of the church could have maintained itself to anything like its pristine extent, once it felt the strength of Christian opposition; but what we learn about it from medieval writers and from the researches of modern folklore may perhaps suffice for its partial and tentative reconstruction.

Of the phases of this cult it is the rituals connected with the wild woman that seem to have been reduced most severely, because these rituals took the form of offerings and thus seemed particularly offensive to Christian sensibilities.[1] All we can offer to prove the former existence of a ritual are a few scattered customs observed in various parts of central Europe: the habit in the Oberpfalz district of Bavaria of throwing some linseed into the bushes at sowing time as a gift for the wood damsels, or the corresponding custom in the Frankenwald of leaving three handfuls of flax for them at the time of harvest. Or finally the isolated custom at the Burgeiser Alm in the Tyrol for children to leave a little stone on a certain rock saying, "I offer this to the wild damsels." [2]

Compared with these attenuated residues the ritual activity connected with the wild man seems to have survived much more vigorously. It consisted of dances, pageants, and dramatic perfomances, in which men in mask and costume played the part of the wild man; and the original meaning of such disguises seems to have been that the performer regarded himself and was regarded as the living recipient of the wild man's power, indeed as the living wild man himself. There was no notion of sacrifice or offering involved and it was thus easier to pass such rituals off as harmless than was the case with those offered to the wild damsels. The church itself, which suppressed the wild-man cults in many places, came to terms with them in others, permitting men dressed to look the part to walk in its processions; and once the wild man had begun to be regarded as funny or pathetic rather than awe-inspiring, as he showed his uncouth figure at festivals, much of the opposition to him was apparently withdrawn.

The wild-man performances of which we have record divide themselves into several categories: those which are connected with only some of his mythological functions and capacities; those which are known as wild-man hunts, in which his entire existence is at stake; and finally those, in which he appears either as the leader or at least as a participant in the activities of the Wild Horde. To these we may add the examples of his marriage with a fairy or earth demon and the great number of wild-men dances held in or out of season and for no apparent purpose other than that of entertainment.

Unfortunately, we cannot always determine which type a certain performance belongs to, this being true of some of the oldest on record. The *magnus ludus de homine salvatico*, the big play of a wild man, which the citizens of Padua put on during Pentecost in 1208, is known only through the few Latin words just quoted, which may or may not indicate that the performance was extended beyond its mythological minimum. Another wild-man play was held in Padua in 1224 and this time we are told that it took place *cum gigantibus*, with giants, whom we may regard as secondary figures in the play. We know no more about the *ludus at virum dictum wildman* acted in 1399 in Aarau, Switzerland. This ignorance is the more regrettable since the Italian plays, at least, are not only among the first instances of theatrical activity in that country since the demise of the Roman theater, but also the first documented examples of wild-man plays. But we shall note at least that these performances took place in Italy and in the part of it that is contiguous to the Alps, and thus help to confirm our surmise regarding the origin of some wild-man sagas there; and that, symbolic of this influence, the next reference comes from Switzerland, which has preserved some of its wild-man cults to the present day.[3]

As might be expected, the least influential among the wild-man performances were those which show him only in a partial aspect. There seem to be no medieval examples of these. From more recent times we have the repeated prohibitions by the Bavarian government as well as by local police authorities against the habit of quacks and salesmen of popular medicines of either appearing as wild men or taking a "wild man" along with them to substantiate their lore.[4] When these orders were issued, in 1727, 1739, 1783, and 1800, the wild man's knowledge of herbs was apparently taken for granted, at least by the more ignorant part of the population; we may perhaps surmise that after 1800 enlightenment in league with modern police facilities put an end to this phase of ancient superstition. In certain parts of Austria, such as Aussee and Ebensee, a similar custom seems to have lingered on somewhat longer, for it was not so long ago that folklorists recorded how the "wild man" there came out of the forest and busied himself with his ointments, as a fitting accompaniment for the performance of a sword dance.[5]

The circumstances attending the dairy business in the mountains of Switzerland furnish another pretext for a wild man's disguise and a small performance, both practiced today but perhaps of considerable age. The wild man acts as the protector of cattle feeding in the high mountain meadows during the summer months. It is his day of honor, consequently, when the animals are brought back in September, unharmed and festively decorated. In the ensuing celebration the "Tschaemmeler," as he is called, participates all clad in lichen and twigs, contributes his own humorous sallies, and is rewarded by gifts of candy and cake. In some places such as Vitznau and Wäggis in the central cantons of Switzerland a wild woman may share the honors with him. It would seem likely that the wild-man dance still practiced in Oberstdorf in the Bavarian Alps * was originally also a cattleman's celebration, for although it takes the form of a battle with clubs, it preserves its ancient date: September, when the cows return from pasture.[6]

More important than these festivities in which a particular trait of the wild man is made manifest are the seasonal wild-man plays which embody a hunt. We saw that the capture of the wild man is one of the most frequent stories in his mythology, and can now add that such stories may often be mere variants upon a ritual that was in the mind of the narrator: it is in the nature of the relation of cult and mythology that the former contributes the lasting framework upon which the latter hangs its shifting phantasms. Folklorists have noted such wild-man hunts in areas as far apart as the German and French parts of Switzerland, the southern Tyrol, the Italian Alps, lower Austria, the eastern border of Czechoslovakia, and Thuringia; and to this modern testimony we have to add that of Pieter Brueghel the Elder, who recorded a similar custom in Flanders, and of Boccaccio, who located a wild-man hunt in Venice.[7]

The core of the ritual is simple enough: a wild man is either stirred up in his cave or in the forest or he may appear spontaneously, roaring and snorting and spreading mock terror and apprehension among the villagers. A hunt ensues which ends either with his being loaded with chains and dragged away or with the pretense of his being killed by shooting or by piercing a little bag filled with blood and attached to his side. Sometimes he is carried away on a bier or, finally, a puppet impersonating him is thrown into the village pond.[8]

This central ritual is subject to certain modifications: instead of

* Fig. 13.

being killed the wild man may be merely put before a "board of justice" that is to try his "case." [9] Or, as recorded by Pieter Brueghel,* the hunt may take place in the presence of higher secular authority: in addition to the wild man performing his uncouth dance and the hunter aiming his crossbow at him, Brueghel's print shows the emperor himself with crown and scepter, as well as a female figure clad in a wide coat and a bowl-shaped hat who holds out a ring to the wild man as if to lure him away. Brueghel has recorded the same scene a second time † in the background of his picture of the battle of Carnival and Lent; and this time it is quite clear that the emperor and his executioner are closing in on the unsuspecting wild man, while he follows the lead of the female figure with the ring. She is apparently a man dressed in simple woman's garb and wearing a white mask. Both in the painting and in the print the little troupe presenting the performance solicits gifts from onlookers, a fact that makes it likely that the show was repeated before inns and the houses of various citizens. Similar itinerant performances, although not as complete as Brueghel's, are on record from Thuringia.[10]

Another variant of the wild-man play, akin to Pieter Brueghel's in that a woman played a vital role in the capture, was performed in the nineteenth century in Marling near Merano in the Italian Tyrol. The wild man absconded to a cave in the nearby mountainside together with two of his "sons" who, like him, were dressed in lichen and twigs. The curious novelty was that, instead of being hunted and buffeted about by men, the wild man was found by little schoolgirls got up in their prettiest dresses, who tied a red ribbon upon him and brought him captive to the village.[11] We shall see later that this version of the game, according the capture to feminine innocence, has its important parallels in medieval poetry and art.

Finally among the variants of the wild-man hunt are those in which the creature loses its name and becomes a bear: a transformation easily arrived at considering that the bear — the "man of the woods" — may stand upright in its tracks like a man, while the wild man resembles it in his close-fitting fur. In the rituals with which we are concerned, the distinction between man and beast is not always

* Fig. 16.   † Fig. 14.

rigorously maintained, so that, for instance, the ceremonial in the Uri canton, Switzerland, differs from that held in the Valais canton only in that the "victim" to be chased and killed is in the former a bear and in the latter a wild man. There are places where even this distinction is not recognized. The inhabitants of Eger, Czechoslovakia, refer to their annual ritual, which is a hunt of the wild man, as the killing of the bear; and in Hesse, where the custom prevails, as it does in other parts of central Europe, of leading a masked and furry human being through the villages as a popular entertainer, the creature is called synonymously "the wild man" or "the wild bear." [12]

It is not surprising to find after this that the wild-man ritual recorded by Pieter Brueghel has its close parallel in a particular group of bizarre and archaic modern customs, with the only distinction that the central figure in the ceremony is a man rigged up not as a wild man but as a bear. In several of the remote and little-known valleys in the Pyrenees, in Andorra, Arles-sur-Tech, and Vallaspir, a play is enacted in the time of the Carnival, in which the protagonists are a bear, a man dressed as a girl, and a group of hunters. In Arles-sur-Tech where the most elaborate version is given, the bear is caught as he tries to throw himself upon his feminine decoy and prospective mate, Rosetta; he is then chained, brought to town, and allowed to invite Rosetta into his cave, a plaster structure erected for him in the town square; he regales her there with cake and wine, while the town people rejoice over the "wedding." Then the bear is shot to death, but immediately resuscitated by a doctor, so that he may renew his clumsy attentions upon his mate. A final shot finishes the sequence.[13]

The similarity of this play to the ritual recorded twice by Brueghel is apparent, particularly if it is remembered that in Brueghel the marriage is implied by the feminine mask holding out a ring to the wild man, who follows her in awed fascination. Obviously, no matter whether the masculine role is played by a wild man or by a bear, the mating of the two protagonists is an essential part of the ritual — a fact to remember when we come to deal with the erotic symbolism of the wild man.

The ritual in question seems to be a very ancient one, for as early as the ninth century Hincmar of Reims found it necessary to inveigh against what he called *turpia ioca cum urso*, reprehensible plays with the bear, which, of course, could not have been mere innocent exhibitions of a dancing bear, since such cruelty to animals would not have bothered a medieval churchman. "One should not allow reprehensible plays with the bear nor with woman dancers [?] to be performed before one," he urges, "nor should one permit the wearing of demoniac masks popularly known as talamascae." [14] Referring as he does to bear, woman, and demons as part of one total program, Hincmar leaves no doubt as to the ritual character of the performance which he is combating. It may, in fact, have been very similar to that still practiced in the Pyrenees.

A century later Regino of Prüm repeated Hincmar's admonition.[15] But other medieval records reveal that the efforts of early ecclesiastics to uproot the pagan ritual had been in vain. In 1142, according to the *Mirabilia Urbis Romae*, a bear was killed in the very capital of Western Christianity under circumstances that imply a human victim in mask and fur; for the killing of the bear was part of a Carnival pageant, in fact of the first one which is described under that name.[16]

In later records "playing with the bear" had become "playing with the wild man," for this is the expression used in a Dutch document of 1364 dealing with the compensation received by men who had participated in the ritual.[17] Or the two games were combined into one hunt upon both wild men and bears. It was the citizens of Venice who, if Boccaccio is not maligning them, engaged in this pleasant but heathen pastime.[18] At least we are told that it was possible there to tell a man that a hunt on bears and wild men was taking place on the Piazza San Marco, to urge him to escape from a house, where he was being held, in a wild man's disguise, and then to expose him to ridicule by removing his mask after having tied him to a column.

Thus in Boccaccio's imagination the slaying of the wild man had become an occasion for ribald jokes and clever schemes of revenge. But the fact that it could be abused cannot hide the serious implications that, originally and for a considerable time, the slaying of the wild man must have had. What was its meaning and purpose? Was it a fertility ritual bringing with it the promise and assurance of immortality after death? Or was it merely meant as the removal of a personified obstacle to the return of spring, a winter demon who had to be killed so that his icy breath would not impede the sprouting of greenery? Both interpretations have considerable evidence to support them.

There is no denying that the oldest *ludus de homine salvatico* was a spring festival held at the time of Pentecost, and that even today some wild-man festivals are celebrated in June and culminate in a resurrection effected through the efforts of a quack doctor. It is impossible, therefore, to rule out the opinion that this hopeful version of the ritual preserves its original intent. It is also true, however, that most of the wild-man rituals are held in the time of the Carnival and thus at the period of the year which can be interpreted as terminating the winter as well as opening the door for the new season. If slain in January or February, the wild man is usually not brought to life, for he and his equivalent, the bear, are declared to be personifications of the Carnival itself, whose execution is meant to signify the removal of the period of exuberance. The performance in the Pyrenees with its elaborate, but temporary, resuscitation of the bear is a great exception in that respect. It would seem likely, although by no means certain, that the allegorical representation of a mere period in the calender has its roots in older mythology, which had singled out the ferocious and unpredictable wild man as the image of winter and death and had decreed his slaughter for the good of all. The dual nature of the wild man as a harbinger of fertility and as an embodiment of the returning dead is thus reflected in the ambiguity of the rituals accorded to him.[19]

There is another interpretation, not in terms of nature cults but in terms of social relevance, which one may want to consider. Why should anybody have exposed himself to the ordeal of impersonating the wild man, considering the rough treatment that his role implied? It appears in some instances that the wild-man plays were discontinued, not because of any interference by church or state, but because nobody could be found ready to be chained, chased, and buffeted about under an anonymous guise. Was there, in former times, any reward for having undergone the trial? The answer to this question involves a jump into the dark, for if it is correct, our sources would have every reason for either not knowing the facts involved or for withholding them. But the ritual itself is suggestive:

the masking and subsequent submergence of personality, the effort demanded in terms of running and dancing, the rough treatment against which no complaint could be made, finally the slaying and death, and the injunction to play dead while lying on a bier: all this is familiar from initiation rituals, as they have been practiced over a large part of the world. In a characteristic way the wild-man hunt combines the features of an endurance test and of a metamorphosis through death — and it is in keeping with this suggestion that, as he undergoes all this, the initiate's face is hidden under a mask, making it impossible for anybody but his intimates to guess his identity.

The reward for being hunted in the guise of the wild man consisted, if our interpretation is correct, of the reception into a society or esoteric group; and we may deduce from the nature of the initiation that the society would be a secret one, at least in the sense of its members being protected against identification while engaged in the group's activities.[20]

The existence of such societies, at least in the period after the Middle Ages, seems to be well established, in spite of obvious obstacles to proving what those who were best informed must always have tried to conceal. We possess, of course, no literature on the subject from those who had the inside knowledge, for they had to fear ecclesiastic and secular authorities and sometimes also revenge from their fellow members.[21] It is much more disconcerting to discover that outsiders, impressed by strange and frightening rituals, found it often impossible to distinguish clearly between genuine ghosts and demons and groups of masked persons impersonating them; so that their reports may be marked by a strange ambiguity, as if it were beyond their capacity to draw the line between phantasms and persons of flesh and blood. In spite of this, enough material has been collected from police records, the statements of eye witnesses, and the accounts of others who heard such statements, to make it certain that pagan societies existed far into modern times.

We shall draw the outlines of what is known in a few bold strokes: the participants met several times a year at predetermined places where they donned their masks, the outstanding periods for their meetings being Twelfth-night and the Carnival time in February. In addition there may have been other meetings at other times of the year and some that took place at intervals of several years.

The activities that then began were almost always marked by an extreme of unreasoning frenzy, a throwing off of all inhibitions, that makes the reading of these accounts a hair-raising venture, particularly for us today who have witnessed the organized resurrection of a similar spirit on a national scale.

Unusually well documented are the meetings of such groups in the Baltic countries, where the participants transformed themselves into werewolves and then proceeded to ravage the countryside alone or in gangs.[22] Much more recently the members of the Bavarian "Haberfeldtreiben" used their anonymity to brand those who had incurred their displeasure by some infraction against village rule. And, to use an example from the area that interests us most because of its faithful preservation of wild-man cults, in the Lötschenvalley in Switzerland young men not very long ago were still in the habit of donning furs, masks, and bells at Carnival time and of raging through the village, while all who were not part of the gang hid in their houses behind bolted doors.[23] In the seventeenth and eighteenth centuries these wild groups were not satisfied with merely frightening the villagers, but used their clubs — the wild man's weapon — to break into houses and carry away whatever food they could lay their hands on. The only justification that could have been given for such violence was a religious one: the maskers felt themselves to be the living embodiment of the Wild Horde and thus to be obsessed by the spirit of the dead — while at the same time their appearance may also have served the purpose of warding off ghosts.

It is certain, at any rate, that Twelfth-night and the time of the Carnival, when these societies were on the rampage, were also the periods in which the wild hunt took place.[24] It is revealing that the numerous accounts of its fury range all the way from tales about ghosts to tales about human mummers. The Carnival itself preserved traits derived from the wild hunt for many centuries, even after it had become a popular amusement in a city environment.

After a glimpse of the reward that could be obtained by agreeing to wear the wild-man mask and going through death on his behalf, let me add that it should not be implied that the wild-man hunts were the only initiation rituals of their kind, since the beliefs and observances in question were much too varied to have allowed such restriction. It does seem certain, on the other hand, that to be initiated and to belong to a society did entail definite social advantage, particularly if it is true, as has been suggested, that as they expanded and accepted Christian rule many of these societies developed into recognized civic groups.[25]

As far as the wild man is concerned, his occasional connection with the Wild Hunt and the Wild Horde has been mentioned in the chapter on his mythology. It will be no surprise, therefore, to hear that he had a place in Twelfth-night and Carnival entertainments. Most of the wild-man dances, if they were not part of the celebration of a prince's entry into a city, took place after Christmas or in February. And even when the wild-man dance had become a court entertainment, its connection with the yearly cycle was not forgotten: witness the dance held for Henry VIII of England in the Great Hall in Greenwich, which was part of a Twelfth-night entertainment; and witness also the disastrous "Bal des Ardents" * — a wild-man dance held in 1392 at the court of Charles VI of France, when several revelers were burned to death — which took place on a January 28th. Of the civic celebrations involving a hairy human disguise, the so-called "Butcher's Jump" in Munich and the pageants of the insignia of Klein-Basel and the "Schembartlaufen" in Nuremberg all took place at Carnival time,† and we shall note in passing that all three of these were put on by civic groups, the first by the butchers, the second by one of the so-called "societies" of Basel, while the third was a masked dance evolved out of the need of guarding a dance held, again, by the butchers' guild.[26]

At celebrations of this kind the wild man found himself in strange and disreputable company whose presence is to be explained only by considering that he was one among the demons — human, composite, and animal — that constituted the motley crew of the wild hunt. Sebastian Franck, sixteenth-century reformer and writer, describes such a pageant of mummers in his *Weltbuch* of 1534.[27] In addition to the wild man's masks there were people who ran about naked, others crawling on all fours, and men impersonating storks, monkeys, and fools. The wild man's closest associates were bears, a fact that requires no further elucidation, and devils, whom we find for the first time explicitly associated with the wild man.

* Fig. 23.   † Figs. 12, 15.

There is every reason, however, to believe that this association or identity would have been proposed to us long before this time were not most of the medieval material examined written by secular writers — that is, not for edification or spiritual improvement, but for entertainment. The association, once established, was a firm one and outlasted the sixteenth century. As late as 1695, at the court festivals held in Dresden at the court of the Arch-Elector Friedrich August of Saxony, the wild man walked in the pageant between the mask of a stag and those of "disorderly [*liederlich*] spirits who vexed people and beat them," probably devils of some kind.²⁸

The theological expression of this relation is to be found in Geiler of Kaysersberg (1445–1510), who devoted part of his book of sermons, *Die Emeis* (The Ant), to a discussion of the wild man. His twentieth sermon, held on Saturday after Reminiscere, dealt with this topic as well as with the "awesome man of Bern," the wild hunter in a then popular guise. On the previous Thursday he had spoken "of the raging horde" and on Friday "of the devil's ghost," while the Sunday following the exposition of wild-man lore was devoted to the "twelve kinds of damage that the devil may wreak." Apparently there was no doubt in his mind that the Wild Horde, devils proper, and wild men belonged together as variants of the same demoniac denomination. It reveals a curious involution in his thinking that in the sermon on wild men the devils appear again, but now not as the species of which the wild man is a part, but as his subspecies, the unspoken argument being that all hairy and demoniac creatures of human form who live beyond the pale of Christian society have "wildness" as their common characteristic.²⁹

Of the civic festivities in central Germany the "Butcher's Jump" in Munich bore some essential features of a fertility cult, since the butcher's apprentices who performed the ritual not only had to dress in animal skins but also had to jump into the fountain in front of the town hall; and the same would be true of the festivities of the civic societies in Basel, were it not that the boat trip down the Rhine which the wild man was to undertake was a feature added in the early eighteenth century.³⁰

The Schembartlaufen in Nuremberg, held at Carnival time intermittently from 1449 till 1539, preserved the features of the Wild Horde more faithfully, in spite of embellishments and variations of costume which the rich patrician mummers introduced in order to manifest their affluence and inventiveness. Hans Sachs in his "Schembartspruch" compares the Nuremberg pageant with the Wild Horde, and for good reason, for the noisy behavior of the mummers was sometimes quite demonlike. A Nuremberg police order of the fifteenth century complains about the habit of "wild men and other mummers" of shouting, chasing people, "scuffling with them, throwing, beating, and scratching them or damaging and offending them in other ways." When these orders were issued the peaceful atmosphere of city life combined with the beneficent influence of the church had apparently not succeeded in eliminating the yearly recurrence of such fits of the *furor teutonicus*. Even when these excesses were avoided, the impact of the masked gang upon the public must have been shockingly great, for the mummers appeared running at an urgent pace, shooting off fireworks out of cone-shaped bundles of evergreen, and clanging bells sewed to their waists shook with every step — the same bells which are the mark of personified demons in carnivals over a large part of the European world.[31]

It is interesting to note that in the police orders mentioned it is mainly the wild men who are charged with and warned against creating a disturbance of the peace, for it would appear that this mask more than any other was looked upon by the mummers as a charter for noisiness and violence. The wild men were prominent in the Nuremberg Carnival, in the conventional form of bearded and hairy men with their wives and children, and in such variants as were dictated by artistic flair and the desire for florid display.* Among those who donned *raue Kleider*, rough cloth, in addition to their human masks, were those who came with little mirrors or pine cones hanging from the tufts, those who replaced the tufts with rows of dice and little dolls, and those who had made for themselves costumes entirely composed of chestnuts. While all these variants were derived from the wild man's original shagginess, other costumes reveal a different origin: beside the hunter there are the demons participating in the hunt, and thus beside the wild man in the Nuremberg pageant there were impersonations of outright devils, of goat, stork, and pig demons, all in furs combined with

* Fig. 15.

animal masks. Even these creatures showed a marked similarity to the original wild man, creating the impression that it is not always easy or even possible to distinguish between demons of human form and their animal counterparts.[32]

The mummers in Nuremberg carried sheaves of evergreen in the midst of which lurked a kind of gun so constructed as to let out fireworks: a simple contrivance so excellently suited to the nature of the wild man, demon of storm and lightning and dweller in the midst of greenery, that we may assume he was the first to be fitted out with it and only later conceded its use to other maskers. The purpose of the fireworks was to keep off the crowds and so to guard the dance of the butchers from interference. This view is confirmed by English pageants wherein the wild man is frequently charged with keeping order and uses fireworks to attain this end. The St. George's procession of 1610 in Chester, for instance, was headed by "two men in ivy with black hair and beards, very ugly to behold, and garlands upon their heads, with great clubs in their hands, with fireworks to scatter abroad to maintain way for the rest of the show." [33]

For tasks of this kind the wild man was supremely suited because of his bearlike strength; perhaps also it may have been customary to choose for the task the strongest and tallest individuals. Therefore, even where he had no fireworks to frighten insistent spectators, he may yet have played the role of festival police, using his ugly countenance and, if this was of no avail, his strong arm and club to maintain order: to this day he can be seen thus employed at the Schemenlaufen in Telfs in the Inn valley. He plays the part of the sexton in the play of St. Evermarus performed outside of a church in the neighborhood of Tongeren in Belgium; and in the great Corpus Christi processions in Barcelona, which in the fifteenth and sixteenth centuries were the most gorgeous in Europe, including kings and officials of every rank and once even the Emperor Charles V himself among the celebrants, the wild men formed the rear guard. They carried staves, which they could lengthen and shorten, and used them to shut off the street to keep back crowds.[34]

Wherever there were heavy objects to carry or to heave into place, there seems to have been a tendency to rely upon the brawny wild men for the task: in Cervantes' *Don Quixote* they build the castle of love, which other maskers are to conquer, and carry the wooden horse on which the hero is to ride.[35] It seems at least possible that the habit in late medieval art of entrusting to wild men the holding and exhibiting of coats of arms may be due in part to the custom at tournaments of thus dressing up the servants or lackeys who guarded the shield in the challenge preceding actual combat.[36] It is certain, however, that this relegation to a subordinate position is not what the wild man had been accustomed to, and that he assumed these various menial duties only after having been demoted from the part of leader or prominent participant in pageants and festivals to one of mere helper and guardian.

In a number of small towns in southern Germany, Switzerland, and the Tyrol, the figure of the hairy man still is part of the traditional winter Carnival, although not usually called by the name of wild man. There is the Plaetzlimanli in the Aargau canton, Switzerland, artfully fitted out with small bits of rags sewn on to a garment, so that he may look his name which means "man in little rags." In the neighborhood of Garmisch, Bavaria, there is the corresponding disguise as Flecklegewand, or "man in patched garment." There is the Haensele in Ueberlingen on Lake Constance, who wears a fringed suit, a belt of cowbells, and a black velvet mask with a snout. In Rottweil, a town a little farther north, there is the Fransenkleidle, who like the others imitates shagginess through the fringes on his costume. There are the Hudler and the Zottler (meaning again "fringed people"), similar figures in rags which appear in the ancient small towns dotting the bottom of the upper Inn valley near Innsbruck. The names may differ according to local dialect, but their meaning is constant, since over this entire geographic area the incarnation of the Wild Horde would be incomplete without the participation of the fringed revenant.[37]

The wild man himself, if exception be made of his police duty in the Schemenlaufen in Telfs, appears only once in these modern rituals, namely in Gastein, Austria, where his redoubtable company consists of witches, a bear with his leader, and a group of persons whose costume is all hidden behind closely hung ropes giving the same general effect as patches. Finally there are the so-called Schuddigs in Elzach, Württemberg, persons all dressed in brownish-reddish costumes and fitted out with masks half human, half bearlike. They are divided into the "bear faces" and the "dead faces" thus manifesting the same connotations which we found universally associated with the figure of the wild man. The Schuddig's contribution to the noise of the carnival is, accordingly, a snort resembling the sound made by a bear. Other mummers in other towns roar, shout, and clang their bells as they jump and thrash about furiously like persons obsessed and beside themselves. Remnants of similar customs were preserved until recently in England, where bands of mummers in costumes covered with fringes and streamers used to visit various houses at Christmas time to perform a traditional play involving a fight between two men and the resurrection of the vanquished.[38]

As for wild-man festivals in France, it will be remembered that in the Carolingian or pre-Carolingian period men believed in a demon named Orcus, a relic, it would seem, from Gallo-Roman times whose impersonation by masked dancers was forbidden in an early penitential. It appears that in France this figure which we equated with the wild man was lost sight of in the course of the Middle Ages. Its place as the leader of the dead was taken by the Germanic demon Hellekin — or Herlekin, Herlechin, Harlekin — who carried on some of the functions of Orcus, although, because of the French preoccupation with theology, regarded as a devil outright.[39]

We meet him for the first time in the *Ecclesiastic History* by Ordericus Vitalis (1075–1143?), in a famous passage that relates how in January of 1091 a priest in Bonneval, near Chartres, had the bad luck to meet the entire Wild Horde as he went across country to visit a sick person: he saw an endless procession of damned souls, men and women, clerics and laymen, some carrying household instruments, others clad in black and burning armor, all of them miserable and tormented; at the head of this procession of what Ordericus calls Hellekins was a giant carrying a heavy club, which he raised in order to force the priest to stand, as the procession rolled by. His kinship to the wild man is indicated by his size, by the nature of his weapon, and particularly by the fact that, like the wild man, he has the task of keeping outsiders from interfering with the proceedings.[40]

It is not surprising to find that in later literary references Hellekin is usually described as a creature of extraordinary ugliness, accentuated by the presence of an untended beard which covers most of his face.[41] As the leader of the Wild Horde he plays the role reserved in other countries for the wild man or for Dietrich of Bern, and thus is found to associate with the same demoniac vermin, human and animal, which we observed in the Nuremberg Carnival. And just as the Wild Horde in Germany is not only a matter of awed hearsay, but of actual performance by groups of masked and raving men, so we find that Hellekin-people are sometimes very human indeed, although their abominable behavior suggests that one need not be disembodied to act like a demon.

The mythological Hellekins are even at times engaged in the storm demon's pastime of pulling out trees as lances or clubs for a Brobdingnagian tournament. This scene was represented in a humorous print by the "Master of the Housebook." * The French version, also meant to be humorous, occurs in the thirteenth-century "Lay de Luque la Maudite," which tells about the marriage of the cursed witch Luque with Hellekin, chief of the devils. As she dies in the city of Rouen, Luque utters a last wish to be married to Hellekin, who accepts her offer with glee. Thereupon he and all the devils rise out of hell at Cape Antifer in Normandy to receive her and then engage in an orgy of destruction which, the poet tells us, is unique in the annals of Rouen; they blast windmills, lay church towers low, drink the wine in people's cellars, throw about the ships in the harbor of Rouen as if they were mere sticks of wood, and end with blasting the doors of the cathedral and destroying the bishop's residence. As they passed the forest of Tret,

> They organized in a moment
> The most powerful tournament
> That ever is or was.
> Their lances were of wood,
> Of such wood as they could find.
> Very well did they try their strength,
> Each embraced a tree
> To use as a shield and tore it out,
> Then they had their tournament.
> One of them fled.

* Fig. 11.

The others were always behind him
Pursuing him closely
Always with the noise of the hunt and with raging speed
Until into the forest of Brotonne
They chased him always in wild pursuit.
There he made a stand
And delivered battle to all.
You should have seen the great fight.[42]

Behavior such as this is of course the privilege of genuine
demons, since their human imitators cannot marshal the physical
force required to wreak so much havoc. But French literature tells
us that the demon impersonators came as near to the standard set by
their prototypes as possible — a group of determined and frenzied
persons using every device of noise-making, senseless movement,
and fantastic, shocking getup to create a disturbance. In the fourteenth-century "Roman de Fauvel," the description of the so-called
charivari, a noisy serenade offered by human Hellekins to an unpopular newlywed, spares our sensibilities even less than does
Sebastian Franck in depicting the Carnival in Germany. Some of
the capering members of the charivari are nude, while a great many
are all or partly covered with animal skins, combined either with
the corresponding head mask or with a mask in the form of a human
grimace. The miniatures accompanying the romance * depict persons got up as lions and bulls, with all that these disguises entail,
and others who, while clad with fur, retain their human shape. The
mummers are shown engaged in a curious swaying giddy dance well
suited to convey the idea of extreme intoxication. The leader of the
gang, like the leader of the horde in Odericus Vitalis, is a giant of a
man. He comes shouting, dressed in green like the wild man in
Brueghel, and mounted on a miserable nag, while a little witch, also
in green garments, accompanies him. We are told that he is Hellekin
himself.[43]

Charivaris such as this one seem to have been frequent occur-
rences in France during the last centuries of the Middle Ages, in
spite of indignant protests against their appalling excesses launched
by secular and ecclesiastical authorities. It is comprehensible that
these protests should have no more than dented the custom, when

* Fig. 18.

one realizes that the king, supposedly the standard of courtly virtue, found it not beneath his dignity to engage occasionally in this nefarious pastime; it is a gauge of the pressure of formalized living upon those who were supposed to be its foremost paragons, that it seems to have been necessary at times to open the valves and to let the agonized fury of "natural man" take its unhampered course.

We hear, at any rate, that Charles VI of France, at best not a man of too well-poised equilibrium, could not deny himself the pleasure of participating in charivaris when the opportunity arose; and that when he did so in 1389, on occasion of the marriage of one of the ladies in waiting, he found himself attacked by the officers of the queen, who, not recognizing him under his mask, treated him to a sound thrashing.[44] Much more tragic was the outcome of a second charivari that he engaged in, not having learned his lesson after the first. In 1392 again a lady in waiting was to be married and a nobleman from Normandy proposed a charivari. This time it was decided to have a wild-man dance in the presence of the ladies, who were assembled for a dance and who could hardly be expected to object to a performance given for their benefit and amusement. The king and five of the highest nobles of the crown were dressed in close-fitting, shaggy costumes, chained themselves to each other, and then proceeded with their romp. In spite of previous warnings to the effect that all torches should be kept away from the dancers, the Duke of Orleans took a flare to examine the mummers as they were going through their romp on the other side of the room. Their costumes caught fire; chained as they were to each other, the revelers had no means of disengaging themselves and four of them perished miserably.* The king was saved only because his quick-witted aunt, the Duchess of Berry, threw the train of her robe over him in time and smothered the flames. The king's precarious sanity broke in consequence of the shock.[45]

One would have thought this experience would have ended the vogue of charivaris or wild-man dances, at least at court. But this was not the case. A Burgundian tapestry of the fifteenth century in the church of Notre Dame de Nantilly in Saumur † shows what can only be described as an aristocratic wild-man masquerade, which differs from those just related mainly by the fact that this

* Fig. 23.   † Fig. 19.

time, instead of being mere onlookers, the ladies themselves participate in the disguise. It is impossible not to recognize a process of
greater and greater familiarity with the demoniac mask. At first the
king had taken part incognito and without knowledge of the queen
in a hubbub outside of his palace. Then, as the animal demons were
transformed into wild men, the proceedings were brought into the
royal residence and thus allowed to become legitimate court entertainment. Finally the ladies, who had stayed aloof from the frolic,
seem to have decided to take a hand. But, if our tapestry is a reliable
witness, they demanded a characteristic concession: if it was to be
graced with their presence, the wild man's dance was to be a fashionable entertainment in which the shaggy fur would serve as a mere
basis for further accouterments; and we may surmise that the ladies
made it a further condition for their participation that the primeval
savagery of the original event be somewhat toned down.

The Burgundian tapestry shows men and women in the most
fantastic getup imaginable, some in the usual court costume, most
of them however in animal furs, and wearing over them rich embroidered coats with gemmed borders and, in addition, the high
hats for men and the hennins for ladies generally worn at the time.
The ladies have their eyebrows plucked and their hair pulled back,
again according to the most recent dictates of fashion, and thus
seem to have refused to wear masks. In the intimacy of the court
family this must have seemed indeed unnecessary.

As the tapestry depicts it, the dance takes place on a meadow
in the open air, and to the strains of music. But a strange tune it is,
for three of the performers, in normal court dress, play conventional recorders, while others, of the wild denomination, blow upon
winding horns, releasing what must have been ugly, braying, bellowing sounds. In the same way the dancers are divided into ladies
and gentlemen and their wild counterparts, but well shuffled
throughout. There are two caves in the picture, one of which is
filled with older and bearded wild men, while out of the second
come the young couples holding hands and sashes and all ready for
the dance. There are even wild children dressed like their elders
and, as a reminder of the subhuman character of the spectacle, a
monkey. Before a tent a man and woman are getting ready to clasp
hands in an intimate and solemn gesture that may indicate that they

are the couple whose marriage is the occasion for all the activity; at any rate, the other couples seem to be moving toward them and the nearest extend their hands to them as if offering felicitations.[46] The total impression is one of bizarre luxury coupled with a savage primitivism that is highlighted through incongruity rather than tempered through moderation. Looking at this strange product of wild-man fancy one can well understand that, when the tapestry was woven, the vogue for wild-man pageants was far from having run its course.

After the early instance at the royal court of France records of wild-man dances in that country follow each other in rapid succession, usually as part of civic festivities celebrating the visits of princes. When the young Henry VI of England entered Paris for his coronation in 1431, the Parisians put up, among other things, "a scaffold with a kind of forest on it, on which three wild men and a wild woman fought a continuous battle, as long as the king and his gentlemen were there to see them." Seven years later, the citizens of Valenciennes arrived on their annual visit to the tournaments in Lille "all dressed up as wild men carrying clubs and big sticks, their heads disguised with the skins of strange animals, which was astounding to see." At the head of the procession there were wild men playing trumpets and horns, and a herald in a bearskin who carried the escutcheon of Valenciennes. Even the horses had been transformed into fantastic beasts by throwing over them the skins of lions, tigers, and dogs and decorating them with feathers. The visitors were received by a delegation of their hosts all dressed in feathers and led by the king of the carnival in skins and plumage, his steed garnished with mirrors and peacock and swan feathers.[47]

In 1437 when Charles VII of France entered Paris, there were "in front of that city and at the Fontaine de Ponceau wild men and women, who fought each other and went through several acts, and besides there were three very beautiful young girls impersonating sirens," who said little motets and bergerettes, while the fountain ran with wine and hippocras (a popular cordial). In the pageant held in 1496 for Joanna, later known as the Mad, wife of Philip the Handsome, the citizens of Brussels showed fourteen wild men together with a Moorish woman and a fool. And at the entry of the Holy Roman Emperor Charles V into Bruges the citizens of that

town seemed to have heard accounts of the performance of 1431 in
Paris or another one very much like it, for there was again a forest
on a scaffold and wild men dancing in it, only that the learned men
of Bruges claimed now that these savages impersonated the first
historic inhabitants of the region before the founding of their city.[48]

From Basel comes the account of a wild-man dance held in 1435,
when persons from all of Europe were assembled on the occasion of
the great church council there. Behind the musicians twenty-three
persons entered dressed as *uomini selvatici*, with their hair, half red,
half green, falling to their feet. They took up their shields and
clubs, which were made of linen and stuffed with tow, and proceeded to perform a lively dance, pretending to bash in each
other's heads. Later, at a repetition of the dance, several of them
fell down as if dead. When the wild men departed, there followed
social dancing that lasted till the early hours. The account, which
comes from an Italian visitor to the council,[49] is interesting since the
dance was given at a time when Basel and its neighborhood were
the hub of wild-man representations in art. It is revealing also that
the account should antedate any mention of the wild man's dance
in connection with the festivities of Basel's civic societies. Their
pageant is first mentioned in 1598, with the implication that it was
then an ancient custom. The societies themselves date back as far as
the end of the fourteenth century. It would seem possible therefore
that the civic pageant had existed for some time before the dance
was added, and that those who arranged it decided to borrow its
central feature for their private entertainment.[50]

There is little record of wild-man dances in Spain, although
they were by no means unknown there. When Cardinal Silíceo was
instated in 1545, the various festivities at Toledo were terminated
by a *danza de salvajes*, besides an exhibition by *seises*, the boy
dancers who then as now performed in Spanish churches.[51] The
introduction of wild men into secular festivities is attested by
Cervantes, in that chapter of his *Don Quixote* in which he describes
the opulent marriage of a rich Castilian peasant and the allegorical
masque which graced the occasion: to the wild men fell the minor
task of building the castle of love without participating in its ensuing
siege.[52]

In England there is a reference to *capita de woodewose* in a

masque of 1348, which suggests the existence there of a wild man's
disguise earlier than anywhere else in Europe, with the one exception of Italy.⁵³ It is possible that the introduction of the wild man's
disguise into France at the end of the fourteenth century, when it
sometimes replaced Hellekin may have been due to the English
influence that was strong and on the increase throughout the
period. After the years of the Black Death there is in England a
silence on the subject which lasts throughout the time of the Wars
of the Roses. When the wild man reappears, in the sixteenth century, he is there to stay for a long time; he passes from the royal
entries into the yearly Lord Mayor's Show in London and is given
his place in masques and civic processions.⁵⁴

The persistence of medieval traditions in a country where they
had lasted longer than elsewhere thus gave birth to a late flowering
of wild-man disguises. And since, when this Indian summer began,
the Renaissance had come to England, the wild man now found
himself surrounded by a host of Roman woodland divinities, sylvans,
satyrs, and fauns who posed as his relatives. The Twelfth-night
celebrations of 1515 for Henry VIII retained their medieval character: "Eight wyldemen, all apparayled in green mosse with
sleved sylke, with ugly weapons and terrible visages. . . there
foughte with eight knyghtes" and after long fighting the armed
knights had drawn "the wild men out of their places." In 1547
Valentine and Orson together welcomed the ill-fated boy Edward
VI on his coronation. But when Elizabeth came to Kenilworth in
1575, the cultural situation had changed. The wild man came out of
the wood appareled as of old in moss and ivy and bearing a small
oak plucked out by the roots. When he began, however, to address
the sovereign, he found it necessary to call upon "his familiarz and
companionz, the fawnz, satyres, nymphs, dryades and hamadry-
ades" to bear out his eulogy.⁵⁵ In the same period in France, at the
court masques for Henry IV and Louis XIII, the wild man had
altogether lost his position to fauns, satyrs, monkeys, and Pans.⁵⁶

In Italy, whence these changes came together with the Renaissance, the wild man was vigorous in the fifteenth century. He was
seen in Viterbo in 1462 at the festivals ordered by Pope Pius II and
appeared in Pesaro in 1475 at the marriage of Costanza Sforza to
Camillo d'Aragon. He helped in 1487 to celebrate the marriage in

Bologna of the local potentate Orazio Bentivoglio to Lucrezia d'Este. In Milan in 1491 he participated in a festivity arranged and directed by Leonardo da Vinci for Galeazzo San Severino.[57]

His demise in Italy began with the high Renaissance and its insistence upon a more literal and wholehearted return to the ancient divinities than the fifteenth century had regarded as necessary. In 1507, at the carnival at Belluno, the conquest of the love castle, a typical medieval pursuit, was undertaken by a swarm of satyrs, fauns, and other *selvaggi*, with the ancient woodland divinities obviously in the lead. And from then on, in carnivals and popular comedies, the wild man was reduced to rather minor parts. We find him, however, still dancing a *moresca* in the performance in 1506 of Castiglione's eclogue *Tirsi* in Urbino. His power of survival is attested by the fact that in 1616, at the entry of the Prince of Urbino into Florence, there appeared alongside the wagon of Thetis "eight giants in form of so many neptunes," large naked creatures, whose derivation from the ancient wild man is manifested by their apparel, wreaths of leaves around their loins and around their bearded heads. And, as if to make sure that their identity be not mistaken, the next wagon, whose astronomical company included Sol, Atlas, and the signs of the zodiac, was guarded by "eight Ethiopian giants" got up in the same way and armed with clubs and with bows and arrows. Together with the rest of the mummers the wild men were depicted in a series of etchings by Jacques Callot.[58]

A last radiance from the Italian carnival flickered up in the second part of Goethe's *Faust*, the first act of which is the finale of all Renaissance and Baroque pageantry. Along with many other maskers, allegorical or gallant, and embodying traditions from the most diverse quarters, the wild men appear, exuberant in their pristine strength:

> "The wild men of the woods" — their name,
> In the Hartz Mountains known to fame.
> In nature's nakedness and might,
> They come, each one of giant height,
> A fir-tree's trunk in each right hand,
> And 'round their loins a bulging band,
> Apron of twigs and leaves uncouth;
> Such guards the Pope has not, in truth.[59]

We have followed the wild men's masquerades into their remote historic ramifications. There remains the precarious task of tracing their origins. The creature whose checkered career we have attempted to trace has not always been known by the familiar terms of wild man, *homme sauvage*, or woodwose. The name is absent from the impersonations of the Wild Horde in the Baltic countries and in Switzerland as well as from most of southern Germany. In France, from the eleventh century onward, it is often replaced by that of Hellekin or Harlekin, the Germanic leader of the Wild Horde. We found, on the other hand, that the first wild-man play to be chronicled under its own proper name took place in the thirteenth century, while the vogue of wild-man dances did not come into its own before the second part of the fourteenth century.

The conclusion to be drawn from this array of dates would seem obvious: the belief in the Wild Horde and its impersonation by masked revelers must antedate the introduction of the forest-dwelling woodwose into it. We must assume that the latter had been an independent mythological figure, when his affinity with the "human" participants in the Wild Hunt allowed him to take their place in the festivities; and that, consequently, the ritual figure of the wild man, as it existed toward the end of the Middle Ages, owes its existence to a mythological convergence. We cannot go far astray when we surmise that the fusion between the two took place sometime in the thirteenth or fourteenth century.

Our final task will be, accordingly, to trace as well as the scanty material will allow the history of the fiery and shaggy demon of the winter nights, that mythological component in the personality of the wild man which was mainly responsible for turning him into a theatrical figure. This demon, whom we may call the leader of the Wild Horde, was at home in the Alps, whence the belief in him seems to have spread to southern Germany; and from a very early time onward he was known as Hellekin in medieval France and England. Nothing would be more natural, therefore, than to assume, as most folklorists have done, that in him we are beholding a native figure arisen out of the soil of Germanic paganism.

Yet the assumption is false. For the furry or shaggy demon occurs not only in central and western Europe, but also in present-day village festivities in Bulgaria, Rumania, and European Turkey, in Dalmatia, Montenegro, the north of Greece, on some of the Aegean islands, in Morocco, and in some instances even in Asia Minor. The mummers in question are usually dressed in fur, sometimes to the extent of having even their faces covered, with holes only for the eyes. They wear a wreath of bells around their waists. Their appearance is limited, as in central Europe, to the time of the Carnival or of Twelfth-night, unless it is to lend zest to a wedding. And as in the Germanic festivities the hairy men show themselves usually amidst an array of other figures, among them often a feminine mask, who acts as the hairy man's bride, a number of satiric masks, and animals.[60]

The relation of these disguises to those still practiced in and north of the Alps is thus beyond reasonable doubt, and this in spite of the fact that the program for these entertainments may be considerably more lavish than that undertaken anywhere in central Europe. In Morocco, where its pagan features are best preserved, the festival contains, among other things, a ritual of purification, the slaughtering of a sacrificial animal, whose fur the main actor then wears, and a coarse play performed by the hairy man and his mate with the assistance of numerous other players. In the Balkans the performance may take the form of a pageant or a play, the latter sometimes an extended popular drama, in which the hairy man named Kuker is killed, lamented by his wife, and finally resurrected, in what can only be judged as a spring ritual. Characteristically several of the plays, as performed in Bulgaria and European Turkey, involve even a ceremonial pulling of the plow, a sure sign that the securing of abundant crops is one of the chief purposes of the observance. How far, if at all, the motive of initiation into a secret group or society has contributed to the preservation of these rituals, I have been unable to find out.[61]

It is sure, at any rate, that the widespread distribution of these rituals — over the Balkans, Greece, Asia Minor, North Africa, Gaul, and southern Germany — is a key to their origin and age, for it cannot be a matter of chance that their geographic dispersion should coincide as it does with the limits of the Roman Empire. It is even possible to state with considerable confidence which were the centers from which these observances spread to the surrounding countryside, assuming, of course, that what are today backward agricultural superstitions were once ideas accepted in the great centers. A map of the rituals in question shows clearly that they are most vital and prolific in the European areas adjoining Constantinople, and that there are secondary centers near or at Salonika and on the Dalmatian coast.[62] If we add to this the consideration that the Alps can be regarded as the hinterland of late Roman centers such as Milan in Lombardy and Aquileia in Venezia, we arrive at a picture of the spreading of the carnival which involves a historic date. For Constantinople, Salonika, and the Italian towns in question flourished in the period of the Roman decline after Constantine and in the Byzantine period: a time in which, in spite of the prohibition of pagan cults under Theodosius, the ideas of paganism had by no means been driven underground and could boast a considerable popular following.

Now it is interesting to see how the writings of church fathers in the East as in the West, as well as the decisions of Eastern church councils, do indeed document the contemporary existence of pagan pageants which correspond in important details to the later festivals in the Balkans and central Europe. According to writers of the fifth to the eighth centuries it was customary in their time for pagans and lax Christians to celebrate the periods known today as Twelfth-night and Carnival by dressing up as animals, monsters of all kinds, old women, or demons, who in this period of lingering classical ideas bore the names of the chief pagan divinities of the recent past.[63] The wearing of animal fur was a general habit, as was the alternative of appearing in ragged cloth. With the furs animal masks were often worn, but these seem to have been discarded at times for human likenesses.

Caesarius, Bishop of Arles (d. 542), tells us that some of the mummers "clad themselves in the fur of their cattle, others put on the heads of animals." Other writers who preserved these facts for us are a Bishop of Ravenna, St. Peter Chrysologus (d. 450), and Maximus, Bishop of Turin, as well as the aforesaid Caesarius in Provence.[64] One would be tempted, therefore, to regard the custom as purely Western, were it not that in Constantinople the same pagan abuses persisted quite as tenaciously. The second Trullan Council of Constantinople in 692 decreed against the still continuing pagan carnivals; and as late as the first part of the tenth century the Byzantine emperor Constantine Porphyrogenitus observed that it was still customary in his time to celebrate Twelfth-night by revels in the streets which included a sword dance performed by men in masks and animal furs. Even "playing with the bear" was as germane to the East as it was to the West, as attested by the fact that the Trullane Council found it necessary to prohibit it. The one surviving artistic representation of the scene, which allows us to identify the bear on his chain unequivocally as a human being in fur and mask, is a relief from Tusla in Asia Minor, thirty miles southeast of Constantinople. It appears that if any part of an early bear cult survived into modern times, it must have been powerfully strengthened and modified by trends which emerged in late antiquity.[65]

The case is thus clear: the figure of the hairy or befringed man in the Carnival and Twelfth-night rituals, medieval and later, traces its origin back at least as far as the pagan pageants of early Christian times. Even though the history of these pageants is not sufficiently recorded to allow us to trace it through the centuries at any given locality, there is a general continuity of customs East and West which speaks for itself. It is possible that some of these festivities may have been due to a cultural transplantation from Byzantium to the dependent and barbarous West: the medieval "bear hunt" in Rome, for instance, with its attendant tournament and pageant, is so strongly reminiscent of Byzantine custom as described by Constantine Porphyrogenitus that one is led to suspect that, in this province of culture as in many others, the former capital had become dependent upon its more brilliant rival on the Bosporus. Similarly, the fact that in central Europe it is so often the butchers who are privileged to conduct the Carnival may have some historical connection with the corresponding liberty accorded to the same social group in Byzantium. Bear hunts and masquerades in the eastern Alps, such as those only recently observed in the Mur valley in lower Austria, may in some instances have more affinities with observances in the Balkans than with others further west.[66]

In most places, however, the continuity is likely to have been a local one, made possible by the firmness with which the rituals held their place in the yearly calendar. It would not seem to be entirely due to chance that the first wild-man play known under that name should have been held in Padua — not very far from Ravenna, whose pagan pageants had been castigated centuries before by St. Peter Chrysologus — and that neighboring Venice should have been the scene of a wild-man hunt. Similar continuities may have existed in many places; and even when the ritual would seem very barbarous and archaic, as in the case of the spring ceremonies in the Pyrenees, the likelihood is that we are beholding a crude rendition of pageants whose prototypes in neighboring centers may have long ago withered away.

At an early time the pagan pageants seem to have spread beyond the areas near the Mediterranean, where they had first been instituted, to regions further north. The burden of leading the battle against them, which had first weighed upon the shoulders of ecclesiastics in Lombardy and the south of France, was taken up by such northern dignitaries as St. Eloy of Noyon and Theodore of Canterbury in the seventh century, and, in the eleventh century, by Burchard of Worms.[67] It is true that the sort of thing these men wrote on the subject, like much early medieval literature, consists of almost literal excerpts from earlier authors and thus is rather a vehicle for the exhibition of scholarship than a document of contemporary mores. But they would hardly have taken up the cudgel had there not been some kindred local abuse worthy of their scorn. By the thirteenth century, at any rate, observances related to those with which we are concerned had spread to the very confines of the former Roman Empire, where they could hardly have been known in early Christian times.

A pageant conducted at Pentecost of 1224 in the Flemish town of Huy included not only the masks of emperor, king, duke and other dignitaries, but also of men dressed in fur for a sword dance. In the words of our witness, Albericus Trium Fontium: "Some were armed with harnesses and shining helmets, the furriers appeared with naked swords in hand and dressed in gray and fox furs with the hair to the outside; and all the others, as best they could, were adorned in the manner of women." [68] The celebration was very generally attended and our witness relates that all the masculine citizens of Huy participated, regardless of age. Similarly the celebration of Pentecost of Padua, of which the wild-man play was a part, brought out a large part of the population, "men and women, nobility and common folk, old people and young," united in joy, "as if they were all brothers, all fellows, all unanimous and linked by a chain of love." Apparently Christianity had at last absorbed the pagan festivities and permeated them with its distinctive spirit.

Festivities such as those held at Huy, occasions for popular revels and city-wide solidarity, bear little resemblance to the more sinister and exclusive performances limited to the winter nights, which are known to us as the Wild Horde or the Wild Hunt. At Huy there seems to have been little of the deadly and infernal urgency which was always connected with the Wild Horde. Nor was there, if our text does not deceive us, that mood of fear and terror stirred up by the threat against the safety of the majority which was held over it by the members of a secret society. Unlike the carnivals described, the onrush of the Wild Horde was a performance so insistently pagan that it was not possible to bring about its adaptation to a Christian society by the simple device of extending it to the community as a whole.

If we are to understand the rise of the Wild Hunt, we will have to assume that there was a new thrust of pagan forces instilling virulence into customs which otherwise would have been slowly neutralized. And it would seem probable that the incorporation into the Wild Horde of details similar to those exhibited in the pageant at Huy — hairy garments and military trappings — was due to a desire to adapt the demoniac dispensation to existing customs.

The history of this second pagan movement, which must have been naturalized in western Europe by the time of Odericus Vitalis in the twelfth century, is known only fragmentarily and opinions about it among scholars vary widely. It is possible that at first this movement brought with it neither disguises nor orgiastic rites, consisting as it did of a mere belief in periodic supernatural visitations.[69] The incarnation of the dead in the figures of masked and raving men may therefore have been a secondary development, and we should not be too surprised to find that the Wilde Horde, when brought down to earth, tended to embody itself in the figures of the traditional late-winter carnivals.

The Wild Horde itself was a complex phenomenon whose origins lose themselves partly in the prehistoric past. There was the assembly of ghosts under the leadership of a feminine divinity,

Hecate or Artemis in ancient Greece, Diana or Herodias, the mother of Salome, in the Latin West. This gathering of feminine spirits which later swelled into the crowd of evil hags at the witch sabbath was well known to theologians of the first millennium who in vain flung their anathema against it. The belief that there are "women who ride in the night upon animals with the goddess Diana and with Herodias and with innumerable women" was known to the author of the (apocryphal) Latin acts of the Council of Ancyra. Other attempts to lay the same specter and thus to defend the Christian community against the nocturnal incursions of the cursed Diana were made by the author of the *Vita Damasi Papae*, by Regino of Prüm, and by Burchard of Worms.[70]

As usual the effort was in vain. For as late as 1484 the Austrian Stephanus Lanzkranna reports in his "Hymmelsstrasse" about the exploits of the Demon Dyana, whom he identifies with Herodias and with the local demons *frawe Percht* and *frawe Holt*. Herodias herself rides to the present day with the Wilde Horde in large parts of Italy and in the eastern Alps. Nothing could testify more strongly to the defeat of ecclesiastic prohibitions by native thought than the fact that ritual performances meant to embody the ghosts of the defunct — a feature not mentioned by writers for the first millennium — have survived over a large part of the eastern Alps under the name of the Percht, a feminine demon in whom the spirit of the Carnival is incarnated. Local opinion informs us that she is to be identified with the wild woman.[71]

The belief in the masculine Wild Horde, which disputes with its feminine counterpart the dominance over central Europe, is usually regarded as of Germanic origin and thus as prior to any influence from the Mediterranean world: whether rightly so it is hard to say, since the history of the motive previous to its first explicit appearance in the chronicle by Odericus Vitalis can only be inferred from philological evidence. Suffice it to say that, in the Alps at least, where the two traditions meet face to face, the leadership of the Wild Horde is accorded almost as often to the wild man, a figure of the local mythology, as it is to the demonic leader of the Wild Horde. It is the wild man for instance, who is believed in Carinthia to be accompanying the Percht in her rapid procession and who at times may be allowed to monopolize her place. It is possible or at least worth considering that the wild man as demon of death may be hidden behind the various figures of the Germanic leaders of the Wild Horde, and that what now looks like the encounter of two rival traditions in central Europe was in reality the birth of a Germanic motive out of its Mediterranean counterpart. If there is any answer to this question — and there may not be — it will have to come out of a pooling of all relevant history, folklore, and philology on a scale such as has not yet been undertaken.

There remains the question about the origin of the Byzantine observances whose fusion with the Wild Horde gave rise to the later European festivities. It is evident enough that the time when these revels were held, Twelfth-night and the period of the Carnival, links them with two classical Roman dates for New Year's Day. The older date, March first, originally meant to mark the beginning of spring, was moved backward into February to adjust it to the exigencies of the Christian year, more particularly to the beginning of Lent. The more recent date, January first, introduced by the Romans in order to have the first day of the year coincide with the accession to office of new political appointees, came between the Christian festivals of Christmas and Epiphany. In both instances the rites originally marking the beginning of spring were retained in the form of observances, merrymaking, and the offering of gifts. Also, on January second there were masquerades and races.

While it is impossible to make out anything about the costumes and masks worn at that time of the year, there is one Roman custom which we must mention although its calendar date was March fourteenth rather than March first: on that day a man dressed in furs was led through the city, beaten, and finally chased out of town, presumably into enemy territory. He was called Mamurius Veturius, the old Mars; his expulsion is best interpreted as the abolition of the old year and of its dying winter season, and thus as a ceremony of the same kind as the killing of the carnival bear and of the wild man. The somewhat surprising date for the ceremony, the fourteenth instead of the first, has been explained as a survival of an ancient lunar calendar and thus seems to testify to the high age of the performance in question.[72]

And now it is interesting to note that at the same date when these so-called Mamuralia were celebrated, there took place a second festivity in honor of what seems to have been a feminine impersonation of the year, Anna Perenna. Ovid has left us a charming account of this celebration: amorous couples, apparently of the lower classes, used to assemble on the banks of the Tiber river, to build themselves light huts of foliage and twigs and then to sing and dance and drink to their heart's delight. The mythological reason given by Ovid for these lighthearted revels was that on that date the goddess Anna had played a successful prank on Mars, putting her own aged body in the place of that of the goddess Minerva whose favor he had hoped to obtain with her help. It would seem fitting that as the representative of the passing year she should be conceived as aged. What interests us is the fact that the two together — the man in furs and the shriveled hag — form the same couple that appears in the spring Carnival in the Balkans and in central Europe. We are tempted to believe that in these twin Roman festivals we behold one of the remote sources of origin of later medieval masquerades.[73]

Before leaving the subject of this chapter, we will have to attend to the sartorial question of transforming an ordinary mortal into his wild counterpart. The modern wild-man dances still performed in peasant communities such as Oberstdorf in Germany are carried out by men dressed in lichen, brushwood, or hay, so that the whole body is covered and only abrupt, uncouth movements are possible. This guise is completed by a wooden mask of generally ugly and frightening countenance. The age of this method of disguise is attested by Pieter Brueghel's picture of the battle of Carnival and Lent in which the wild man appears dressed all in green. Since he is a woodland creature, such a reminiscence of the garb of fertility divinities seems adequate enough.

It is certain however that such costumes are not the oldest with which European communities fitted out the wild man, for in medieval documents he is shown dressed not in vegetable matter, but in fur. He is thus described in Chrétien de Troyes' "Yvain" and in the free translation of the epic by Hartmann von Aue; [74] and we have seen how the equivocation of wild man and bear was caused by the furriness of both. Most medieval artists, from the very inception of the conventional wild-man representations in the second part of the thirteenth century, rendered him as a person closely wrapped in fur, rather than greenery.

The conventional wild man is often shown with his knees and elbows free from the fur that covers the rest of his body; the wild woman bares her breasts.* Assuming that these representations dealt with the wild man not as freely imagined, but as observed in dances and pageants, the artist would have seen or realized that such active performance might require cutting holes into the animal fleeces at the places corresponding to human joints; otherwise the performers, pressed and sewed into close-fitting skins, would hardly have been able to budge, much less to jump and bound as their roles demanded. The exhibition of the women's breasts may have been in imitation of wood damsels. Evidently plays and dances set the rule for the representation of the wild man in art; the preëminence of these rituals in the Middle Ages could not be better illustrated than by this fact.

As in modern times the performers wore masks which we have to imagine as ugly as possible, for our sources comment frequently on how ghastly they were, calling them *terrible visages* or *orrende in viso e spaventevole*, "faces horrible and frightful to behold." [75] We find them well rendered in the illustrations to the "Roman de Fauvel" and, at a stage much further removed from their original frightfulness, in the Nuremberg Schembart books.† These masks, like the demon disguises among primitive people, were a congenital part of the cult and could not be doffed without endangering its validity. It is a sign, therefore, of the transformation of the ritual into a sophisticated pastime that at some of the court dances held toward the end of the Middle Ages the masks seem to have disappeared. The Bal des Ardents, if we are to believe the visual commentary by some of the miniaturists who illustrated the chronicles of Froissart, was still executed in costume and facial mask,‡ whose presence caused the fatal gesture — holding out a torch for identification.[76] When we come, however, to the fifteenth-century tapestry at Saumur, we find that the faces of the revelers are freely shown.§

It may also be a sign of deterioration in the religious signifi-

* Figs. 15, 30.   † Figs. 15, 18.   ‡ Fig. 23.   § Fig. 19.

cance of the ritual that occasionally the fur covering was abandoned and other materials substituted. In Boccaccio's story the wild man, while correctly fitted out with mask, cudgel, and chain, is provided only with a workable imitation of a wild man's costume, consisting of feathers plastered on to his body with honey; and in the context this seems feasible enough, for the disguise is an improvised one and the wild-man hunt supposed to take place in the Piazza San Marco is only a pretence and instrument for an act of revenge. Costumes similarly contrived were worn, however, as late as the nineteenth century at carnivals in the Hérault, the Aude, and the Lauragais districts of France.[77] And sometimes, as one may very well imagine, the feathers came to be attributes of savages from foreign lands such as American Indians. The "wild man" in the carnival at Bar-sur-Aube, a creature pretending to feed only on raw meat and distinguished by the presence of a crown on his head and of feathers around his loins, is much more like the savages from distant isles and continents than like the native man of the woods.[78] One may regard him as a relative of Papageno, the bird man in Mozart's *Magic Flute*.

More frequent than the replacement of the fur by feathers was the use of close-fitting tights and bodices covered with little bits of colored rags or flax to simulate tufts. We have a precise description of the manner in which such garments were made in Froissart's account of the preparations for the Bal des Ardents: a thin undergarment was cut to measure, rubbed with pitch, and then strewn with ample amounts of flax, to give the impression of hair; into this garment the mummer had to force his body and then be sewed in.[79] One advantage of this method was that one could give to the tufts whatever color was desired, instead of that naturally possessed by animal skins — an aesthetic improvement that could be appreciated wherever the wild man's dance had passed out of the jurisdiction of pagan cult societies. The wild men who performed their revels in Basel in 1435 wore green and red tufts; and the wild men and women rendered on the Swiss tapestries of the same period wore fluff of any color that might enhance the rich and gay effect of the whole.*

The final outcome of this development may be anticipated: the

* Figs. 34, 41, 42.

sartorial tradition of the wild man and his demoniac relatives and associates was inherited by the Harlequin of the modern stage, who is no other than the funny devil Herlekin acclimatized to a baroque environment.[80] His costume consists of multicolored rags sewn to a close-fitting garment; on the attire worn today, which dates back to the eighteenth century, these rags were systematized into interlocking triangular or lozenge-shaped patches, but the original Harlequin of the seventeenth century wore them at random, in a manner similar to a wild demon's garb. It is in the Harlequin's disguise of our ballets and carnival entertainments that a last fleeting visual memory of the wild man and the Wild Horde survives into the cultural milieu of the present day.

4

The Learned

Aspect

We have presented the history of the wild man as if the Middle Ages had been only a time of lingering folkways and persisting pagan beliefs. But the Middle Ages was also a period of diligent encyclopedic scholarship and reverent preservation of traditions from classical antiquity. Unless we give heed to what was known from books, as well as to native customs and ideas, we will have drawn a very onesided picture of wild-man lore.

We will have to find out what the Middle Ages knew of legends from the Mediterranean past and then gauge the influence of these upon folklore, art, and imaginative literature: a task of whose hazards we are aware, since it is very difficult at this distance to know how far the lore of the bookmen penetrated into popular consciousness and how it was transformed as it left the scholar's study. It is likely that the knowledge preserved by clerks and the beliefs held by the multitude were often regarded as either unrelated or antagonistic.

Classical antiquity like the Middle Ages, had its wild men, creatures whose manner of life was incompatible with civilization and who were relegated therefore to uninhabited places or to positions distant in space and time. They were regarded as demons if their habitat was close by, as representatives of fabulous races if they resided in faraway countries, and as specimens of prehistoric man if they were believed to have died out in the distant past. However far apart in space and time, all these wild men have one thing in common which links them with their relatives in medieval folklore: their bodies are naked and in many instances covered with a dense growth of hair.

The existence of such creatures was assumed in Greek literature from its very beginning, for appearance and manner of life mark the Cyclopes and their leader Polyphemus, in the *Odyssey*, as a giant breed of sheep-tending wild men. It was Herodotus who, first among known writers, localized the wild men in a well-defined but distant geographical area, thus inaugurating a custom of billeting them in faraway quarters that was to last for two millenniums. His wild men and women inhabit western Libia in company with great snakes, lions, and human monsters with dog heads or with eyes in their chests — associates that were to remain with them throughout the rest of their literary history. Who or what these wild people were it is impossible to say, given the shortness of Herodotus' statement, which is obviously based on hearsay rather than his own travel observations. The likelihood is that he meant to refer to members of a savage tribe, such as may very well have inhabited parts of Libia or Tunisia in his time, if indeed the creatures are not altogether as fictitious as their monstrous company.[1]

After Herodotus the localization of the distant wild men underwent a sudden and drastic redirection, for not long after his death a book on India was published by Ctesias, who as former royal physician at the Persian court had had opportunity to study Asiatic lore at the source.[2] Upon this first glimpse of Eastern marvels there followed the conquests of Alexander, which brought India for a short period into the orbit of Greek political and cultural interest. The result was that from then on India was the chief receptacle of fantastic geographical lore, a no man's land of the imagination, said to be swarming with cynocephali, headless men, people with ears so large that they could sleep in them, giants, and satyrs. And since for a long time after that few Westerners had the opportunity to study the fabulous country on the spot, these stories throve and lasted, to be repressed only when the combined impact of the age of discovery and the critical method of science had changed the tenor of European thought. It is doubtful whether a close acquaintance with India before the introduction of the scientific method would have changed matters very much, since many of the figments about fabulous races seem to be derived from genuine Indian traditions transmitted to Greek visitors and by them frequently misunderstood.[3]

Ctesias' account of India was amplified in the third century B.C. by Megasthenes — ambassador of Seleucus Nicator to the court of the Indian king Chandragupta — who listed among the creatures living in India a monster with its heels in front and its instep and toes turned backward. The wild man, as he is expressly called, was caught and brought to court, where he refused to take food and died in captivity. Also wild, according to Megasthenes, was a race of forest people afflicted with the strange deficiency of being unable to take in food, having no mouths, and subsisting rather poetically by the smell of roast meat, fruit, and flowers.[4] *

Other statements, on the basis of somewhat sounder observation, were put down by historians of the conquests of Alexander and repeated by Roman collectors of facts and oddities. According to Pliny there existed in India a race of so-called Choromandi named *silvestres*, that is wild, creatures possessed of hairy bodies, yellow eyes, and canine teeth, who were incapable of speech and could let out only horrible shrieks.[5] These creatures may not have been altogether fabulous, since their description fits a large monkey such as the eastern gibbon.[6] It seems to be generally true that whatever little was known in antiquity about the large anthropoid apes did not suffice to identify them as animals, so that they were usually described as hairy, speechless humans and thus, by implication, as wild men. Pomponius Mela, Latin geographer of the first century A.D., repeated the ancient account by Hanno, a Carthaginian explorer, of how he discovered what appear to have been gorillas in the equatorial region of Sierra Leone; the females, which were killed and flayed, he called hairy women. And Pliny, identifying them with other creatures whom Mela mentions in the same context, is convinced that what Hanno saw were altogether demons, namely the ugly Gorgons of ancient Greek mythology. Before this, in the second century B.C., Agatharchides had described in his book

* Fig. 17.

on the Red Sea what may have been chimpanzees, calling them tribes of Ethiopian seed-eaters and wood-eaters. They are identified as monkeys only through their great agility of body, their promiscuity, and their dexterity in using both hands and feet when climbing through the trees.[7]

To return to the story of Alexander, the historians Arrian and Curtius Rufus insist that he met at least one savage tribe, the fisheaters, inhabitants, it would seem, of the coast of Baluchistan or northern India, who were clad only in animal skins and ate their catch after merely drying it in the sun. Curtius Rufus relates that these creatures, having for long had no intercourse with neighbors, had become quite squalid in their habits, appearing with nails grown long and hair shaggy and unshorn. Later, when the story of Alexander had developed into a collection of fantastic tales, these "Ichthyophagi" were often relegated to the bottom of the sea, where Alexander, in a transparent diving bell, could inspect them along with other creatures of the deep. They are thus shown in a miniature of the fourteenth century in Brussels,* where they appear naked and hairy, intent upon devouring the fish they have just caught. Alexander himself sits enthroned in his glass barrel surrounded by fish and sea monsters including huge leviathan himself; while, far above, two men in a boat hold the ropes which connect his diving bell with the upper world.[8]

It was not, however, the legitimate historians who contributed most to the expanding lore of the Indian wild men, but the fantastic compilation known as the "Alexander Romance" and in it the spurious letter of Alexander to his mother Olympias and his teacher Aristotle. Here we are told how Alexander, in his search for the fountain of life, traversed a dark and dangerous area that teemed with monstrous creatures: a reminiscence, it would seem, of similar quests and perils in earlier Oriental literature. Among the human monsters encountered were giant-sized humans with hands and feet like saws; other giants with lion heads, hairy bodies, and red scalps; and a creature, bristly as a pig, which, when caught and given a woman for its enjoyment, carried her away and proceeded to eat her. When set upon again, the creature let out a shriek, whereupon its fellows appeared on all sides, barking like dogs as they attacked

* Fig. 21.

the Greek soldiers. It requires little persuasion to convince ourselves that the prototype of this imaginary wild man was not human, but an ape. Alexander's letter to Olympias and Aristotle contains also a description of the men with eyes in their chests; like regular wild men they were now said to be furry, a characteristic they retained for many centuries.[9]

It cannot be our task here to follow the Alexander traditions in their long and intricate course through the medieval literature of East and West. Suffice it to say that in the European Middle Ages the contents of the romance were regarded as real history, since it was believed to have been written by Callisthenes, one of the historians who had accompanied Alexander; consequently, the tales of wild and monstrous races took on an air of authenticity which caused them to be repeated almost literally. It was this reputed authenticity which enabled the fabulous races to enter into world histories and encyclopedias as well as into medieval accounts of contemporary Eastern history; and the same firm belief, that these fabulous races did really inhabit the legendary East, caused great travelers of the late Middle Ages, from the Dominican and Franciscan monks of the thirteenth century to Columbus, actually to find some of them in the countries they visited and to describe them with complete conviction and sincerity.[10]

To modern readers the chapters in medieval books dealing with fabulous races are as monotonous as they are absurd, for the belief in the scientific truth of Alexander's letter to his teacher and mother kept the guardians of this heritage from using their imagination to tamper with it. There were, however, some modifications in the tales of the Indian wild man, most of them tending to bring him closer to his indigenous medieval counterpart. In the tenth-century "Historia de proeliis," by Archpresbyter Leo, the most influential of medieval Latin versions of the romance, the monkey with the fur like a pig's is called *magnus homo agrestis*, a large wild man; and in the same version the Indian giants have become vegetarian wild men, *homines agrestes*, who live on fruits from the trees in a dense forest which is their habitat.[11]

In later versions of the Alexander story, Latin and vernacular, the epithet "wild man" is even more liberally applied, even to human beings of definitely monstrous aspect.[12] The wild woman also

makes her appearance, huge and bristly and forbidding, and practicing her familiar vice of devouring humans; like her medieval
sister she is so ugly as to be staggering, for she has the teeth of a
wild boar, a long tail, and a covering of "fur" like an ostrich or a
camel.[13] The writers of the romance seem to have lifted her from
the spurious "Letter of Fermes to Hadrian," itself an early medieval
compilation of the fourth century.[14] Even the marine wild men
occur in a late version of the romance as "nude men and women
whose whole body was furry like that of animals and whose habit
it was to live in the river and on land." [15] While these amphibious
creatures are probably remote descendants of the fish-eaters of
Baluchistan, the manner of life attributed to them is even more
reminiscent of the sirens and aquatic wild men in native medieval
romance. There was thus a gradual approximation of native and
Greco-Roman traditions about wild men.

The Alexander saga was, however, not the only vehicle for the
transmission of legends about Indian wild men from antiquity to
the Middle Ages, for its historical information was supplemented
and confirmed by the more properly geographical lore of the Roman encyclopedists. Both Pliny and Solinus have their say about
the fabulous men of the East, whose improbable attributes they
accept without a flicker of criticism. And from their widely read
writings the information passed to Martianus Capella, writing in
northern Africa in the fifth century, and to the fact-devouring
pantologists of the early Middle Ages: to Isidore of Seville (seventh
century), Rabanus Maurus (ninth century), and Honorius of
Autun (early twelfth century). Their miscellaneous collections
served in turn as sources of supply for the more ambitious and more
systematic scholars of the twelfth and thirteenth centuries.[16]

The information about wild men that was passed on through
these channels was substantially the same as that contained in the
Alexander manuscripts, although in some of the later encyclopedias
it was carried separately: in the work of Vincent of Beauvais the
fabulous human beings appear twice, once in the systematic exposition of God's creation in the "Mirror of Nature," and another
time among the adventures of Alexander the Great in the "Mirror
of History."

The unique interest of the encyclopedic tradition lies in the fact that the encyclopedic treatises seem to have been originally supplemented by miniatures, the nature of which it is still possible to reconstruct with a small measure of certainty from copies still extant. Illustrations in a manuscript of Rabanus Maurus of about the year 1000, formerly at Monte Cassino, seem to repeat in much deteriorated form earlier illustrations for the writings of Isidore, and perhaps through them a still older prototype. Unfortunately, the quality of the illustrations is so low, their manner of execution so infantile, that it is difficult to learn anything of real significance about the manner in which Indian wild men might have been drawn in antiquity. All that one can say is that they appear in the miniatures as naked, upright, and without fur.[17] Another series of illustrations, also based upon much older prototypes, is to be found in three English manuscripts of the late tenth to the twelfth centuries reproducing the "Letter by Fermes to Hadrian" under the name of "Marvels of the East." [18] Here the wild men are clearly rendered. The fish-eaters appear as repulsive naked giants with long beards and hair that falls to the ground, and the huge men who devour human beings are shown ghoulishly bent over their prey and exposing bristly spines and arms.[19] *

When these pictures were drawn, the image of the conventional wild man with his overall covering of fur had not yet been created. They represent, therefore, an early stage in wild-man iconography and may help us discern the creature in other phases of pre-Gothic art. Wherever in Romanesque art we find representations of naked giants without a narrative context to justify their presence, there is the possibility that wild men are meant to be rendered. An excellent example from the early years of the eleventh century is carved on a capital in the crypt of St. Aignan in Orléans,* showing the ungainly bearded creature surrounded by two ferocious animals, his wards.[20] Although the composition is derived from the well-worn theme of Daniel between the lions, the nakedness of the human figure together with his long unkempt beard make it unlikely that the Biblical scene is intended. A similar creature, dressed in a short fur and with a fish and a bowl in his hands, is to be found on one of the capitals in the crypt of Canterbury Cathedral, and may be

* Fig. 20.   * Fig. 22.

interpreted as one of the Ichthyophagi from the "Romance of Alexander." [21]

Later, when the conventional wild-man type was established, the fabulous creatures were usually made to conform with it. In the famous *Livre des merveilles* of the Bibliothèque Nationale in Paris, a composite volume of the early fifteenth century containing among others the travel accounts of Marco Polo and the apocryphal Mandeville, the giants and the people living by the smell of fruit are rendered as conventional wild men,* the satyrs as wild men with horns; while the giant man-eaters have no fur, they carry the wild man's weapon, the club.[22] Similarly, in the Alexander manuscripts the various hairy creatures of the romance are usually portrayed as conventional wild men.[23]

We may conclude this short survey of the European view of the wild man in Asia by stating that the Middle Ages had the dubitable luck of finding his existence confirmed by what to all appearances was a contemporary document. In 1164 Prester John, ruler over a fabulous realm in the East, wrote a letter to the Byzantine emperor, Manuel Comnenus, describing himself as a Christian and his Asiatic empire as a region of unimaginable wealth including all the fabulous races and even the terrestrial paradise of Christian tradition. We know of course today that this letter was spurious; it may have been intended to describe a political Utopia. To contemporaries, however, and for several centuries after, Prester John was a historical reality, a man to whom embassies could be sent and whose help could be counted on in the fight against the Saracen infidel. When in the thirteenth century Genghis Khan with his Mongols broke upon the world, it was rumored either that they were the army of Prester John or that the Khan had gained his power from overrunning Prester John's territory.[24]

It is likely that unquestioning acceptance of this fictitious letter was facilitated by the list it contained of fabulous races of whose existence one was sure, for it included centaurs, fauns, satyrs, satyresses, pygmies, cynocephali, cyclopes, giants, and, furthermore, our familiar *homines agrestes*, the wild men.

It was impossible, at any rate, even for the most critical minds to discount the stories about the Asiatic wild men, once such con-

* Fig. 17.

temporary evidence had been provided. Even a man like Roger Bacon, one of the most "realistic" thinkers (in the modern sense) of the thirteenth century, fell a prey to them. In his *Opus majus* he starts his discussion of India and Central Asia with an account of Prester John, from there swings to the history of Genghis Khan, and ventures some quite correct information on Tibet and China on the basis of recent travel accounts. What follows, however, is a piece of undisguised mythology, for he tells us that in the high rocks (the mountains of Central Asia?) there lives a hairy creature of human form, but of ape-like behavior, whom the native hunters overcome by the device of intoxicating him; it is the old story of the capture of Silenus by the Greeks or of the wild man by the Swiss woodsmen, but now transplanted into an exotic environment.[25]

That even the travelers themselves were not immune from the belief in the Asiatic wild man or at least from pretending to believe in him, is shown in a curious little book dated 1590 by an English adventurer, Edward Webbe, who visited parts of the Near East and Russia and was bemused enough, after such preparation, to give detailed accounts of the court of Prester John. He pretends to have seen with his own eyes that there — as well as at the sultan's residence in Constantinople — a wild man was kept chained to a post to hinder him from devouring human flesh, except what he was given on days after capital executions.[26]

It could even happen that a man who had been in faraway lands would try to attract interest and to fill his pocket by posing as a wild man. According to a story from the sixteenth century by Garcilaso de la Vega, a certain Pedro Serrano claimed to have grown fur all over his body, after having been shipwrecked upon an island and spending a long time there in complete isolation. Upon his return to Europe he traveled from Spain to Germany to show his hairy body to the emperor, to retell the story of his privations and, undoubtedly, to cash in on his physical abnormality.[27]

Passing from the distant wild men of Asia to those close by, we find that to the Greeks and Romans these native creatures were no other than the demons of lower mythology, the centaurs, satyrs, and Pan, the fauns and sylvans and Silenus. That these are akin to

the medieval wild men, having perhaps a very ancient prehistory
in common as well as later historic connections, is demonstrated by
a great number of traits, chief of which is the fact that they are
all woodland divinities, most of them lords of the forest and protec-
tors of its animals. Like the medieval wild man the centaurs wield
huge clubs and tree trunks as weapons. The uprooted tree is an
attribute also of Silvanus, who, however, as the lord of gardens,
prefers to be seen not with a giant trunk in his hands, but with a
small cypress sapling which he is about to transplant. Even the
physical appearance of these woodland demons may come near
to that of the wild man, since the part-animal aspect under which
several of them are known is not always retained. Instead of horse
legs and tail the satyr may show only a sensual face and low fore-
head, and he may even be without this reminder of his bestial
nature, when a great Hellenistic sculptor like the one who created
the Barberini Satyr in Munich is given the task of portraying him.
Faunus, usually horned and goat-legged like Pan, may only wear
an animal skin over his human limbs.[28]

The closest relative of the wild man in antiquity is Silenus,
god of the wooded mountainside, who is portrayed in one very
ancient monument carrying an uprooted tree as a weapon against
ferocious animals.[29] While he was soon to give up this manner of
displaying his supernatural strength, Silenus remained riotous and
indomitable, thus deserving the attribute of bestial hairiness accorded to him by painters of Greek vases and again by some of the
sculptors of the Roman imperial age.[30] Since Silenus, like the wild
man, was expected to appear in plays, the alternative to rendering
him as befringed and shaggy lay in showing him in his stage costume, a close-fitting garment with glued-on tufts imitating animal
fur.

To give an adequate description of the survival of the Greco-
Roman woodland divinities into the Middle Ages is impossible, for
unlike the Olympian divinities, who were preserved mainly as
dried-out specimens in the collections of mythographers and encyclopedists, these humbler creatures had a chance to remain alive
among the peasantry and in the yearly calendar of agricultural
festivities, subsisting so unobtrusively that their history has not been
recorded. Only the final results of survival, in the form of a few

specimens of nomenclature and of mythology, are available to us today.

It is fortunate for our sense of continuity that in the learned world of the Middle Ages, whose history we can trace in its products, the satyrs and fauns fared no less well than among the peasants, for they survived not only in encyclopedias and bestiaries, but also in the minds of those lovers of the Roman poets who found pleasure in copying their manuscripts, writing glosses upon them, and trying their own pens at poetic composition in the ancient vein. There was no period in the Middle Ages when the ancient woodland divinities could have been entirely forgotten. And when, in the twelfth century, the general revival of learning brought a heightened interest in ancient lore, it was natural that the satyrs and fauns should profit from it. They sprang into full-blown existence once more, swinging the thyrsus with their ancient bestial energy. In the accented, dancing rhythms of "Phyllis and Flora" in the *Carmina Burana*:

> Fauni, Nymphe Satyri
> Comitatus multus
> Tympanicant, concinunt
> Ante dei vultus
> Portant thyma manibus
> Et coronas florum
> Bacchus Nymphas instruit
> Et choros Faunorum
> Servant pedum ordines
> Et instrumentorum
> Sed Silenus titubat
> Et salit in chorum [31]

Revivals such as this show not only an antiquary's interest in the ancient divinities, but a sense of their pulsating life, possible perhaps only among persons who, like the goliards, were ready to cut themselves off from the benefits of Christian society to devote themselves to the gay and dangerous pastime of resuscitating the ancient past.[32]

What they did in words was accomplished in stone by masons who, like them, had studied genuine remains of classical antiquity. A very lively and credible satyr stalks through the scrolls of a capital of the early twelfth century now in the Musée des Augustins in Toulouse, and on a capital in St. Paul de Varax in Burgundy a correctly rendered faun shows to St. Anthony the way to his hoary brother hermit, St. Paul. In the thirteenth century, finally, the notion of the satyr had become so much popular property that the illuminators began to play with the satyr's mask, inserting it irresponsibly into almost any part of the haphazard creatures of drollery with which they enlivened and ornamented the margins of manuscripts.[33]

It would seem most likely that even the image of the conventional wild man, as it appears in art shortly after the middle of the thirteenth century, may owe its appearance to an *exemplum* from antiquity. We saw how close the hairy type of Silenus was to that of the medieval wild man, who differs from him only by being usually without a tail. It would have been in keeping with all that we know of the artistic methods of the thirteenth century, and the derivation of its drollery from ancient prototypes, for its artists, in order to illustrate a somewhat comical offshoot of native thought, to turn to classical antiquity as the only repertory of models on which they could draw in giving visible shape to the unformed and incongruous.

The most important of the references upon which the Middle Ages relied for their idea of the ancient woodland divinities were found, however, neither in art nor in the Roman poets, but in quotations from the Latin Bible. St. Jerome, in his translation from the Hebrew, had found it feasible to render a word of Isaiah's, regarding the demons who upon the realization of Jahveh's wrath would roam through the deserted ruins of Palestine, as *et pilosi saltabunt ibi*, "and the hairy ones will dance there." [34] Again, in interpreting a similar prediction by Isaiah of the desolation that would reign in the palaces of Edom, Jerome had translated it as *et pilosus clamabit at alterum*, "and one hairy creature will shout to the other." [35] The Hebrew term corresponding to Jerome's *pilosi* was *se'irim*, a word from the lower reaches of Jewish folklore denoting a demon,[36] of which not much more is known than what is implied in Jerome's text; apparently it is a hairy monster inhabiting deserted places. Presumably *se'irim*, like Silenus and the wild men, were demons of the mountains, in which form they survived into modern

Arabic superstition. Like other Palestinian demons they seem to have been propitiated by sacrifices.

To Jerome the term *pilosi* was fraught not only with Hebrew but also with Greco-Roman connotations. He says, in his commentary on Isaiah: "When in the following it is said that 'the hairy ones will dance here' we must understand this to mean either incubi or satyrs or a certain kind of wild men whom some call *fatui ficarii* and regard as of the nature of demons." [37] In explanation of this may it be said that *fatui ficarii* were satyrs known for their insatiable lasciviousness and thus closely akin to incubi, the professional ravishers of mortal women. To St. Jerome all these creatures were unclean spirits and their sexual proclivities only an exaggeration of that pagan immorality which he condemned on all counts. No wonder, therefore, that his description, like those of other church fathers, tended to lay stress upon the phallic character of vegetation demons that formerly had had wider scope for their activities. In the same spirit as St. Jerome, St. Augustine in his *City of God* brackets fauns and sylvans together as incubi, and then proceeds to explain that both "desire women and act carnally with them." [38]

As far as satyrs and fauns were concerned, the effect of the Vulgate translation upon the Middle Ages was a double one: it tended to make writers subsume all woodland divinities under a common denominator, their hairiness; and it tended to make the creatures appear as incubi, ravishers of women, thus lending Christian authority to a thriving popular superstition. Both tendencies left their imprint upon later literature, making it possible for Isidore of Seville to speak of *pilosi qui Graece Panita Latine Incubi appellantur*, "hairy ones called Pans in Greek and Incubi in Latin," and to comment at length on their sexual behavior; or making it legitimate for the so-called "second mythographer" to introduce the fauns as *qui vulgo incubi vel pilosi appellati sunt*, creatures "ordinarily known as incubi or the hairy ones"; apparently at the time when these words were written the new nomenclature had all but replaced the names of the ancient divinities.[39]

Finally Jerome's translation and commentary made possible such treatment of the matter as was given by Bartholomaeus Anglicus in his *De proprietatibus rerum*, an encyclopedic work written about 1230–1250, in the heyday of medieval scholarship. Here, in the chapter on fauns and satyrs, we hear that the *fauni* are no other than *homines silvestres*, wild men, a statement made similarly by Isidore of Seville; [40] and in the chapter *de ficario* the burden of the none too clear argument is that the *ficarii* are the same as wild men, fauns, and satyrs, and that they are in practice identical even with centaurs (*onocentauri*) and other monstrosities. [41] It would appear that in the thirteenth century the differences between the various ancient woodland divinities tended to be blotted out.

In parenthesis we must note that these various identifications, reminiscent of ancient syncretism in its most tolerant and cosmopolitan mood, were expanded further by authors of glosses seeking synonyms in the Germanic languages for the ancient terms. We saw already, on a former occasion, that *pilosus, incubus, faunus,* and *satyrus* became *Schrat* in ancient High German; correspondingly, *wudewasan* stands for the same combination of terms in Middle English glosses. When Wycliffe set out to render Jerome's Vulgate into his native tongue, he found *wodewose*, that is, wild man, to be the most suggestive equivalent for Jerome's *pilosi*. The same situation in reverse arose, of course, when Latin writers attempted to describe in their language the native Germanic cults. It is hardly necessary to point out that the Warasi, a pagan tribe akin to the Baiuwarii (Bavarians), did not really worship "fauns," as the seventh-century legend of St. Eustace asserts, but some other woodland divinity, perhaps identical with the wild man. And in the same way Burchard of Worms merely revealed his linguistic embarrassment when he used the phrase *satyri vel pilosi* for the diminutive house sprites to whom his contemporaries gave little toys and shoes as a gesture of good will. [42]

Although these lexicographical oddities could hardly have had significant effects upon medieval life, there is some evidence that the literate part of the population was apt to think in terms rather similar to those suggested by encyclopedists and writers of glosses. To revert to matters of more vital concern, we find the identity of satyr and wild man connected with crucial phenomena in the history of medieval literature.

The scene is the forest of Brocéliande in Brittany, the enchanted habitat of fairies and wild beasts and favorite of Arthurian poets since the times of Chrétien de Troyes. It will be remembered that

Chrétien in his "Yvain" describes the wild man who lives in the glades of Brocéliande as a huge creature, the only one of his species, who sits on a stump as he keeps watch over the wild animals. It would be unbearable to think of him in the plural, overpowering as he is in his size and ugliness. At variance with Chrétien is the twelfth-century poet Wace, in his "Roman de Rou"; he knows of villeins — that is, a group of wild men — who were once inhabitants of Brocéliande, but they deserted it before his time.[43] The same creatures, whom we may imagine sliding quietly through the glades, occur once more in Walter of Metz's popular encyclopedia, the *Image du Monde*, in the thirteenth century, again as inhabitants of Brocéliande, but now they have tails, like satyrs or fauns, reminding the author that

> Si ra l'eu en France veu
> Un gent qui furent cornu

— "people were seen in France who had horns." [44]

The final outcome is that the wild man himself is given the traits of a satyr. We find ourselves once more in the green glades of Brocéliande and notice a young damsel, who has lost her way on her return from the market and, surprised by dusk, has gone to sleep under a tree. A wild man appears and ravishes her. And we learn later that a child has been born out of this union, himself endowed with many traits of the wild man. He is no other than the magician and bard, Merlin. This is the story of Merlin's birth in "Lestoire de Merlin," written in the thirteenth century. It is interesting to note that preceding this late version of Merlin's birth there is the other in the *Historia regum Britanniae* by Geoffrey of Monmouth (about 1137), in which his father is an incubus — that is, a faun or satyr of the conventional kind. The story of the encounter in the forest of Brocéliande is thus closely related to the sinister one in Robert of Boron's "Merlin" (twelfth century) of how the devils in hell thought out the fantastic conspiracy of undoing Christ's work through a rival virgin birth which was to produce the Antichrist; and how the plan of begetting him through an incubus failed only because the intended victim, the virgin damsel, had too much native goodness in her to bring forth such unmitigated evil. Her offspring turned out to be endowed with preternatural powers, changeable and often mischievous, but essentially on the right side of the moral order.[45]

The story of how the wild man was begotten by a satyr was not an invention by Arthurian poets, but a motive of ancient folklore. The earliest instance known to me is the report by Philostratus in his "Vita Apollonii" in the third century A.D., that he himself had seen a man on the island of Lemnos who was regarded as a satyr's son because his back and part of his chest were as densely covered with hair as an animal fleece.[46] More than thirteen centuries later Edmund Spenser introduced Sir Satyrane, the satyr's son, in the *Faërie Queene* and made him a typical wild man, who had learned from his father the art of dominating the beasts through courage and brute force. His mother, like Merlin's, had been a human maiden lost in the forest.[47]

Between the works of these two authors, one in the third century, the other in the sixteenth, lies the whole fantastic range of incubus lore, perhaps the most appalling example known of the elaboration of a popular superstition into a system of legal concepts. St. Augustine and Isidore of Seville asserted that incubi were in the habit of pursuing mortal women with their usually undesired attentions; the implication being, obviously, that the woman was the victim of demoniac desire and, at worst, or her own carelessness in wandering into the forest unchaperoned. A young lady for instance, whose adventure created a stir in England in 1337, because she had gone out into the forest to meet her swain, only to find out that she had made a date with a demon in his guise, could hardly be accused and condemned for not having been able to recognize the deception.[48]

But as the incubus changed from a wood demon into a devil the story of women's relationship with him was decisively modified. For now a moral choice seemed to be involved in the proceedings. The intercourse between woman and devil was now conceived as a conscious act of apostasy by which the witch, who had sought such contact, sealed her compact with the evil one.[49] As the delusion of witchcraft developed in the closing centuries of the Middle Ages, the intercourse with Satan and his emissaries, the "familiar demons," became part of an elaborate ceremonial of initiation and was looked upon as confirmation of the witchs' trade. The development culminated in the witch's sabbath with its perverted act of worship, its consumption of children's flesh, and the teaching by Satan of the *maleficia* with which the witch was to harrow the human community. The original nightmare, which may have spawned both satyr and wild man, had indeed taken on monstrous proportions.

Concomitant with this expansion of the witchs' assumed activities was the codification by the scholastics — and even great saints like Thomas Aquinas and Bonaventura had a hand in it — of a theory of the incubus and the succubus: a theory half physiological, half metaphysical, which assumed that the devil, who is sexless, could take on male or female form at will and substitute himself in place of the actual partner in the sexual act.[50]

Inquisitor and scholastic combined thus in severing incubus lore from the lore of the wood demon and replacing the former by organized Satanism. From then on there were to exist two kinds of incubi: one, a demon under orders from hell, subject to codification by the pseudoscience of demonology; the other, much more harmless, a creature from the woods subject to no higher rule than that of his own overbearing passion. While it is true that in the course of time the wood-demon incubus came to be absorbed by his infernal brother, there was a time, covering mainly the last two centuries of the Middle Ages, when the two lived side by side. Indeed it may be assumed that the concentration of fundamental evil in the scholastic incubus gave the lecher of the fields and woods a lease on life, since his habits had now been exempted from infernal implications.

We return to the medieval renditions of Greco-Roman mythology to register one last curiosity: the representation of Hercules as a wild man. The identification here is made not on mythological but merely on visual grounds, for in Greek and Roman art Hercules is shown carrying a club and clad in the skin of the slain lion of Nemea. Given the medieval indifference to the distinction between a man clad in fur and one endowed with it by nature, it was a natural consequence that the various attributes of the strong Hercules should have coalesced into those of the conventional wild man. A bestiary in the Bibliothèque de l'Arsenal in Paris tells us that in India there lives a peculiar species of horned wild men who have to climb in the treetops for fear of their various animal foes;

they go naked, unless they have succeeded in killing a lion and can clothe themselves in its skin.[51] While the name of Hercules is here not mentioned and the reminiscence farfetched, it is definite in a miniature of the fourteenth century representing a scene from Seneca's *Hercules Furens*. Here he is shown as a beast with tail and claws on his feet, yet standing upright and endowed with human hands.[52] Finally, a marginal drollery in a manuscript of poems by Robert of Blois (late thirteenth century) * shows Hercules, now quite the conventional wild man, running with his club after Hippolyta, the mounted queen of the Amazons, who flees but sends her spear after her pursuer. She is a chaste and elusive antagonist to a figure which may have appeared to the medieval beholder as a symbol of satyrlike lust.[53]

The last type of Greco-Roman wild men with which we have to deal owes its existence, unlike those examined heretofore, not to mere abundance of mythological imagination, but to a definite moral or, if you will, historical valuation. This wild man is a primitive or savage, and his claim upon the attention of writers lies in the fact that his manner of life, in its stark simplicity, is regarded as a paragon of virtue lost in the unfolding of civilization. His image is the compounded creation of what Freud calls man's uneasiness in his civilization and what should be termed more bluntly his abhorrence of and revulsion from its injustice and recurrent bouts of organized violence.

Since violence and fear through all the ages have been the accompaniment of advanced social organization, we find that the dream of the simple life and of men privileged to lead it undisturbed is as old as history itself. It is expounded in one of the earliest Sumerian documents, while modern man has inherited this idea of the "noble savage" from his ancestors in the eighteenth century and through them from classical antiquity. The lost paradise of man's innocence may be imagined either to have existed in the historical distance of a golden age or to survive in the geographical remoteness of an untouched island. What matters is that in almost all periods man has found it necessary to construct for himself the image of a

* Fig. 27.

country or an age to which the corruption under which he suffers has not penetrated and where his brother can live in his — very hypothetical — goodness. It is thus that civilization provides an imaginative escape from itself. But dreams of innocence and simplicity do not solve man's problems.

The history of this dream in classical antiquity and the arguments then brought forth against it have been presented elsewhere in a detailed and exhaustive study; [54] we can limit ourselves here to those phases of it which may fairly be assumed to have influenced ideas about the wild man in the Middle Ages and in the Renaissance.

But this much must be said in a general way: the nature of primitive man as developed by Greek and Roman writers amplifying or expounding Hesiod's myth of the Golden Age shows certain common traits, although these may not all be simultaneously present in any one specimen. Negatively speaking, primitive man abstains from the luxuries of sophisticated life and thus finds it easy to do without the arts that make it possible: the arts of war, of mining and metallurgy, and of navigation. In a positive way this abstention from all that enriches life materially shields primitive man from the vices of avarice and trickery and bellicosity. Since even agriculture and cattle breeding are unknown to him, he finds himself leading a life without possessions but also without toil and burden. As a means of livelihood Virgil and Juvenal allow him the hunt, while most other writers make him a vegetarian, following Empedocles' assertion that in the Golden Age man was on affectionate terms with the animals and birds and thus could not commit the disloyalty of slaughtering them. Acorns and fruit are thus all he can afford, and it is assumed that they suffice for his needs. Indeed, this diet favors his health and he may expect to live to a ripe old age.[55]

From the beginning this image of man without his latter-day frailties was a mythological one, little affected by contact with the realities of primitive life on the outskirts of the Greco-Roman world. With the expansion of the frontiers of Greek and Roman civilization the ancient chronological primitivism merely blossomed forth into its geographical counterpart, which did not always adhere to what we today call "facts" and sometimes found itself inventing races of noble savages. The mythological character of the theme found expression in the association of historic ages with presiding divinities, such as Cronus or Saturn for the Golden Age.

The savages themselves had a way of associating with fauns and nymphs that would indicate that they were made of similarly potent material. Virgil, in the *Aeneid*, says that the same groves that bore primitive man were the dwellings also of wood divinities. And Ovid, in the *Fasti*, insists that the ancient Arcadians, although "their life was like that of beasts unprofitably spent," devoid even of the vestiges of civilization, worshiped Pan.[56]

Correspondingly, the wild men of the Golden Age show many traits of woodland divinities. In the *Aeneid* Virgil speaks of "a race of men born of tree trunks and hard oak who had neither a rule of life nor civilization"; again, "and who fed themselves from trees and the rough fare of the huntsman." The same origin from tree trunks is claimed for prehistoric man in one of the satires of Juvenal in which it is said that in these days "men lived otherwise than now, those who had no parents being born of riven oak and compounded of mud." It is interesting to compare with this the statement of the seventh or eighth century in the "Anonymus de monstris" that "Fauns are born of worms between the wood and the bark of trees and proceed from there to the ground" and "become wild men." A rationalization of this primitive belief is in Servius' commentary on Virgil, in the fourth century: "this figment arose out of the old living quarters of man, who before there were houses resided either in hollow trees or in caves; thence when they vacated or took their offspring with them the impression was created that they had been born there." The picture drawn by Servius is one worth remembering, considering the importance of his commentary for the interpretation of Virgil in the Middle Ages.[57]

It is only natural that a race of men raised the hard way, as these people were, should have excelled in physical vigor, thus again approaching the medieval type of wild man. Ovid, in his *Ars Amatoria*, speaks of them as having *merae vires et rude corpus*, "strength unabated and their bodies rough," so as to render them fit to live in the woods, sleeping on beds of leaves and subsisting on herbs. And in the *Amores* Ovid even gives them their proverbial hairiness: "The hairy rustics parched no corn, nor was the word 'threshing floor' known on earth, but the oak, man's first oracle, bore acorns; these and the tender shoots of grass were man's food."

Juvenal attributes this same rude strength to the wild woman of the past, painting again a picture of primitive family life foreshadowing that of her descendants in the late Middle Ages: "The mountain wife spread down a sylvan bed of leaves and stalks and skins of the neighboring beasts." Then, in a sally against contemporary failure of nerve: "Not like you, Cynthia, was she, nor like you, whose shining eyes a dead sparrow clouded. But she bore breasts to feed great children and was often shaggier than her acorn-belching mate." [58]

Thus Juvenal, Ovid, and Virgil supplement each other in describing man's hard but hearty life in the period which we may describe in modern terms as the Stone Age; and it will be noted that among the writers quoted there are the two Roman poets most generally revered, cited, and commented upon throughout the Middle Ages, so that no notion bearing their august names could have a chance to be forgotten.

But the idealization of the primitive past proposed by Hesiod and elaborated by Roman poets was not generally accepted; even Ovid's own description in the *Amores* is influenced by a reaction against the admiration of primitivism. The opposing faction maintained that man's early life had been nothing but squalor, ignorance, and misery; and it attempted to construct an ascending scale of human evolution, in which man with the help of the gods and sometimes of great inventors gradually overcame his primitive stage, learning how to till the soil, build houses and cities, develop the arts and crafts, and submit to the restraining influence of law. This philosophy of enlightenment had among its adherents Horace, Vitruvius, and Pliny, and thus could not fail to cast its spell upon later ages.[59] Isidore of Seville, for instance, subscribes to it and writes of primitive man as nude and defenseless against wild beasts and the rigors of weather until he learned to take refuge in caves or to build huts out of intertwined twigs.[60] For us the most important adherent of the theory, because of his influence upon the later Middle Ages, is Prudentius (348–*c.* 410), whose sarcasm regarding the original condition of man seems not to have been always appreciated in its satirical intention.[61] When he speaks of original man's acorn diet, his use of furs from animals he has slain, and of the cave that serves him as a refuge, he means to contrast this squalid condition with man's later heightened estate. It was not his fault that his ironic description agreed as perfectly as it did with what the Middle Ages believed they knew about the life of the wild man, and thus served to confirm and to expand native lore.

It is not, however, the historic or chronological form of ancient primitivism which had the greatest influence upon the Middle Ages, but its geographic variety. And for good reason: to thinkers brought up in the Christian tradition the ideal state of nature was epitomized in the life of Adam and Eve in Paradise, and any legend about man's goodness in past ages was thus apt to conflict with fundamental doctrine. We find in consequence that the Middle Ages preferred to transfer the objects of their anthropological daydreams to distant areas and to locate them in India or Ethiopia, in the vicinity of other almost incredible marvels.

The beginning of this trend is to be found in antiquity itself, in the proclivity of writers to criticize the culture of their own day and age by extolling the shining virtues of savages. Thus the Scythians, the Ethiopians, and the Germanic tribes came in for admiring descriptions of their dispositions and institutions.[62] And an old tradition claimed that the Arcadians were not only ancient in lineage and backward in custom compared with other Greeks, but also renowned for their extraordinary virtue. It goes with this that they, the companions of Pans and fauns, wore skins for cloth and that they were believed to be living on a diet of acorns.[63] The tradition that the Ethiopians were particularly hospitable to the gods goes back to Homer,[64] who was responsible also for the location of their eastern and western branches in opposite sections of the universe, and thus implicitly for the later confusion of the Eastern Ethiopians with the Indians. To Homer the Ethiopians were merely "lordly." For Agatharchides, however, writing in the second century B.C., the Ethiopian Ichthyophagi had become a people of ideal disposition, worthy of the Golden Age, indifferent to power and thus averse to strife, and content with a life without luxuries.

The legend of the virtuous Ethiopians was passed on to the Middle Ages through the *Periegesis* of Dionysius and continued strong throughout the period.[65] Of other noble savages from antiquity the Hyperboreans, a legendary race of the far north, can be traced down to Petrarch and into the *Imago Mundi* by Pierre d'Ailly (fifteenth century), one of the books which influenced Columbus; [66] and the Jewish sect of the Essenes, a monastic order described by Pliny and other Roman writers as a tribe of virtuous men, appear in the same guise in the *Livre du Trésor* by Brunetto Latini (thirteenth century) and later also in Mandeville and Christine de Pisan (fifteenth century).[67] It is from books such as these that the generation of the great geographical discoverers drew their ideas. Very naturally, therefore, the seafarers looked for the survival of the Golden Age long lost to Western man among the unspoiled inhabitants of the Caribbean islands, praising as symptoms of a beatific state their lack of private property, their ignorance of books, and the apparent absence among them of organized law.

The legend of the ideal life of the Hindu Brahmans, like other medieval reports on India, has its roots in the observations, detailed and this time at least in part trustworthy, by Megasthenes, who treats them as a community of philosophers; he was the first to acquaint the West with the various Brahman sects and with their practices, describing the self-castigations of yogis and the extreme primitivism of other groups of Sadhus called by him Hylobii, forest dwellers (and later known also as gymnosophists, the wise men who go naked), who subsist on leaves and wild fruit and clothe themselves in the bark of trees. It was Megasthenes also and after him Strabo who related how even kings, even Alexander the Great, had to comply with the refusal of these Hindu ascetics to leave the place of their retreat, and thus either were forced to seek them out in person or to send messengers to them, in order to profit from their wisdom. It could happen then that the Brahman, secure in the knowledge of his own composure, would rebuke the king, exposing the emptiness of his claim for total power. Occasionally, according to Strabo, one of the Brahmans, such as Calamus, would deliver himself of a sermon about the lost Golden Age that had been forfeited through luxury and insolence, and would threaten an even greater loss of prosperity and happiness if the mighty continued in their course.[68]

The Christian version of the ideal life of the Brahmans, now mistaken for an Indian tribe rather than a caste in Hindu society, arose in the fourth century, its simplest form appearing under the name of Palladius, Bishop of Helenopolis (368?–431?), as *Commonitorium Palladii* and a related reading under the name of St. Ambrose.[69] In this new guise the legend repeated some of the staple attributes of the noble savage: his rudeness, his lack of agriculture and cattle-breeding, and his vegetarian diet, the latter a trait in accord with the real habits and beliefs of the group described. Furthermore the Brahmans are said to be God-fearing and pious, so much so that worship and prayer fill most of their days. It is a striking piece of Christian presumption that in spite of their exemplary holiness the Brahmans are said to know little about God.

The version in question had considerable circulation during the Middle Ages. Roger Bacon for instance, usually careful about his sources, quotes it in full in his *Opus Majus*, choosing the pseudo-Ambrosian reading, as he says, *propter maiorem certitudinem* because of its greater certainty. Even Petrarch relies on it in the chapter of his *De Vita Solitaria* devoted to the life of the Hindu ascetics, although his humanist sense of style leads him to suspect that the attribution of the booklet to the great church father could not withstand literary criticism.[70]

An older and much longer form of the *Commonitorium Palladii* passed into the Alexander legend and thus into the main body of medieval lore.[71] It appears to have existed in two distinct versions, one contained in the *Res Gestae Alexandri* by Julius Valerius (fourth century), the other anonymous one under the name of *The Letter of Dindymus* or *The Correspondence of Dindymus with Alexander*. Both had great and lasting influence upon medieval thought because of their connection with the legend of Alexander, upon whose achievement they level their devastating commentary. We choose the *Letter of Dindymus* for an abridged presentation here.

Dindymus is king of the Brahmans and his letter is a reply to Alexander's inquiry about the manner of life practiced by the Brahmans. Although it is easy to show that Dindymus' harangue is derived from the similar one by Calamus and through it from earlier classical prototypes,[72] the letter is, in its own right, a powerful denunciation of the ideal of living dangerously at other people's expense and a fitting vindication of primitivism.

The letter begins with the contemptuous statement that it is written with little hope to impress, since the world conqueror has his mind too full of military plans to find time to read. There follows a description of the Brahman's life in its primeval simplicity, its nudism, communism, vegetarianism, and pacifism. Like the wild man the Brahman, devoid as he is of needs, lives in the forest or in mountain caves and sleeps on the ground, leading a frugal life which serves to preserve his health. He speaks seldom, shortly, and the truth, since his time is taken with the praise of God and the admiration of His universe. Philosophy and oratory he shuns, knowing that they only divide minds and requiring no doctrine to keep on the path of righteousness. And since he regards all men as his brothers he can dispense with courts of law, and allows himself no such luxury as the possession of servants or slaves. With all temptations removed, he finds it easy to lead a life without weakness or sin.

Alexander's life, in contrast to this, is the epitome of all the offenses which civilization has foisted upon man: its insatiable cupidity, its recourse to war to gain its ends, its adultery and fornication, and, in the case of the Greeks, its torture of animals to propitiate the gods. Rousseau or Tolstoy could hardly have spoken more passionately.

The expanded version of the letter, known as the *Collatio Alexandri cum Dindymo per litteras facta* contains Alexander's reply, partly an *argumentum ad hominem*, and certainly inferior in tone; its burden is that man should enjoy the riches which nature has spread before him, and that not to do so is a sign not of wisdom, but of pride aspiring to godlike self-sufficiency. Also that the Brahman's refusal to plow or to build is caused not by conscious resolve, but by the lack of iron, and thus by technological backwardness.

Dindymus' reply rises to a further height of passionate conviction and takes on a definitely Christian character: it is the Macedonians who are inflated into subjective godlikeness by their overgreat prosperity, while they, the Brahmans, regarding themselves as strangers in a world from which they are sure to be taken by death, are trying no more than to live according to God's will. Thus, knowing that they are walking in righteousness, they can have no other sentiment for the misguided Greeks than pity.

Now thoroughly aroused, Alexander throws out a final retort: in the last letter he compares the land of the Brahman with a prison and their manner of life with that imposed in civilized lands as a penalty, ending with: *Verius ego confirmo quia non est beatitudo vita vestra, sed castigatio et miseria* — "I assert, with greater truth, that your life is not happiness, but castigation and misery." He has the last word. The reader, however, knows that this ultimate self-assertion has only been required to salvage an ego defeated in argument.

We have accorded broader space to the correspondence between Alexander and Dindymas than we have to other literary documents because we believe it to be of great intrinsic and topical interest. In addition to this however it had considerable influence upon medieval literature. It appeared fused with the text from Julius Valerius in the "Mirror of History" by Vincent of Beauvais. It (or its rival version by Julius) was in all likelihood the cause for the inclusion of the Brahman in the letter by Prester John to Emperor Manuel Comnenus; and its content entered into the *Liber de Monstruosis Hominibus* by Thomas of Cantimpré (thirteenth century) and through the latter into the most popular travel book of the late Middle Ages, the travels by "Sir John Mandeville." The so-called Mandeville was so impressed with the holiness of the Brahmans that he appended to their description what can only be called an exposition of natural religion, which knows no difference between Christians and devout infidels. He concluded quite plausibly that, to be as good as they were, the Brahmans must indeed be in the love of God.[73]

As far as artistic representation is concerned, in the Alexander romances the Brahmans were sometimes rendered as furry and scaly wild men, as was fitting for forest people braving the weather in complete nudity.[74] In the illustrations to Mandeville's travels they are usually shown scantily but decently dressed, having lost the attribute of nudeness to a special group among them, the Hylobii or gymnosophists. A good example of both conventions is to be found in the *Livre des merveilles* in the Bibliothèque Nationale in Paris.[75]

Like the older Greek and Roman versions of man's original beatific state this later tale of the perfections attained under a tropical sky ran into criticism from believers in more moderate ideals. Petrarch, who loved nature with the poignancy that Christian ascetism had added to the pleasant bucolic emotions of the Roman age, found it necessary to repudiate the extreme primitivism attributed to the Brahman in the name of a more humane temperance. In his *De Vita Solitaria* he expounds his version of the good life as one of voluntary retirement from the turmoil of cities into a lonely scholar's refuge somewhere in the woods, where circumstance and environment would not detract from intellectual pursuit.[76] Because he knew so well what solitude, rightly conceived, could contribute toward a scholar's bliss, he had to defend his worldly heaven against the extreme claims of primitivism. He found the Brahmans' nakedness discreditable, however well defended on climatic grounds, and was displeased with their "beastlike indifference toward food and shelter, lest the effort to escape the worry and scheming of civilized life lead to the opposite extreme." To spend all day and night under the open sky appeared to him "more fitting for a bear than for a man, no matter how much the Brahmans may pride themselves of having the sky for a roof and the whole earth for a bed." [77]

While his training in the literature of ancient stoicism prevented Petrarch from crediting flagrant departures from the golden mean, it was his Christianity, that made him revolt against the Brahman's claim of sinlessness. "It is churlish pride," he writes, "for them to claim that they are without sin, seducing themselves and giving the lie to the Holy Spirit, who dissuaded this kind of insolence through the mouth of the Apostle John and invited us to confession and penitence." [78]

Only after having registered these strong objections does Petrarch allow himself to find any good in the Brahman attitude. With his conscience salved and his taste explained, he now ventures all the way. "I like," he writes in his intensely personal way, "the contempt of the world, which could not be greater; I like the solitude and the freedom, the greatest that any nation enjoys; I like the silence, the leisure, the quiet, the intent thought, the integrity and security, provided the pride be taken out of it. I like the peace of mind, the singleness of attitude, the fact that there is neither fear nor desire, I like the dwelling in the forest and the closeness of springs from which, as it is written in the book, they drink as if they were suckling at the fresh uncorrupted bosom of mother earth." [79]

Since he affirms these aspects of primitive life, Petrarch could not but endorse the Brahman's criticism of civilized society with its criminality, its "hatred of all and contempt for God"; he enumerates its sins and follies in a long litany taken from Dindymus' strictures against the Greeks and ends with an account, perhaps contemporary, of a sylvan, naked Hindu guru, a man of few words but of profound wisdom, whom even kings approach with reverence and whose sayings are treasured by all. It is perhaps useless to speculate on the identity of this sage although it is not impossible that his short account contains a faraway reflection of the hallowed figure of the Gautama Buddha.

To gauge the influence of the literature on the noble savage upon the interpretation of the wild man in the Middle Ages is not easy, since as a figment of native thought the wild man almost always lacks at least two of the attributes of his classical counterpart: his pacifism and his vegetarianism. That there was, however, a transfer of features from the ideal men distant in space and time to the mythical creatures close by, may be seen from the example of the dwarf in "Ruodlieb" (eleventh century) who, when caught and reproached for harboring the proverbial malice of his race, throws out an ill-tempered rebuttal to the effect that it is the human race rather than his own against whom the reproach should be leveled.[80] It is men, not dwarfs, who habitually talk with cunning in their hearts and thus, by a queer process of causation, deprive themselves of the longevity which dwarfs enjoy; while his own people believe in veracity and frugality and thus, though uncultured, outlast their human competitors. We have here one more philosophical harangue like those of Calamus and Dindymus, although an abbreviated one since, in deference to the mythology of the dwarf, only veracity and longevity have been singled out among the list of primitive perfections.

We will have to go as far as the sixteenth century before again coming upon such a clear example of native mythology molded in the form of the noble savage of antiquity, for in the intervening period the wild man reigned supreme. Even when we meet the wild man of the Renaissance in Spenser's *Faërie Queene*, ennobled and made more lenient through contact with his classical counterpart, the native element in him proves so strong that only a few traits betray his literary derivation.[81] He is a real wild man, naked, fierce as a tiger when aroused, instinctive in his responses, and expert at the use of his wooden club. Like the most debased specimens of his race he has never learned the use of human speech and crawls through the forest on all fours. Yet considering such bestial rudeness his habits are remarkably gentle, forbidding him to use his great strength for the killing of animals. His loyalty to the man whom he chooses for his master is as unswerving as a dog's. And when an accident in Spenser's plot brings a wounded knight and a maiden who has been roughly handled into his forest empire, emotions of compassion are aroused in him which in their purity would do honor to much finer breeds. Indeed Spenser, aristocratic as he is in fundamental approach, concludes that his wild man's suprising gentleness of heart could be explained only through the presence in him of noble blood obliterated through tragic circumstance. Spenser's wonder at his creature's humanity is none the less genuine:

> In such a salvage wight, of brutish kynd,
> Amongst wild beastes in desert forrests bred,
> It is most straunge and wonderfull to fynd
> So milde humanity and perfect gentle mynd.[82]

The clearest exposition of the noble proclivities of the wild man when allowed to live his life according to his conviction is to be found, however, not in English literature, but in the pithy German of Hans Sachs, who had inherited his town's and country's rich wild-man lore and yet chose to combine it with the Greco-Roman encomium of primitivism. His wild men are such perfect examples of humanity cleansed of its meaner passions and preoccupations, that Hans Sachs could use them as mouthpieces for his own moral admonitions. The *Lament of the Wild Men about the Unfaithful World* is a tract, which, like many others by its author, was printed as a broadside to reach a wide reading public.[83] A large-scale woodcut by Schäufelein, designed to attract attention, shows the wild-men speakers as a hairy male and female in the classical pose of Dürer's Adam and Eve, together with their child and dog.[84]

The poem itself belongs to a category frequent in Hans Sachs's works of complaints over the evil ways of the corrupt world and lists them with impressive and monotonous insistence in a litany of eighty-five verses, each a complete statement of some aspect of evil. At last, after having exhausted the appalling catalogue, the wild men are ready to explain how they have handled the problem of evil: "Now since the world is thus immersed in cunning and unfaithfulness, we have decided to forsake it and to escape to where its falseness cannot reach us. We keep house in the wild woods together with our uneducated children. We feed on wild fruit and roots, drink the clear water of springs, and warm ourselves by the light of the sun. Our garment is mossy foliage and grass which serve also as our beds and bedspreads. Our house is a stony cave, from which none will drive out the other. Company and pleasure we find in the wild animals of the woods, for since we do them no harm, they let us live in peace. Thus we live in deserted places and there bring forth our children and grandchildren. We exult in brotherly love and have never had any strife among us, for each does to the other as he would want him to do to himself. Nor do we care for worldly goods, gathering our food each morning, taking of it a scant minimum and no more, and praising and honoring God for the gift. If illness or death befalls us, we know that they were sent from God, who orders all things for the best. Thus we spend our time simply and with humility, awaiting the great change, when in all the world everybody will be loyal and pious, and poverty and simplicity will prevail; only then will we leave the forest to dwell among men again." [85]

This is indeed a comprehensive program of escape, and one which omits few of the literary clichés from antiquity. It is curious to see that this prolonged picnic without the food baskets should have been dreamed up by a member of a Christian society accustomed to the much harsher demands of the monastic orders upon man's ability to deny himself fleeting satisfactions for the sake of a higher good.

We note, furthermore, that in Hans Sachs the ancient dream of the Golden Age has been made accessible to all, for his wild men do not live at a distance that puts them and their manner of life beyond man's reach, but at an undefined place which may be close by. It is this closeness which made possible the complete fusion of the native wild man with the noble savage from antiquity. It may have been, on the other hand, the same proximity which kept the wild men from playing the role as a receptacle for all unrequited dreams, as the noble savage of distant lands and periods did in antiquity and again in the eighteenth century. For people living north of the Alps the dream was all too obviously ruled out by the climate.

It is clear, at any rate, that, as envisaged by Hans Sachs, the wild man's place on the scale of moral values has been completely reversed. When we met him first, he was a creature of rage and violence, destructive and a cannibal, in short a devil, as he had been labeled by Hans Sachs's older contemporary, Geiler von Kaysersberg. Hans Sachs himself knew the creature as a member of the Wild Horde in the Nuremberg Carnival. Nevertheless the wild man whom we now behold is a paragon of virtue, gentle and enlightened, and above most ordinary mortals in having succeeded in practicing without difficulty what he preaches. The bane of original sin does not extend to him, so that he finds it possible to be good without effort and without invoking supernatural help. We are reminded of Rousseau, when we realize that this revamping of man's personality is not due to any inner process of purification, but merely to a change in his social environment, a return to the natural life, which, through a strange and inexplicable alchemy, proves capable of transmuting man's soul and wiping out evil. We must not forget that Hans Sachs's wild men are not demons, but people like you and me who have fled to the woods.

As might be expected, this thoroughgoing revaluation was not due merely to the presence of immediate literary examples, but was based upon the existence of a tradition and of a gradual growth of thought. We possess a number of tapestries, love caskets, engraved tomb plates, and prints, most of them from the Rhine region and Switzerland, bearing the message of the idyllic wild-man life and its ethical superiority over civilization's trickery and unfaithfulness.[86] The earliest of them date from the last years of the fourteenth century, while the most recent were executed toward the end of the fifteenth century, not long before the time of Hans Sachs. If we add to them the satyr families depicted by Dürer, Altdorfer, Urs Graf, and Lucas Cranach, all of them representing the same theme in terms made fashionable by the Renaissance, we can say that the subject was carried into Hans Sachs's own time.[87]

The burden of these accumulated artistic messages is that the wild man may well be regarded as a model for human conduct, because of the intimacy and cordiality of his family life and the unanimity and complete solidarity with which wild-man groups tackle the various tasks which their habitat imposes upon them. Theirs is an atmosphere of peace and contentment, in spite of the fact that at any time the group may have to defend itself against the onslaught of bears or lions or boars or dragons. And we find that this inevitable enmity against the fiercest of forest monsters does not of necessity extend to other animals, for the wild men seem to be on excellent terms with stags and unicorns, riding them with ease and confidence; at times they mount even lions, as a token of their overwhelming mastery.

This intimacy with the animals, which the wild men often lead on chains as if they were dogs on leashes, is expressed in inscriptions contrasting their present felicity in the company of the dumb creatures of the woods against the misery of existence among men. *Disse tierlin wil ich triben und wil on die welt beliben*, says a wild man on a Swiss tapestry of the fifteenth century, in the museum in Klagenfurt: "I shall drive these animals and do without the world." And he is echoed by a second saying: *Das han ich wol empfunden, zu disen dierlin han ich mich verbunden* — "This I have felt strongly and thus have decided to stay with these animals." A third one takes up the theme: *Mit disen dierlin sun wier uns began die welt git bussen lon* — "With these animals have we consorted, for the world gives evil reward." And a forth one harps upon the same subject again: *Die welt ist untruwen fol, mit dissen dierlin ist uns wol* — "The world is full of treachery, but we feel at ease with these animals."

On another wild-man tapestry, formerly in Sigmaringen, we find the expression of similar sentiments: "Nobody can escape the great evils of the world," and "Thus we bring complaint to our princes that there is neither loyalty nor steadiness," or "She and I, we complain that the world is so treacherous." [88] Several of these phrases belong to the stereotyped expressions of an age which regarded the utmost gloom and despair over the affairs of the world as a matter of good style and propriety.[89] It is characteristic, nevertheless, that these phrases should have been attributed to wild men, who thus are made to resemble children unfairly scolded by the grownups, and prompted to bring their complaints to their faithful mute companions.

Hans Sachs's litany of the evils of the world spoken through the mouths of wild men thus stands revealed as an expanded compendium of thoughts and sentiments which had been popularly associated with the wild men's escape into the woods for more than a hundred years. In the tapestries, as we shall see, this longing for escape was sweetened and justified by lovers' desire for a flight into intimacy from a society harassing them — a motive which goes far in explaining the emphasis upon a happy and contented family life. In Hans Sachs's version this theme has been dropped; and it speaks for the strength of his allegiance to the Greco-Roman tradition that he should have been willing to forgo an essential part of his medieval heritage in order to present the lovers' complaint about the unfaithful world as a mere exposition of the superiority of wild-man life over civilization.

The minds of those who specified the themes of wild-men tapestries and love caskets may, in turn, have been sensible to the spell of the classics, although their foremost attention was on the correct rendition of native lore, especially the wild man's habit of hunting and slaying savage beasts. It may have been a remote reflection of ancient doctrine that caused these patrons to insist upon the friendship between wild men and animals. And even when they allowed the wild men to bear down with their clubs upon some of the savage creatures of the forest, they could claim for their version the authority of the ancients, for Virgil and Prudentius had described primitive men as hunters. When it is considered that, according to the commentary by Servius, original man lived in trees or caves with his wife and children, we arrive at a picture of the classical savage so close to the representations of wild-man life in the fifteenth century as to make it hard to believe in mere coincidence. Virgil's works together with Servius' commentary on the *Aeneid* were a must for any self-respecting library of the classics, so that the reference was almost certain to be available, even before the great church councils of Constance and Basel attracted a confluence of learned humanists to the upper Rhine.

A detailed analysis of the works of art referred to will have to be reserved for the next chapter, since in most of them erotic and escapist motives are closely intertwined. But before we close this chapter, we must mention the one artist who, unlike the servants of utopian sentimentalists, was able to treat primitive life as a reality because his own instincts drove him toward rejection of contemporary civilization and toward a pronounced bestialism: the Florentine painter, Piero di Cosimo (1462-1521).

His biographer Vasari relates that "he saw everything in wild [*salvatico*] terms, because such was his nature," and proceeds to furnish us with a list of the painter's neurotic idiosyncrasies, among them his insensate love for animals contrasted with his loathing for human society, his delight with rain and storm, and his insistence that everything around him stay in its state of natural disorder.[90] Nobody was to interfere with the untended growth of his garden or even to pick fruits in it. Through a strange coincidence this natural wild man who, according to Vasari, "led a life more bestial than human," was also an unusually gifted painter. As a result we find him prompted at times to lay aside the conventional themes and to engage in the pleasure of producing meticulous and powerful renditions of life in the primitive ages of which he regarded himself as a belated citizen.

It is an interesting comment on the influence of environment even on those who profess to reject it that Piero chose among the many available interpretations of primitivism one in which man's history is not looked upon as a fall from original goodness as in Hesiod's myth, but as an ascending scale of evolution, in keeping with the generally optimistic mood of Florence in the fifteenth century.[91] Piero himself may have preferred the primitivism of close contact with nature to that of unredeemed savagery. Selecting Vitruvius [92] as his text and combining it with others, he traced in a series of panels the evolution of man from appalling brutality to the acquisition of a rudimentary civilization, showing how he tamed the fire and at last was taught the arts and crafts by Vulcan.

The later stages in this ascent do not interest us here. In the early panels, however, and particularly in the first one, Piero succeeded in fusing the traditional wild-man lore with the teaching of Vitruvius into a picture of raw passion and violence that has few parallels in Italian art. Man's earliest stage, according to this, was marked by a chaotic struggle of all against all, reminiscent of the most unfavorable renditions of wild-man life north of the Alps. Among the participants in this battle there are not only nude men and animals, but also, in accordance with Roman tradition, satyrs and fauns, who appear as savage combatants armed with spiked clubs and tree trunks. The burden of such savagery is only slowly lightened as man learns, according to the second panel,[93] to engage in elementary coöperation and to get along with women, while in the third he is shown at the point where he has mastered fire.

Through all the pictures runs the sensitive and unruly temperament of a man who, perhaps in order to compensate for childhood experiences, seems to have patterned himself after the traditional image of the wild man and so found it congenial to represent him in art. One may ask oneself, in view of this strange predisposition, whether Piero, whose sympathies with northern art are well known, did not derive part of his inspiration from prints (and tapestries?) dealing with the wild man and known to have been in Florence during the fifteenth century.[94]

In Piero's art, for the first time, the primitive life is again a matter of the mythological past, as it had been for the classical writers, while in the Middle Ages this distance in time had been allowed to lapse under the influence of theology and folklore. The moment had come for the reintegration in visual terms of Hesiod's conception of man's early stages, a task solved in Signorelli's "Rule of Pan," with its assemblage of perfect human bodies in a perfect landscape.[95] For Lucas Cranach, first among northern painters to try his hand at the theme, the Golden Age was one of childish happiness, when man exulted in his pagan paradise, dancing round-dances with innocent abandon, playing in springs and lakes and enjoying the peaceable company of the animals. Man's progressive deterioration, which began with the Age of Silver, is shown by Cranach in terms of an internecine war of all against all, fought in the nude and with clubs * as in the first age of Piero di Cosimo's optimistic series. It is curious to realize that in Cranach's art both the peaceful and the warlike phases of primitive life have their parallels and perhaps their prototypes in conflicting interpretations of the life of the wild man.[96]

* Fig. 29.

We return once more to the native wild man to point out the influence which the reëstablishment of the time dimension in the mythology of the Golden Age had upon opinions about him. It was in the Renaissance that the wild man of native folklore, who had so faithfully accompanied his civilized brother through the involutions and contortions of his history, found himself for the first time relegated to the past and treated as a creature that had become extinct; a view which originated in scholarly circles, but gradually percolated to the peasants and burghers who were the mainstay of wild-man lore.

This opinion was held by the scholars who prepared the program for Charles V's entry into Bruges and who presented the wild man as the earliest inhabitant of Flanders. The same idea is expounded in *Gorboduc*, a pre-Shakespearian drama, where the wild men are identified with the early Britons prior to the Anglo-Saxon invasion.[97] And it was later expanded in the light of nineteenth-century historicism, when in the millenary celebration of 1886 in Ripon, England, the wild men were allowed to show themselves as the earliest prehistoric aborigines, the antecedents even of the Druids and Romans.[98] Wherever this view was held, the mythology of the wild man was emptied of all pristine valuations and these were replaced by local pride or nationalist sentiment. No wonder therefore that in modern time, with its romantic regard for prehistory and its disregard for value, this attitude should have won adherents, not only among Swiss and Tyrolean villagers, but also among a few scholars as well.[99] After what has been said about the origin of the wild man and his mythology in general, we need not insist that this explanation is, to put it mildly, implausible.

5

The Erotic

Connotations

The wild man's attitude toward life, and consequently his civilized brother's attitude toward him, encompass divergences of mood and feeling far beyond anything possible within the range of character of a real personality. It requires little psychological insight to infer from the violent ambiguity imputed to him that the wild man's attitude toward women would also be far from simple or coherent. The wild man is, as it were, a focus of man's various instincts and desires; as a consequence, his actions reflect to an absolute degree those impulses which normally make their compromise with the demands of reality. He approaches women with raw lust, or with bleak hatred, or again uses their company to act out an idyllic picture of sexual harmony within the sympathetic framework of a forest environment. The only major attitude toward women which he cannot adopt, without losing his character as a wild man, is that humble adulation and worship which the Middle Ages demanded from the well-trained knight, for this attitude implied the ability to restrain appetite for the sake of a civilized ideal. The wild man, whose ways were always impulsive, could not be expected to be capable of such self-control. And we find, therefore, that wherever women enter in, the wild man is conceived

as the actual antagonist of the knight, and the two fight it out for
the possession of the lady. As long as the knightly ideal remained
untarnished, the victory in this battle of human principles was invariably accorded to the knight. It marks a major turning point
in the history of European civilization that, as we shall see, the wild
man is sometimes allowed to win in works of art describing the
conflict after the middle of the fourteenth century.

The story of the battle is described on some of the French
ivory caskets in which fair ladies of the time used to keep their
trinkets and toilet utensils.* There we see the knight, on horseback
and in full armor, gallantly piercing the giant wight, while the lady
in distress lifts up her hands in supplication to her rescuer. We
may assume that there used to be considerably more objects with
representations of this kind than we possess today, for in the inven-
tory of the property of Louis d'Anjou, regent of France during the
minority of Charles V, the entries of 1364–65 include two enamel
basins, in the bottoms of which was rendered in color the battle
between a knight and a wild man who had abducted a lady.[1] As the
theme was expanded, it took on the character of a short romance.
In a French ivory casket, again of the fourteenth century, the duel
takes place before the battlements of a castle, where ladies and
gentlemen behold it as if it were a prearranged tournament.[2] We
see in succession two wild men laying hands on the lady, a fight
between knights and wild men for her possession, another similar
encounter, the departure of the two human lovers on the rescuer's
steed, and the subjection of the wild man, whom the lady leads to
the castle on a chain; finally we see the lady present her rescuer with
the keys to the castle, where the two lovers appear once more,
happily united, and looking out beyond the battlements. In representations of this sort there seems to be little intention beyond that
of presenting an extensive narrative, although the chaining of the
wild man was capable of definite moral implication.

It occurred to somebody, however, in the opening years of the
fourteenth century, to make of the abduction and its aftermath a
moral example in the manner of the erotic casuistry practiced at the
contemporary courts of love. We possess two closely related series
of marginal miniatures of that period, clearly meant to preach a

* Fig. 37.

lesson to the ladies, for the vice to be castigated is feminine ingratitude for man's help and generosity. In the first series, which decorates a manuscript of the decretals of Gregory IX, the sequence, extending over the margins of many pages, relates how a damsel was rescued from a wild man's clutches by a knight, whom she was reprehensible enough to spurn, giving her favor to another; and how this luckier suitor was slain by a third, while the lady, now alone and helpless, was attacked by bears and perished miserably.[3]

The second series, in the so-called Taymouth Hours, tells a similar story through miniatures and inscriptions.[4] Here the maiden is beset and carried away by a big and hairy woodwose, whose intentness and cupidity are admirably rendered.* In the nick of time an elderly knight appears and rescues her, but fails to win her affection, which she callously bestows upon a younger man. In the ensuing duel the man of her choice is killed, and her rescuer, now free from moral obligation toward her, decides to leave her to her fate. In the last miniature she is shown in helpless distress, as two bears close in upon her. It would seem likely that both series of miniatures reproduce a lost literary prototype built upon the central motive of the abduction of the lady.

The final transformation of the motive may be studied in two wooden love caskets made by one master somewhere in the region of the lower Rhine and dating in the third quarter of the fourteenth century. Here, more clearly even than in the ivory casket previously described, the story of the abduction of the maiden by the wild man is rendered in terms of human erotic behavior, so that its allegorical meaning grows out of it instead of being extraneously imposed upon it. The wild man is interpreted as a symbol of unruly passion, with its corresponding impetuous and unreasoning conduct, while the knight is consciously treated as the protagonist of the opposite maner of life. Even the lady has been raised in allegorical status. Although still the pawn of battle, she is presented with a choice of principles, and makes her preference known through gesticulation.

On the first of these caskets † the knight wins his prize in spite of interference by his wild competitor. Both lovers woo the lady, who rejects the wild suitor with determined gesture, whereupon

* Fig. 26.   † Fig. 31.

he takes the law into his own hands and abducts her, only to find himself challenged to a duel, in which he is defeated. The knight now lifts the lady on his horse and carries her home. In the last scene she honors her champion by graciously placing a wreath upon his hair, as a reward for his perseverance and courage.

The young citizen of the Rhineland who sent this casket to his ladylove intended to further his ends by protesting figuratively that his intentions were respectable. Nothing could better demonstrate our thesis — that the story of the abduction had by now become a conscious symbol for conflicting types of love — than the fact that if certain safeguards were taken, it was possible to adopt the opposite approach. The young man who ordered the second casket from the same workshop intended to manifest his sensual desire, while protesting that, once granted his request, he would be a submissive and courteous lover. He saw to it, consequently, that the box which he was to place in his lady's hand would show the wild man winning the duel, only to be tamed by the ennobling influence of womanhood.*

The casket exhibits on its first panel a pensive wild man, the young lover himself, sitting morosely on a tree stump, as a messenger arrives and excites him into action, for a little further we see him trotting away on his horse. Apparently he is on his way to his lady, whose affection for him he overestimates. On the next panel we behold him laying hands on her forcibly, while she tries to escape into the arms of a young knight holding out a ring to her. By now battle has become inevitable. We see it being fought on the third panel, with both the knight and his shield-bearer riding in headlong pursuit, while the wild man's retreat on horseback is also covered by a riding companion. It may be the same companion who on the last panel is shown holding his club with a defiant gesture, as if detailed to guard his friend against trouble, for, right behind him, we behold the fierce wild man tamed by his prey. Instead of continuing to molest her, he sits, hairy as he is, with legs crossed to signify unconcern, playing chess with his lady while holding a falcon on his fist, in the manner practiced by the best society.

After what has gone before, this is a somewhat surprising denouement, and we cannot help feeling that it presupposes some-

* Fig. 32.

thing that has remained unsaid. It is, after all, neither the knight nor the wild man who emerges victorious from this battle, but the young damsel, who has been able to overcome through her charm the vehemence of her wild suitor. She has, to use the medieval term, captured him to subject him to her quieting and civilizing influence. Therefore, to make the sequence complete, there should have been a picture of the capture of fettering of the wild man by his lady, such as we saw on one of the French ivory caskets and also on a number of other works of art. Only by submitting to the radiation of her love can the wild man be expected to forgo his savage ways and to adopt the code of his civilized antagonist.

We are thus presented with the necessity of explaining another artistic motive, the intent of which amounts to a rather thoroughgoing modification of those values which had led to the representation of the battle between wild man and knight. Before we do so, it will be necessary, however, to analyze the mythological implications of the battle itself. What are we to think of the tempestuous wild man whose lack of self-control is the cause of his allegorical exploitation? Is he a satyr or incubus? Or will it suffice to think of him as the ordinary creature of mythology, primarily, though not entirely, a revenant and demon of death? It is plain that the works of art examined do not provide the key to the question, since they cannot explain the intention of the wild man's assault. It will be noted, however, that only in the last two caskets described is the relation of the wild man and damsel a definitely amorous one, and that, consequently, while there is ample testimony for the wild man's proclivity to carry away bundles of feminine innocence, it is not quite so easy to establish the sexual intent in the act.

By following up this lead and combining it with the cues contained in what literary examples of the scene we know, it is, I think, possible to exclude the identity of the wild man as raper with the incubus. For, as befits a creature of nightmare, the incubus is conceived as a passing visitor, who obtrudes himself into the life of his victim without requiring a change of residence. He comes and passes away. Even the familiar demon of the witch trials, an incubus adopted in permanence, behaves as the secretive third in a love triangle rather than as a captor. In contrast to this, literature describes the wild man as determined to bring the damsel to his abode in the forest or in the mountains, and there to make her his wife rather than to obtain momentary sensual gratification. He acts not as a lecher, but as a kidnapper. And the maiden's adventure must, therefore, be described as a visit to the other world, like the experience of innumerable other fair captives in medieval fairy tales and romance who are detained by giants and ogres and must be liberated.[5] When whisking the lady away to his residence beyond the great divide, the wild man acts thus as a demon of death. Whatever erotic implications the scene may contain, even though prominently displayed, are secondary.

A good example of such literary treatment of the theme, from the same fourteenth century that saw the chief artistic representation of it, is "Gismirante," a short epic of the Arthurian cycle, by the Florentine poet Antonio Pucci (1309–1388).[6] There the damsel is stolen by the wild man as she rests her head in the lap of her sleeping lover. She is imprisoned in the wild man's castle in the woods, a doorless structure to which there is no entry by ordinary means, just as there can be none to the underworld. And the task of her prospective rescuer is thus made possible only by her pretending to make love to her wild man captor *in buona fede* and extorting from him the secrets of the castle as well as of his own enchanted existence, in order to communicate with her rescuer. It is of interest, in view of the wild man's close kinship with the beasts, that, like many creatures in fairy tales, he has his heart concealed in the body of an animal, which the hero must kill in order to dispatch his adversary and to effect the liberation of his lady.

This literary example of abduction by a wild man is thus a tale of a maiden's sojourn in the afterworld and of the magic obstacles that her rescuer has to overcome to bring her back. The theme is, of course, not limited to wild-man mythology, for giants, ogres, and dwarfs — in fact, the whole variegated population of fairy-land — all have a desire to obtain mortals in marriage and to enshrine them in their strongholds. The battle of knights with such creatures is, therefore, a constantly recurring phenomenon in medieval romance, and one may very well ask whether the wild men of the love caskets are really meant to represent this one mythological species or whether they are to stand for the whole host of their uncanny companions.

In the majority of cases it is very difficult to decide this, for the superhuman stature of the hairy creature on some of the French ivories or in the Taymouth Hours my be the property of an over-size wild man just as well as it could be of a giant. There exists, however, one work of art — Flemish, of about 1355 — which is plainly intended to show in the guise of wild men their diminutive relatives the dwarfs.* There, on the grave plate for Gottfried and Friedrich von Buelow in Schwerin, we see again the scene of ab-duction, with the maiden high on the wild man's horse and with the knight riding out of the castle doors in belated pursuit. This time, however, the wild man has not undertaken the theft to suit his own passion or fancy, for there are others to benefit from his deed. A second wild man, his fellow conspirator, stands ready to receive the prey, and beyond him a wild king in his tent makes the usual gesture of command, indicating that he is the instigator and prob-able beneficiary of the plot. The implied close coöperation within a political organization is something of which the solitary wild men are quite incapable, although it is commonly imputed to the dwarfs. And if there be any doubt as to the identification pro-posed, it will be dispelled by viewing the other wild-men scenes shown on the same plate — a banquet attended by the king and his retainers, a kitchen scene and a bath scene, with a wild man seated in a wooden chair, while attendants help to wash his head and feet. It is a commonplace in the mythology of dwarfs that they love to cook and bake, and when occasion presents itself give lavish parties to which they may invite their favorite human beings, and also that they take delight in cleanliness, washing and bathing at frequent intervals.[7] Popular hearsay has it that isolated mist is the visible trace of their subterranean heated furnaces and that a muddied spring is the sign of a dwarf having used the water for a bath. No such details are reported in the mythology of the wild man.

To clinch the proof, it may be mentioned that the abduction of the maiden by the dwarf king is a frequent motive in Middle High German epics. The dwarf king Laurin, in the poem of that name, takes hold of Dietlieb's sister Kunhild and hides her in his subter-ranean empire, where she has to stay until her rescue can be effected with her own surreptitious help. And a similar adventure is related

* Fig. 33.

of Hertlin, daughter of the king of Portugal, who is held in bondage by the dwarf king Goldemar, and released only when Dietrich forces his way into the subterranean and otherworldly realm of his adversary.[8]

The abduction of the lady, while always plainly conceived as an enforced visit to the other world, is thus not the wild man's unique prerogative. It is consistent, therefore, that in ballads, which present the medieval material in comparatively modern popular form, the identity of the kidnapper may vary from what appears to be a well-defined wild man to that of dwarf king, elf king, hill king, or merman. All these variants occur in the North German and Scandinavian versions of the ballad of "Hind Etin." It is only in one of the Scotch versions that the creature who carries the maiden off on his horse is a "forester," that is, a wild man and protector of the woods, who uproots tall trees to build a bower for his love. In other versions he may, dwarflike, confine her in a cave. A central motive, different from those so far described, connects the various forms of the story. The hind (workman, employee) elopes with the maiden, obtaining her loyalty and love, and lives happily with her and their children in wild-man fashion in the faraway woods, "for what he makes of prey," but he loses her again when, after years of heathen gratification, her Christian upbringing asserts itself in a natural desire to go once more to church. When, won over by the memories of her childhood, she overstays her time, he presents himself, this time quite the enraged demon of doom, carries her back by main force, and so is the cause of her death.[9]

The ballad presents thus a concatenation of motives usually separate in wild-man lore, notably those of abduction and happy love life in a bower made possible through hunting forays by the wild man. It may be mentioned that, according to most versions, the first departure of the damsel is undertaken of her own free will, and that as a motive it is thus similar to one represented in a fourteenth-century French love casket whereon the human damsel is seen climbing a ladder to a tree house, while a giant ensconced in it reaches out to receive her.[10]

If there is any need, after what has been said, of proving that the wild man as kidnapper is not an incubus, but a demon of death, such demonstration is afforded by a series of tales in which the demon seeks out the lady not in order to marry her, but in order to kill her outright. The victim, in the modern legends, is usually a moss damsel or blessed damsel, and the pursurer more often the wild hunter with his dogs than the wild man. But the near-identity of the hunter with his hairy relative is by now known to us. And as far as the wild damsel is concerned, medieval tales present her as a well-brought-up young lady, in order to enlist the listener's sympathy on her side, so that, in total effect, the scene is almost indistinguishable from the bridal rape by a demon with which we have dealt up to now. Modern folklore in regions as far apart as the Austrian Alps, Sweden, Denmark, and England relates how wild women of every variety suffer persecution from a hunting and riding demon who chases through the countryside alone or in rowdy company, and ends, when he has found his victim, by tearing her apart. Even if she escapes murder, the wild woman will be thrown over the demon's horse, tied down with her own long hair, and carried away by force. Human onlookers who demand a share of the prey may, to their horror, find half of a dead wild woman nailed to their stable door. It may be added, in order to demonstrate the connection of these legends with the main theme of our interest, that again in regions as far apart as Carinthia, the Tyrol, and England, the part of the wild hunter can actually be played by the wild man.[11]

The wide distribution of these stories argues for their age. And it is to be expected, therefore, that they were well established before the high Middle Ages, when writers had the opportunity of acquainting themselves with them. The persecution of the damsel by the wild hunter is mentioned by Vincent of Beauvais and by Caesarius of Heisterbach, who has preserved so many other items of the folklore of his day.[12] In the contemporary "Eckenliet," written somewhere in the Alps, the wild hunter is introduced under the name of Fasolt and made a giant, proprietor of a vast stretch of mountainous territory.[13] Claiming the wild woman as his game — *min wilt*, he calls her — he chases her relentlessly with dogs until challenged and overcome by her protector Dietrich. The triangle of human interests which we found operative on the love caskets is established again, and it is revealing to see the author make his concession to a courtly atmosphere by introducing the wild woman not only as very frightened, but also as a rather comely young lady whose character is made apparent by her masterly and merciful use, on the wounded Dietrich's behalf, of the healing arts.

One further step, and the wild woman becomes a richly clad lady of noble rank, as in the Tyrolean epic, "Der Wunderer," where the contrast between the pursuer and his prey is sharpened by presenting her as gentry, while the wild hunter is a man-eating fiend. Finally, in the epic of "Virginal," again of Tyrolean origin, the victim is a queen of dwarfs, while the hunter, an ogre and cannibal who uses dogs for the chase, reveals his identity by his name: he is called Orkise, an only slightly modernized version of the mythological terms "Orcus," which, it will be remembered, is the oldest name for the wild man as a demon of death. It must be added that in both these epics the victim is released from her anxieties through the energetic interference of Dietrich of Bern, who kills the wild hunter in battle and then proceeds to reward himself for the deed by marrying the liberated queen.[14]

About the mythological meaning of the hunt of the wild woman the scholars are divided, for one group maintains, in accordance with the old-fashioned theory of nature mythology, that the scene is meant to signify the maltreatment of the lower vegetation by storms, while the other, oriented sociologically, believes the scene denotes the extermination of witches by persons and groups bent upon liberating society from their obnoxious influence.[15] Neither explanation is satisfactory, the first because it ignores the human element, the second because it distorts it by forgetting that the wild hunter and his group are demons themselves, and that to entrust to them the removal of poisonous influence would be like driving out the devil with Beelzebub. The same wild hunter who treats the wild woman at times as his prey is equally ready at other times to ride with her in the Wild Horde, and is indeed her substitute as its leader.

One would be tempted, therefore, to regard the chase of the wood damsel by the wild man simply as a consequence of their habit of furious activity, on the assumption that they tend to pass from hunting together into hunting each other when there is no outer goal to attract their energies. But this too is of no avail, since, if it were true, the male hunter would have to be the victim some of the time, which is not the case. It is possible, however, to evade and perhaps to settle the issue of mythological meaning by concentrating upon the origin of the scene and upon the range of related ideas in areas adjoining central Europe. It is striking that, corresponding to the chase of the wild woman in the Alps, there exists a group of similar modern beliefs in Yugoslavia, where, in fact, only the names are changed. Here the wild woman, incredibly ugly with her long filthy hair and hanging breasts, yet capable of rapid transformation into an image of seductive youth, is called "Vila," "Striga" (witch), or "Vjèštica." Her pursuer, a hero but also a sorcerer, appears under the name of "Marco" or, in Slavic, "Komjen." And it may be significant, in view of her similarity to Artemis, to be discussed forthwith, that Vila, as she tries to escape, can take the form of an animal or ride on one, her favorite steed being the stag.[16]

Considering the geographical proximity of the regions in question, we must regard it as likely that the beliefs held in the Illyrian areas on the rim of the Adriatic are related to those endemic in the Alps. It is perhaps not incautious to suggest that the transition was made at a time when classical paganism in the general region was still a living force and thus capable of being transmitted to those new ethnic groups which were to settle there. If such reasoning is correct, it was the Baiuwarii (Bavarians) who were impregnated with native pagan beliefs when, at the end of the fifth century, they settled in Raetia and Noricum (a region covering parts of modern Austria, Germany, and Switzerland). We would have to assume then that, just like the Wild Hunt and Horde, which had a similar history, the related phenomenon of the chase of the wild woman spread from its Baiuwarian pivot in the Alps to other parts of central and western Europe.

Behind the Illyrian world looms ancient Greece. There are, it is true, no examples of the persecution of the feminine demon from medieval or modern Greece, and it may be assumed that the legend had died out there at a time when it was still vital in the culturally dependent barbarian regions to the north. But it can hardly be accidental that to the chasing of Vila, Striga, or the wood damsel there corresponded in classical times the chase of Artemis by a masculine demon, who forces her to precipitate herself from a rock and thus brings about her death. Tales to that effect were widespread in Argolis, Arcadia, and in Crete; and in the neighborhood of Troezen a yearly festival, the Saronia, was celebrated to commemorate the hunting of Artemis by her pursuer, Saron.[17] Perhaps the latter was an important local hero and "Artemis" originally the appellation given to an otherwise nameless local divinity. It is striking, at any rate, that the tale of the demise of a woman demon at the hands of a male foe should have been told of the same goddess Artemis who, as Hecate, was the whip and leader of rampant souls and who, as Diana, later in the Middle Ages, became the Latin eponym of the wild woman as mistress of the Wild Horde. It is obvious that there must be a historical connection. And since, to my knowledge, the motive was not known to the Romans nor to the Italians of medieval and postmedieval times, it could have been transmitted only through those regions of Dalmatia and Istria which have remained cognizant of it right to the present day.[18]

What holds of Diana is true also of her alter ego, Herodias, the woman demon whom the Middle Ages believed to be condemned to leading the souls of unbaptized children into all eternity. Herodias, it will be remembered, in a document from the early Middle Ages is cited as the leader of vagrant souls and, according to various sources, holds this position right into modern times. It is significant, therefore, that her name should be substituted for that of Vila, of southern Slavic folklore, as she runs for her life to escape her demon foe, and that the same should be told about her in parts of the eastern Alps.[19]

We are now ready for one last move in the uncertain but fascinating game of mythological identification. For if it is true, as put forth here, that the rape of the lady by the amorous wild man is akin in intention to his murderous onslaught upon the wood damsel, then one would have a right to expect that the two motives would attract each other, as such motives always do in mythology, and that personalities from one cycle would pass over into the other. This is indeed the case. The ground on which they met was the classical myth of Pluto and Proserpina. In order to understand what occurred, it may be well to recall once more that, as a demon of death, the wild man was known under the name of the Roman god of the underworld, Orcus, whose mythological kinship to his

Greek analogue could not but obtrude itself to persons acquainted with the classical tradition. And it will have to be added that, by the very nature of her myth, Proserpina is not only the maiden torn out of her innocent activities by Pluto's violence, but also the terrible and threatening goddess of the underworld, daughter of Styx, and identical image of Hecate. This conception, which was the oldest Greek one, was never quite lost sight of, even in the Middle Ages when the tendency was to transform simple tales such as this into fairy tales and thus remove their sting. It is clear at any rate that both Pluto and Proserpina had aspects of wild-man mythology, and that it was not necessary to resort to farfetched contrivances to translate the classical myth into native folklore.

A first inkling of how this could be done is given in the Taymouth Hours, where, according to the description, the lady is overcome by the wild man as she is gathering flowers, that is, when engaged in the same activity in which Proserpina was interrupted by Pluto's tempestuous attentions. Assuming that this is a sign of the author's acquaintance with the classical story, we have a specimen of the transformation of myth into moral exemplum that appealed to the medieval mentality. Not long after the writing of the Taymouth Hours, Berchorius gave an entire allegorical interpretation of the rape of Proserpina, claiming that Pluto was the devil, Proserpina the Christian soul, her mother Ceres the church, and the flowers the vain temporal attractions of the world.[20]

We would not dare, however, to insist upon the identity proposed, were not the rather tenuous allusion in the Taymouth Hours confirmed by a literary document, which goes all the way in proclaiming the fusion between native folklore and ancient myth. Here, in an English epic of the early fourteenth century, "Sir Orfeo," it is the classical myth which is the ostensible theme, but the writer, enamored as he is with the light creatures of the native glades, undertakes to translate the myth into a fairy tale, spicing it with a few details from the contemporary scene.[21] In his hands the tragic lover Orpheus becomes Sir Orfeo, a knight and minstrel singer, Pluto a fairy king, and the rape a magic sleight of hand. It is all the more shocking to discover, in the midst of such harmless playfulness, that the place of Proserpina, whose name does not occur, is given to one of the darkest and most sinister figures in the medieval vocabulary, Herodias, here named Queen Heurodas. We have here a medieval example of the killing of Herodias — of which we have mentioned modern Alpine and Slavic instances — only that the murderous assault has been transmuted into one of those amorous abductions into fairyland which we ventured to interpret as similes of death. We are forced to assume, therefore, that the author, although he gives no outward sign of it, was acquainted with the mythology of the Wild Horde and, by inference, of the wild man.

It fell to Albrecht Dürer to produce the final synthesis of native folklore and Greek myth, not by allowing them both to degenerate into harmless caricatures of themselves, but by stressing their common dark and sinister reality. His etching * of the abduction of the lady, an image of unrelenting force vainly resisted, is known as the rape of Proserpina, and rightly so, for at the time when the print was produced (1516), Dürer was under the full sway of humanist influences, which would surely have prevented his preoccupation with native superstition for its own sake. It is striking, however, and has of course not gone unobserved, that the details of the turbulent scene hardly serve to bear out its humanist meaning. The classical story asserts that Pluto, when overcome by his passion for the daughter of Demeter, rose out of the earth on his carriage and lifted her on his vehicle before dragging her away.

In Dürer, however, the abductor rides on a shaggy unicorn, and, while the scene lacks none of the bleakness and violence which the ancient tale demanded, the presence of the monster imparts to it a fantastic air which could have come only out of the medieval heritage. Dürer himself arrived at the full intensity of his vision only gradually, and in a preparatory drawing that has come down to us introduced a horse instead of the unicorn.[22] It is clear that in placing both abductor and victim on the back of equine creatures Dürer followed a tradition other than the classical, a tradition of which the artistic side is embodied in older miniatures showing both Proserpina and her pursuer astride a galloping horse,† with Pluto rendered as a devil, befitting the king of the underworld, and Proserpina as a lady fully dressed, rather than the nude struggling woman in Dürer's print. The indebtedness of Dürer to works of this kind is apparent, nevertheless, since his departures from their

* Fig. 28.   † Fig. 25.

type are obviously due to his effort to translate the conventional rendition, of which alone medieval art was capable, into the classical medium, which knows neither devils nor modest maidens. In doing so he endowed the scene for the first and only time with the passion and impetuosity which both the medieval and the classical myth demanded.

It is most likely that the abduction on a horse, as shown in the medieval miniatures, is itself a concession to native mythology, and that the model of the mounted Pluto is no other than the leader of the Wild Hunt carrying the wood damsel to her death. It is significant in this connection that Pluto, the fairy king, in the epic of "Sir Orfeo," rides, as do all his knights, on a white steed.[23] But Dürer, while showing acquaintance with this tradition, went far beyond his medieval prototypes by introducing the wild man's steed, the unicorn. This detail, too, he took from artistic prototypes. For in prints, love caskets, and tapestries of the fifteenth century the opinion had found expression that, apart from fair ladies who tamed the unicorn by the magic of their sex, the wild men were the only creatures capable of overcoming its ferocity, though not by blandishments, but by force.[24] Alone among human beings they maintained themselves on the unicorn's back. And Dürer was thus in the position of acquainting himself with one of the motives found in his etching by examining prints by his forerunners, the "Master E. S.," and the "Master of the Housebook." * It is typical of the synthetizing power of his genius that he should have thought of equating the mythology of the wild hunter with that of the wild man, and of asserting the equivalence of both traditions with the classical myth of Pluto and Proserpina.

We return to the motive of the wild man tamed and fettered by his lady, which, it will be remembered, was shown on one of the love caskets of the fourteenth century. Other works of art exhibiting the same theme, this time alone, include a fresco formerly in the Swiss castle of Liebenfeld, a Swiss tapestry, the boxwood handle of a German ornamented dagger, and a German love casket.[25] The history of the motive previous to its appearance in art

* Fig. 24.

shows a convergence of ritual and amorous interests, the final coincidence of which seems to have been the cause for its visual emergence. Of these, the ritual of the capture of the wild man through the instrumentation of a fair lady has occupied us before. It will be recalled that in Marling, near Merano in the Tyrol, the capture of the savage creature was entrusted to schoolgirls, who may have taken the place of their older sisters, since at their age they could not possess an aura strong enough to captivate a wild man. We found furthermore that a related performance was the Flemish one recorded by Pieter Brueghel,* where the mask of a woman was used as a decoy to lure the wild man into an ambush; and that in the modern observances in the Pyrenees a similar snare waited for the bear and prepared the way for his killing. We may add, in order to complete this list, that in the Swedish province of Dalecarlia the young bridegroom in a marriage is called "the bear," the marriage fireworks, "the shooting of the bear," and an engagement, "a play with the bear," implying a parallelism between a successful courtship and the ritual killing of the beast.[26] The observances in question were a general European phenomenon, and the artists who recorded similar scenes had a great fund of folklore upon which to draw.

It would have been possible for them, in consequence, to attach their courtly and amorous symbolism to the scene of the wild man's death, as was done in the case of the related theme of the capture and killing of the unicorn. There the motive, when used in its secular context, revealed the miraculous transformation of a creature living in a state of passion and ferocity into one living in a state of love; and, therefore, the unicorn, symbol of generative power, had to die in the lap of the virgin, as man's strength does in the sexual act, to be reborn, content, tame, and relaxed, ready to bear the fetters of love.[27] In the case of the wild man there is no such death and rebirth, for, as we shall see, he is the individual lover who had been wild and was tamed, and thus must show in his person the continuity of spiritual states. Therefore, when interpreted in terms of human affection, the ritual of the capture of the wild man is abridged and deprived of its sting by omitting the scene of his death.

* Fig. 16.

This tempering of an otherwise rather brutal scene was due to the influence of love poetry upon the primordial pagan ritual. In the songs of the German Minnesingers wildness is an image for the state of unruly self-assertion which, if we are to believe the poets, is man's barbarian lot, unless the influence of woman instills in him a gentler habit of mind. It is thus connected with man's estate previous to any amorous engagement. It can be also the unhappy first result of having fallen in love, denoting that feeling of unappeased yearning in which man is engulfed unless his lady relents and admits him into her favor. In neither case does the fact that a man is wild necessarily imply that he is or is about to become a hairy wild man of the woods. The application of the metaphor to art was due to a deliberate fusion of the poetic tradition with the mythological. Indeed, the term "wild" belongs to the poet's stock in trade, a cliché no less than the endless repetition of descriptions of the lady's matchless beauty, or of the delights of May, with nightingales singing and flowers budding under clear skies.[28]

Examples are abundant. Ulrich von Gutenberg, a twelfth-century Alsatian minnesinger, sang: "I was wild however much I sang; her beautiful eyes were the rods with which she first overcame me." [29] The implication is, apparently, that woman has it in her power to tame her wild lover by letting her charms work upon him. Dietmar von Elst, in the same century, asserts that his lady, *benimet mir mange wilde tat*, prevents many a wild deed, by forcing the submission of his heart to her, as if she were the steersman and he the ship.[30] In a later century Heinrich von Württemberg (1448–1519), far more personal than his forerunners, protests his love by asking his lady's forgiveness for having grown wild for her sake: "O you who are the excess of beauty, tender as one might wish, delicately formed; O Treasure, do not let me suffer for having become wild because of you, dainty damsel, and helpless." [31] The image even entered into religious poetry, and Heinrich von Burgus, a friar from the southern Tyrol (about 1300) made use of it in his didactic poem, "Der Seele Rat," letting the soul speak to Lady Penitence quite in the manner of the submissive lover: "Sweet penitence, thou shalt tame me; I have been wild." And later, "I have been wild and have not read many prayers." [32]

Man was, however, not entirely alone in being liable to fall from civilized estate, for wildness could be imputed also to the lady, only that, since it was the lover who was speaking, this undesirable state was in her case a symptom not of passion, which was beneath her, nor of unruly behavior, but of inclemency and cruelty. Instead of falling short of the demands of love by too much impetuosity, as the man did, she sinned against it by her frigidity, which was only an exaggeration of her ordinarily aloof and exalted state. It was in this sense that Cino da Pistoia (1270–1336) complained about his lady as being *una selvaggia crudele*. And Wernher von Homberg (1284–1320) stated with bitterness that his damsel was "wild" toward deserving lovers, while letting the sun of her favor shine upon unworthy ones.[33]

The analogy of the lover's wildness with the manner of life of the wild man is completed by considering that he, like his savage counterpart, can be caught and fettered, and thus forced to abandon his previous state of mind. It is true that the wild man's iron chain and the light red ribbon by which the lover was held are ligatures of different strength, but the amorous captive and the wild man both find it impossible to escape, no matter whether it is physical force or superior fascination which holds them in bondage. And the lover, for his part, will do best not to fret, but to acquiesce in his capture by turning with admiration to his feminine captor. *Forma tua fulgida/tunc me catinavit*, sings one of the Goliard poets in the *Carmina Burana*: "Thy brilliant aspect has bound me in chains." [34] And this metaphor of the lover's loss of free will was repeated by poets of all schools and tongues as long as the courtly sentiment prevailed. For by being bound the lover had passed from wildness into that state of tameness humbly borne and of unquestioning obedience to his lady's whims and wishes which alone could give him title to be initiated into her intimacy. No writer records how much residual or persisting wildness she expected from him, once he had fulfilled the difficult conditions of his courtship.

It is clear, then, that there is a striking resemblance between the amorous conventions of courtly poetry and the mythology of the wild man, the more striking, in fact, since there is no indication of any original connection between them. The two modes of thought were bound to attract each other, although the fusion between them was to be long delayed. The canons of courtly love had to sink from the nobility, which had created them, to the level of the citzens of the town before they could be compared with the pagan rituals that were practiced there. Therefore, the sayings about the lover's wildness, which were common coinage in the twelfth century, had to wait until the fourteenth before they could be attributed to the genuine wild man.

There exists a Dutch poem of less than mediocre merit, but of some interest historically, which contains, perhaps for the first time in literature, the fusion of erotic convention and mythology. It is a didactic opus, tedious in its lengthy insistence upon the commonplace, and we shall spare the reader the perusal of it. Its title is "Van der wilden Man." [35] The author claims to have seen in a dream how a maiden dragged a wild man out of the forest on a chain. In an ensuing conversation he expresses doubt as to her ability to hold a creature as strong and unruly as the wild man, only to be told that after having chased him through many a land she did not intend to give up now; furthermore, that she trusted to the power of her love and to the mild treatment she would accord him to cause her captive to forgo wildness and become faithful and obedient. The author gives vent to his doubts once more, but is told in no uncertain terms that she, the damsel, would not hear of anything but success.

The proof of her contention is not long in coming, for hardly has the uneven couple departed from the scene, when the author hears the wild man intone a happy song in praise of his new estate:

> I was wild, now I am caught
> And brought into the ties of love;
> A maid has done this to me.
> I was wild, now I am caught,
> And though I could, I would not escape,
> For I gave my good faith as a pledge.
> I was wild, now I am caught
> And brought into the ties of love.[36]

Hearing this song, the author becomes pensive, realizing how rightly the maiden had spoken. He begins to think now that a woman endowed with high-minded virtues would find it easier to master the wild man than would "an entire army," for what force could not hope to achieve would be accomplished by sweetness, shrewdness, and courtesy. Then he awakes. And, as if his own thoughts were not enough, he seeks advice from a maiden, this time of real flesh and blood, who adds to his deliberations some of the commonplaces of courtly doctrine, and thus manages to set his mind at rest.

So much for the poem. The reader will have recognized that its doctrine and mythology are built around the wild man's song which is its germ, containing in concentrated form all the action and thought evolved in the other verses. The song has its existence apart, even when read in the context of the rhymes surrounding it, and it is, perhaps, not incautious to suggest that the author found it ready-made when he decided to extend it into his rather fatuous piece of moralized mythology. It is a love song, complete in eight verses with three refrains, and endowed with that well-rounded simplicity which fits a piece of poetry for popular usage. It will be noted that, like the loftier songs of the minnesingers from which it derives its contents, it has as yet none of the references to the mythology of the wild man which the author found dormant in it and amplified.

And now it is interesting to compare the entire poem with the works of art which, like it, are devoted to the capture and taming of the wild man. The situation described in love caskets, paintings, and tapestries is the by now familiar one of the calm and gracious lady, radiant in her youthful charm, holding the untutored wild man on an iron chain. The analogy is completed by inscriptions which correspond to the love song in the Dutch poem and to the metaphors in older poetry. *Ich wil iemer wesen wild bis mich zemt ein Frowen bild* — "I have always been wild until tamed by a lady" — says the wild man in a Swiss tapestry,* using almost the same words as the sinner of Heinrich von Burgus, the lover of Ulrich von Gutenberg, or the wild man in the refrain of the Dutch love song. And the lady who has the creature in her power answers no less obstinately than her Dutch analogue: *Ich frow ich wel dich zemen wol als ich billich sol* — "Tame I will thee, since tame I shall thee." The inscriptions accompanying the fresco in Castle Liebenfeld are variants to these. The wild man asserts: *Ich bin haarig and wild und Fuert mich ain wiplich bild* — "I am Hairy and wild and I am led by a damsel" — and the lady answers by insisting on her

* Fig. 35.

attractions: *Ich zaig dir min anmuot wie min herz fliegen tuot* —
"As my heart flies out to thee, I show thee my charm." More compressed are the inscriptions on love caskets, where there was less
space to develop them. The wild man says no more than: *Zam und
wild macht mich ein bild* — 'It is a damsel who makes me tame and
wild" — or, even shorter, *frowelich bilde mahet mich wilde* —
"A woman makes me wild." [37]

Through all these inscriptions runs as a recurrent theme the
repetition of one or two sententious formulas, derived, it would
seem, from a common stock of phrases easily available. The extreme
shortness of these was balanced by the presence close by of the
image, so that text and picture formed an entirety no less complete
than the poems from which the inscriptions were chosen. Whether
the artistic formulations were based upon literary ones such as the
poem, "Van der wilden Man," or whether the latter was patterned
after a work of art now lost, I would not dare to say. But while
there can be some doubt as to the origin of the combination of
amorous text and mythology, the origin of the inscriptions is fairly
certain: they are abbreviated versions of love songs of the kind
accidentally preserved in the Dutch poem.[38] Such songs retained,
in simplified popular style, some of the metaphors and stock phrases
of older poetry, and thus prepared the way for their penetration
into the amorous life of a wider public. We may be justified in
imagining that some of the metaphors thus singled out became part
of the vocabulary upon which writers of love poems relied when
trying to express their feelings to their ladies. When it came to
protesting their allegiance by the more impressive and perhaps more
obligating display of works of art, the young men of the time found
no difficulty in combining the visual image of the wild man in
chains with the conventional sentiments that went with it.

Corresponding to the lyrical and artistic treatment of the capture
of a wild man by a lady there was also the telling of the tale in epic
form; although it must be owned that, as transmitted to us, the
motive is vitiated by disturbing extraneous accretions. We shall
not go into it too deeply, merely giving its outline without entering
into the intricacies of its development and origin, with which others
have dealt more than adequately.[39]

The tale was a popular one and occurs with various modifications in folk traditions as far apart in space as those of the Abruzzi, Tuscany, and Brittany, and as distant from each other in time as an Arthurian epic of the thirteenth century, Straparola's classical collection of stories of the sixteenth century,[40] and the *Cabinet des Fées*, published in Geneva in 1787. We must add that the chief protagonist is not always a wild man, who may yield his place to a satyr (Straparola, the Breton, and one of the Abruzzi versions) or even to a centaur or a snake; and that a large part of the story is made up of themes such as a queen's unfaithfulness, discovered by the demon, and his superior but enigmatic laughter at various examples of human folly and trickery. Stripped of these accretions, the story merely tells how a wild man or satyr, whichever it may be, was caught by a lady through the familiar device of spreading food or drink before him. It is most probably due to Oriental influence that this lady should present herself at first disguised as a youth, and that the discovery of her concealment should be one of the demon's achievements in clairvoyance.

In the medieval version of the tale, which is contained in "Lestoire de Merlin," and with which we are here concerned, it is the professional shape-shifter and intermittent wild man, Merlin, who acts the part of the demon. He himself arranges his own capture in order to be able to put the wild man's prophetic capacities at the service of the emperor who is his liege. Disguised as a stag, he reveals that only a wild man will be able to explain the emperor's dreams. Then he vanishes into the forest, leaving instructions as to how the wild man may be caught. The capture, of which all the men at court prove incapable, is finally accomplished by the disguised maiden Grisandoles. And Merlin, now returned to the emperor's castle, explains that *Feme mavoit pris par sa poisance et par son engin che que nus homs ne pooit faire de tout vostre pooir —* "A woman took me through her power and cunning, something which none of you men could have done with all your strength" — adding *que Grisandoles est la plus bele Feme et la plus boine de tout nostre terre et sest pucelle —* "Grisandoles is the most beautiful woman and the best in all [the emperor's] lands and she is a virgin." The conditions of the capture are thus plainly stated and, on the whole, the same as those prevailing in ritual and poetry.[41]

It will be necessary now to return for a second time to those two love caskets from the lower Rhine with which this inquiry began. The reader will remember that one of these, composed from the point of view of virtuous knighthood, showed the victory of high principles over mere appetite and lust, while the other, reversing this scale of values, presented the defeat of selfless bravery at the hands of its wild antagonist, while the wild man who administers this repulse is in his turn overcome by the magic of his lady, who is capable of subduing both civilized and savage suitors. In allowing the implied victory of the wild man over the knight, the latter, or the group for which he stands, admits the possibility of a world in which the ideals of chivalry do not reign supreme and can be replaced by their outright denial. Temporarily, at least, knighthood seems to be abdicating and joining a revolt of brute instinct against its rule. One will realize how serious was this about-face when it is considered that the love casket in question is by no means the only document for the change. It was not very long after the casket was made that Charles VI of France joined the highest dignitaries of his realm in performing a wild man's dance, and thus deliberately descending to the lowest level of human life. And, as will be shown later, his contemporary, King Wenceslaus of Bohemia, found it no more embarrassing to have his own image in the guise of a wild man inserted in the pages of an illuminated manuscript, this wild man shown under the spell of a light girl from a bathing establishment.

Such change of sentiment, such outright treason to the knightly ideal, was obviously possible only under the influence of a far-reaching cultural dislocation. In the late Middle Ages the life of the aristocracy had indeed undergone significant modifications. Its usefulness had been impaired by the cessation of the Crusades and its leadership challenged by the rising power of the cities, of capitalism, and of dynastic interests. And while these pressures had not been able to affect the leadership of the knighthood in matters pertaining to taste, polished behavior, and the definition of the good life, they had taken the substance out of its ideals and left nothing but their empty form. The reaction of the knightly class, notably in France and Burgundy, to this unfortunate situation has been described by Huizinga in one of the most sensitive and penetrating books ever written on the history of the Middle Ages.[42] Unable to conceive of an alteration in a mode of life containing so much that was admirable and worth preserving, the aristocracy entrenched itself in the minute observance of its own rules, the mere etiquette of court life, battle, and tournament, elaborating them into an intricate and beautiful game. By thus insisting upon the rigid maintenance of its own identity, the aristocracy deepened the chasm that existed between its conventional behavior and the realities of the political life of which it was part, and ended by adopting, for many purposes, a double standard — of austerity, generosity, and valor for everything pertaining to the shining surface of life, and of political expediency and brute force for its practical machinery.

For this duplicity, though largely unconscious, it paid the usual price in unhappiness, a price particularly heavy since the ideals ostensibly maintained were so high. It was natural, therefore, that the tenor of the age, as exposed in chivalric chronicles, should have been one of gloom, dejection, and despair. Life as really lived, we are told, is a constant betrayal of what it should be, and particularly of those values of loyalty and honorable behavior which were the cement of all feudal relationships, including that between the lover and his lady. So great, however, was the tendency of the age toward artificiality that the sentiment which had its origin in reflections on the pointlessness of conventions without substance was itself overwhelmed by convention and so became only a mere literary exercise, a pose. When the good citizens of Switzerland and Western Germany adopted the general complaint about the unfaithfulness of the world, in selecting inscriptions for their tapestries, they were following a fad which had little basis in their own aspiring lives.

Such a situation cried out for escape, and since the flight into sublimation had been preëmpted by the illusions of the chivalric code, such escape was offered only by a reversion to primitivism. The spectacle is one which repeats itself at the end of great epochs in history, when traditional aims and values have become questionable and forms of life once meaningful have become brittle and petrified. In such periods radical archaism is sometimes an easy way out of a spiritual impasse. Nothing could have been more radical than the attitude of sympathizing or identifying oneself with the

wild man, whose ways of life was the repudiation of all the accumulated values of civilization. It must be added that the prominence
given to the wild man in the latter part of the fourteenth century
and in the fifteenth century was, of course, only an extremist consequence of a movement which had much wider scope.[43] Instead of
playing with the thought of the wild man's superiority, it was always possible to adopt the pastoral genre, rather than the primitivist,
to sing the popular pastorals or *bergerettes*, or even to slip into the
costume of those lower classes whose "villainy" one despised in
practical life. The fifteenth century was as capable of this attitude
as was the eighteenth. And it must have been felt, as in the later age,
that temporary surcease from restraint and boredom was not too
dearly bought at the expense of the semblance of a little Horatian
frugality, particularly if such slight discomfort was offset by the delights of facile love in the woods.

As far as the wild man is concerned, his popularity in the late
Middle Ages is due not only to the faintheartedness of the knighthood betraying its own ideals, but equally to the increasing ascendancy of the citizenry. The very origin of the wild-man stories as
told at the courts and of the wild-man dances there points to the
lower strata of society as the source of such sophisticated diversion.
It is only natural, therefore, that the increasing importance of the
culture of cities, as observed in many facets of life in the latter part
of the fourteenth century, should have led to an increase of interest
in the wild man. The disappointment of fashionable knights and
ladies in their way of life, and the imitation of their attitudes by
others eager to assume their pose, may have been the main cause for
the adoption of the new sympathetic iconography. Its increase in
quantity was in fact due to bourgeois influence. We find, consequently, that France and Burgundy, the hub of all fashionable
sentiment, were peripheral countries as far as the preoccupation
with the wild man was concerned, while Switzerland and the
Rhineland, provincial areas from the western point of view, allowed
it to burgeon luxuriantly. It happened that in these regions a considerable urban growth coincided with abundant local development
of the folklore required.

In consequence of the joint operation of the social factors described, wild-man iconography took an upturn in the latter decades

of the fourteenth century. It was this period which saw the introduction into art of the wild man as shield-bearer, the wild man as captive of the lady, and particularly the various happy scenes of his family life in the woods, all of which imply at least limited approval of his mode of existence. Since by now the wild man was not conceived of as an inferior antagonist of the knight, but in many ways as his equal, it became possible even to recast some of the tales of the romances in terms of wild-man life, turning them into fairy tales by replacing the plate armor of the knight by the fur of the demon.

An example of this procedure is to be found in a Swiss tapestry of the fifteenth century that tells the story of the "Count of Safoy" in terms of shaggy personalities, converting even such dignitaries as the King of France into hairy maskers. A similar earlier tapestry, of Alsatian origin, and again with only hairy actors, may bear witness to the same intention.[44] Its incomplete plot has not been identified. What there is of an originally more extended sequence — a wild king welcomed by his queen, a royal meal, a game of checkers played by the king and queen, and finally the visit of the former to a hermit — reminds one more of the mythology of the dwarfs, who are royalists, than of the wild men. Finally, among the scenes transformed capriciously by dressing the participants in the tufts of wild men, was the conquest of the castle of love, a favorite amusement at pageants and festivals which passed from there into art.[45] In the earliest performances and in works of art dependent on them, the defenders of the castle had been gracious ladies only, and the assailants, armored knights. Love caskets and tapestries show how these polite warriors came to be gradually replaced by impetuous wild men, acting first as attackers, later also, under the influence of the "Roman de la Rose," as guardians of the castle. Wild men were customarily arrayed against a company of knights on the opposite side.

Such fantasies about the conquest of feminine virtue by masculine force or insistence were enacted in pageants before the same theme was given subtle allegorical expression in the "Roman de la Rose." But the law of the mutual attraction of related ideas was operative here as it is everywhere and, as a consequence, the one wild man in the romance, the villain, "Dangers," who is enlisted on the side of the lady's virtue, is now multiplied into a whole group of hairy warriors meant to personify those "wild" proclivities which contribute to feminine coldness and prudery. In an English pageant of 1522, which may well serve to explain similar representations in art, the castle was guarded by ladies "tired lyke the women of India" — that is, as wild women. Their names are largely taken from the romance: Dangier, Disdain, Gelosie, Unkyndness, Scorne, Malebouche, Straungeness.[46]

Even after this partial invasion of the wild men into the courtly scene, the fifteenth-century Swiss tapestries devoted to the subject come as somewhat of a surprise.[47] Here the world of gracious allegory is abandoned altogether; instead, we find ourselves projected into fairyland, with no civilized human figures anywhere in sight. There are in one tapestry only hairy wild men assailing blackamoors, including a black king and queen. And in another tapestry, now cut up and divided among various museums,* we find the attacking armies, their royalty, and the defenders of the castle rendered as wild men whose colored shaggy tufts contribute to the atmosphere of bright and lusty unreality that pervades the whole. There are notched trees, colored in all the hues of the rainbow and set off against a background of shining red. Before them a scene unfolds that seems to be sheer undiluted fantasy: a wild king, queen, and prince are seen dining in a tent, while a wild army, composed of riders on lions, stags, and unicorns, goes forth to attack the castle. The defenders, a lady and a garrison no less shaggy than their opponents, use lilies as their arrows and are assailed with roses, the symbolic meaning of which is obvious. But much more striking, and almost unique among works of art of the Middle Ages, is the sense afforded the spectator of a visit to the land where the unlikely is the commonplace, and where in place of everyday, crude, accustomed sights are the frothy and trifling creatures of fairyland. It would be foolish, before a work of art of this kind, to be too dogmatic about the mythological identity of the wild man, whose task it is here as elsewhere to embody any and all of their relatives among spirits.

The new sympathetic attitude toward the wild man was thus fraught with striking consequences for his position in art and litera-

* Fig. 34.

ture. None could have been as momentous as the fact that, by being set up, as it were, as a kind of final cause for man's suppressed desires, the wild man found himself turned into an exponent of human erotic behavior. It was natural and perhaps inevitable that this should have occurred, for by identifying himself with his savage brother, man had sought the license and freedom from artificial restraint which his own manner of life had not afforded him. Since social barriers against the sway of appetite had been, as they usually are, highest and most formidable in the field of erotic satisfactions, it was there that the desire for escape found its most persistent expression. We studied an example of this new attitude in the artistic representations of the capture of the wild man by his lady. Others come to mind easily and will be studied in their proper place. It will suffice to note here that the new role of the wild man brought him closer than before to his mythological relative, the satyr, and that it prepared the way for the identification of the two in the Renaissance and the final absorption of the former in the figure of his relative from antiquity.

The new attitude expressed itself drastically and sometimes explicitly, creating its own standards of excellence and its own artistic iconography. As one would expect, it skirted not infrequently the limits of what today would be regarded as the minimum proprieties. Almost always it acted as a counterpoise to those values of courtly love which had been the mainstay of the past, aligning itself with whatever sentiments were in favor of a more natural approach toward amorous experience.

Characteristic, for instance, is a print previously mentioned, by Israel von Meckenem,* showing a blossom rising out of winding scrolls and a group of wild men and women climbing through them as they try to reach the petals. The medievalist cannot help feeling reminded, when beholding the print, of the central motive of the "Roman de la Rose," where a symbolic flower is also the goal of man's craving. The courts of France and Burgundy had seen a contentious discussion as to the worthiness of a poem in which the workings of nature in providing for man's propagation had been extolled as unreservedly as they had been in the second part of the "Roman de la Rose." [48] As far as the maker of the print is con-

* Fig. 38.

cerned, the discussion is settled in favor of unabashed naturalness. And we see, therefore, two couples of naked wild men and women helping each other to the enjoyment of the flower by climbing on each other's backs, while other wild men underneath, contestants for the same pleasure, are slugging their rivals with clubs or shooting them with arrows.

This, then, is another version of the conquest of the castle of love, only that, with the courtly technique of amorous delay excluded, men and women may now assist each other in achieving the consummation. As one would expect, where the conditions of nature predominate, whatever postponement there is, is caused not by the actions of the various personified emotions of a chaste lady, but merely by the mutual interference of rivals for her favor. An inscription veils and reveals the engraver's symbolic intention: *Flore pulchro nobili apes melle colligunt Ex hoc vermes frivoli virus forte hauriunt* ("From a beautiful and noble flower do bees collect their honey. From this one, however, do the frivolous vermin extract a stronger potion.")

When a less drastic version of the same kind of thought was intended, the wild men were connected not with mere sexual appetite, but with the nobler principle of unfulfilled sensual desire. "My name is desire," says the hairy wild man and *caballero* in Diego de San Pedro's "Carcel de Amor," and "I am the principal official in the castle of love." He bears out his contention by first appearing to the author's view * with a nude statuette of Venus in his hands, and dragging behind him the unfortunate figure of a lover, who is dazzled and tortured by beholding it. The wild man explains that "with the beauty of this image he inspires affections and with those consumes lives, as can be seen in the prisoner, whom he is conducting to the prison of love." [49] His task is not dissimilar to that of the lady holding her lover in chains. It signifies the less esoteric nature of the wild man's mission that in carrying it out he should invoke the help of Venus, according to medieval usage the embodiment of sensual love; indeed, he is her natural ally and follower. And he appears as such not only in the Spanish work here discussed, but also in the German epic, "Die Moerin," where he makes his entry as the first of her entourage, preceding the others

* Fig. 46.

with a large iron pole in hand.[50] At the pageant performed on occasion of the marriage of Orazio Bentivoglio to Lucrezia d'Este in 1487 Venus appeared with her lion in the midst of forest decoration and surrounded by dancing wild men.

The threats of the *caballero* wild man in "Carcel de Amor" against the safety and happiness of his captive are carried out to the hilt. The victim is dragged to the prison of love, inaccessibly located in a tower on a mountaintop, and there is tortured by allegorical creatures which give him no more surcease than the damned can expect in Dante's *Inferno*. The wild man meanwhile transforms himself into one of the guards of the prison.[51]

Amorous desire and the promise of its prompt fulfillment are cunningly combined in the marginal drolleries in various luxurious manuscripts written for Wenceslaus of Bohemia (1361–1419), notably the magnificent Bible in several volumes, illuminated for his use.* [52] Wild men, sometimes of fantastic types, are liberally scattered over these pages, climbing through the scrolls, rising out of the cups of flowers, or walking proudly, shield and lance in hand. Shocking as it would be, were we not aware of the royal propensities of the time, some at least of these hairy creatures are apparently meant to be incarnations of the king himself. They have a way of obtruding themselves into his intimacy by holding his crested helmet or his coat of arms; but while in representations of this kind a subtle line of demarcation may still exist between the king and the bearer of his armorial identity, such distinction disappears when the wild man is shown as the embodiment of sensual desire. Then we find him caught in the king's own initial W, that is, in a position meant to indicate the captive's unappeased ardors as well as his royal identity.[53]

Nor are we left in the dark as to the member of the opposite sex guilty of having put the king into such straits. She is not a lady — and here the miniaturist departs from an old and honorable tradition — but what today would best be called a bathing beauty, a light-skirted damsel, armed with bucket and broom, of a type that graced the bathing establishments of the day and there took care of man's needs.[54] Sometimes in the pages of Wenceslaus' books we see her multiplied into a whole group of damsels of her profession, who

* Figs. 40, 41.

mock the captive king in his predicament; or again she may tantalize him by appearing in the nude like Venus; or, in a fit of unnecessary cruelty, she may ride on the wild man's back, forcing him to walk on all fours,[55] thus maintaining her dominion over him in the same manner as does Phyllis over her learned, but foolish, lover Aristotle. In short, the bathing beauty is, in almost any sense one would care to adopt, a wild woman, even though she sports a light skirt and sash rather than the usual fur. A learned commentator on the miniatures in question suggested, decades ago, that this unconventional quarry of a king's desires may have more in common with a ravishing siren, of whose kinship with the wild woman we are aware, than with the unapproachable great lady of the courtly past.[56] Both siren and bathing beauty have, in their different ways, intimate connections with water.

The question who may have been the somewhat disreputable lass to whom a king owed such loyalty occupied the good citizens of Prague before it penetrated to the scholar's study. They saw the bathing beauty, along with various other royal emblems, painted and carved on several buildings from Wenceslaus' time.[57] Naturally they enjoyed combining historical explanation with the kind of scandalmongering which brings even kings down to the level of everyday humanity, and so they came up with a romantic but incredible story of how Wenceslaus, caught in the city, had been helped by a bathing girl to hide himself and escape, and how she had been rewarded with love and money.

A little thought will convince us, however, that a king, if he had once lost his bearings, would not be likely to so lose all sense of propriety as to proclaim his disgrace in public, and even to have symbolic reminders of it inserted in the pages of a Bible. The solution of the puzzle lies in another much more surprising direction. As we take another glance at the decorations of King Wenceslaus' books, we find the bathing beauty not only performing the tasks of her calling, but also those of her opposite, the wild man, holding the royal coat of arms or allowing herself to be held captive. Once she appears crowned like the king himself — indicating a more intimate relationship between her and her swain than a mere courtesan could boast.[58] In addition, we find among the emblems the love knot and, most revealing, the kingfisher, symbol of marital loyalty.

There is no escape: the bathing beauty can be no other than the queen herself, extraordinary as such a symbolization of a great and, of course, respectable lady would appear to us today. Since the name of the Queen of Bohemia — second wife of Wenceslaus — was Sophia Euphemia, we find that her initial E appears as often in the manuscripts as does that of the king, sometimes in combination with the latter, sometimes alone. And our surmise is confirmed by the fact that the king and his alter ego, the wild man, are caught in the labyrinthian embraces of the letter E as often as in those of his own initial. For all we know, the E may hold him more strongly than could any magic spell composed only of his own royal name.

The combination of wild man and bathing beauty contains thus the story of passion inflamed and held in abeyance, as well as of its ready appeasement by a loving wife. But conceding this solution still leaves the question how conjugal love could have been celebrated pictorially by what appears to be a slur upon the good name of the wife, or, if you wish, of both lovers. It is all very well to consider, as has been suggested, that in Wenceslaus' time the bathing establishments were frequently used as trysting places, and that a good wife regarded it as a duty to serve her husband in his bath.[59] It would still seem enigmatic that in celebrating the mystery of conjugal love, situations and ideas should have been evoked, which to our way of thinking tend to debase rather than exalt, the relationship of marriage.

To understand the apparent paradox it is necessary to cast a glance at the ideas of courtly love. It had been characteristic of these ever since the first troubadours attempted to win the favor of their ladies, that the relation of the lover to his love was to be extra-marital, or, to put it more bluntly in modern terms, adulterous. Marriage being what it usually was in the high Middle Ages, a matter of convenience, business, and high policy, the lady did not feel obligated to her husband beyond the adequate discharge of the duties which she had contracted or, rather, which had been contracted for her. This being the case, the married lady regarded it as an infraction of the rules of love, if she bestowed upon the person who had the legal right to her those romantic favors that could only be freely given. Marriage and passionate love were incompatible. And since by far the greater emphasis was laid upon that relation which challenged a person's spontaneous responses, love was regarded as the stronger tie of the two.[60]

The theoreticians of love, like Andreas Capellanus, felt that to cherish one's own wife beyond the measure of devotion which Christian charity demanded was a sin, because such behavior abused the marriage sacrament; and in this they were confirmed by the consensus of scholastic authorities, who believed that, while the act of copulation within marriage was without sin, the carnal desire that led up to it was unrighteous since it deprived man of his rational faculties.[61] No distinction was made by scholastics between passionate love inside or outside the marriage bond. Since their reasoning did not extend to the newfangled extramarital passions, they encouraged by their silence the spread of the practice of romantic love. Without restraint, and almost without censorship, the Middle Ages poured the energies of a passionate age into the idealization of a relation which excluded legitimacy.

It will be understood when considering this that, if a man insisted on celebrating his relationship to his wife, as King Wenceslaus did, challenging a tradition established for centuries, it was difficult for him to use those conventions of reverent adulation of the lady which had been connected with polite adultery. If marriage had any merits beyond the economic benefits which the husband could derive from it, they lay largely in the whole and hearty enjoyment of sensuality. Therefore, if a man chose to pay homage to his wife, he could do no better than to acknowledge her merits in this respect. It was a humorous and, according to the lights of the time, a not entirely tactless procedure, when Wenceslaus had his wife portrayed as a lady ready to grant her favors, while he pined and languished for them romantically. Indeed, by allowing any part of the courtly tradition to enter into the portrayal of marriage, as he did in having himself shown wild and in fetters, he was giving to marriage more than its due.

That anybody should have reveled in the delights of the married estate was not quite so extraordinary in German territory, and at the end of the fourteenth century, as it would have been in France, and in the twelfth century. In Germany the French doctrine of the extramarital character of true love, while very widely accepted, had never been adhered to exclusively. The praise of the sweet satisfactions of steadiness and legitimacy, as compared with the surreptitiousness imposed upon unmarried lovers, had been sung there as early as the Hohenstaufen age. A few poets of that period had even dared to endow marriage with the halo of romantic love, or to make of it the reward for a knight's labors on behalf of his lady. In France itself, which in the time of Wenceslaus was still the home of all highly bred elegance, the attractions of courtly love had begun to wane by the latter part of the fourteenth century. Criticism of it, even sarcastic derision, had become widespread precisely in those groups whom tradition would have trusted to be its staunchest champions. It had become almost fashionable to satirize the courtly ideal, or to oppose it, as did Christine de Pisan, on grounds of prudence and common decency. And as courtly love declined in the esteem of those who professed to practice it, marriage gained in prestige, although it would have occurred to very few, not even to those who knew the deep joy of happy marriage, to endow it with those glistening qualities which tradition found vested in romantic relationships. The tenor of the new age is very aptly expressed in Chaucer's *Canterbury Tales*, in which the prevailing sarcastic attitude toward marriage, while fully and boisterously presented, is ultimately rejected for a more reasoned approach based on mutual forbearance and love.[62]

The most important factor was the growing ascendancy all over Europe of the burghers, in whose life marriage had presumably often played a more than economic role; it assumed a solid, permanent, and ceremonious significance which it had not had before, thus influencing the attitudes of other groups. It is a sign of this ascendancy that, from the second part of the fourteenth century, art began to be employed in the service of marriage, solemnizing it through the creation of household chests, platters, tapestries, and embroideries, whose decoration referred in various ways to the married estate. Beside the works of art representing the religious sanctions of marriage or its civic and dynastic aspects, there were always some, like those showing the capture of the unicorn, that were meant to celebrate its sensual gratification.[63]

As far as the wild man is concerned, this growing importance of human marriage as a factor in cultural development influenced his lore in two mutually complementary ways. He came to appear on

.works of art owned by married couples and presumably meant to celebrate the glories of the married estate. And it became fashionable at the same time to show him in the full enjoyment of similar pleasures, no less lasting and satisfactory for not having been sanctioned by the blessings of the church. Indeed, in the works of art in question, notably tapestries with the joint escutcheon of two families united through wedlock, the married life of the wild man is idealized as a life unfettered by convention or by any of the limitations imposed by the demands of organized society.[64] He was particularly suited to take this position, since as a creature of instinct and impulse he could personify those natural forces whose predominance in marriage was emphasized by Catholic theology. We are told, accordingly, by Geiler von Kaysersberg, that the good women of Strassburg had a way of referring to their husbands as "wild men," presumably in dismay and pride over their tempestuous attentions.[65] Interestingly enough, this manner of speaking was current in that region from which came the majority of wild-man tapestries.

We certainly do not claim that all works of art showing the marital life of the wild man were necessarily meant to grace the household of a matron, or that all which allude to his erotic habits show him in the blessed state of wedlock without contract or obligations. The connection between the new social forces and the function of the wild man in late medieval art is nevertheless unmistakable.

In Chapter 4 we attempted to show how this idealization of the wild man grew out of traditions reaching back into antiquity which were continued into medieval times. We omitted, at that time, giving descriptions of works of art, but now that the amorous background has been sketched in, we present a few of the works of art devoted to the ancient and yet so novel theme.

The oldest such representation known to me is one that is not yet connected with marriage. It is a grave plate of the fourteenth century in Altenberg im Düntal (near Cologne), one of those which in the period of the Hanseatic League were exported from Flemish ateliers.[66] In a marginal area we see what from now on will be part of the usual stock in trade of the new iconography: wild men hunting or returning from the chase with the slain beast slung over one shoulder, wild women welcoming the hunters (in this case herself a woman) and presenting themselves with their children in front of the communal cave; and all of this acted out against a background of stylized trees signifying the remote sylvan setting of the scene.

The theme is taken up again in an Alsatian tapestry of the late fourteenth century with joint family escutcheons,* probably a wedding gift, which shows the wild men hunters, magnificent in their size, combative strength, and ferocity, the chief distinctive feature being that the wild woman receives their prey as she sits rather grandly with her children in front of the family cave, like the Madonna receiving the Magi from the East.[67] The erotic import of the scene is gainsaid by the presence, in another part of the tapestry, of the conquest of the castle of love.

A beautiful casket,† made on the upper or middle Rhine about 1500, marks the highest development of this type of subject matter.[68] All sides of the casket are devoted to the dangers and pleasures of wild-man life. The rear side shows the satisfactions of savagery: free love-making in the nude, the hunt, the contented sleep after a day of exertion, and in the middle, all enshrined in the involutions of a leafy scroll, the wild woman suckling her baby. On the opposite side, this idyl is disturbed by the invasion of wild beasts, making the woman start up from her somnolence, while, to the left, a male and female wrestle with a bear, and, to her right, a wild man runs after a griffon to retrieve a baby it has stolen. The final glorification of wild-man life is reserved for the lid of the casket, on which we see a group of nude males passing through the woods with their hunting equipment, their booty, and their pack of eager hounds, while above them the wild woman sits enthroned on a unicorn, splendid in her nudity, the queen and idol of the little group.

To these elaborate renditions of wild-man life we may add others, in engravings and dry points of the fifteenth century, limited to the wild man's fortunate family relations: the wild woman riding on a stag and holding two of her children in a print by the

* Fig. 45.   † Fig. 36.

"Master of the Housebook;" or the print by the "Master b/X Ƨ "
showing the congenial family, father, mother, and children happily
and urbanely assembled in their native playgrounds in the woods.
It is in direct continuation of traditions such as this that Cranach
created his picture of the so-called "Family of Fauns," whose connection with classical prototypes is only indicated by an almost
unnoticeable lengthening of the ears. The father faun poses like a
conventional wild man, club in hand, the lion he has killed beneath his feet; with him are his wild though hairless woman and
her children.[69]

The reader may have noted that in the first three works described — but not in the prints and painting last mentioned — the
social unit is not the family, but what one might call the clan, and
that within it the wild creatures are disporting themselves as if they
had not yet attained the monogamous or, to be precise, the mono-
androus state. The artists show the wild men as considerably superior in number to the wild women; frequently one wild woman
"rules the roost" as a benevolent matriarch, while all around her,
wild men are striving to render themselves agreeable to her. There
is a sense of harmonious coöperation of all, in spite of the presence
of several full-grown males, potential rivals for the wild woman's
attention.

We do not believe, in the absence of literary documents, that
there is an attempt here at showing the wild humans in a primordial state of promiscuity. It may be more to the point to urge that
we here behold a remainder, under bizarrely changed circumstances, from the courtly tradition which made the feudal lady the
superior object of desire for many knights. But even this explanation is not likely to be correct, for the wild woman is invariably
shown with a child or children, and so beyond such preliminary
rivalries.

The truth is probably that the wild woman is given her unique
position because she plays a more important part in the cycle of
procreation than does the male. To make her fit into her new
function she had to be "sensualized" no less than her wild suitors,
and thus was thrown back upon her identity as Maia, demon of
earth and fertility, or as "Salvangga." The polite renditions of her
without the enormous hanging breasts tend to make one forget this

mythological identity. And it is therefore significant for our purpose that, precisely in the regions in which the tapestry was made, the image of the fertile wild woman was preceded by the unmistakable one of her relative, the fertile siren, which has no male counterpart. Representations of the siren suckling her young and taking care of those who have outgrown such maternal attention are to be found in the Romanesque parts of the cathedrals of Basel and of Freiburg im Breisgau. The pertinence to our problem of their presence there will be appreciated when it is realized that sirens can be foster mothers of wild men, as is the siren who nurtures the wild man, Tristan de Nanteuil, in the fourteenth-century French epic of that name.[70]

In contrast to the group of works of art just studied, the next one, consisting of Swiss tapestries of the latter part of the fifteenth century, represents the wild men and women not as members of a matriarchal clan, but as lovers enjoying the delights of life in the woods.* The artists show them closely allied in body and spirit, unwilling to separate themselves from each other very far or for very long. Since the situation is one of love in its early fruition and felicity, the wild men — most of them, at least — are now shown without their more elderly attributes. The long beards have disappeared, and instead we encounter mere boys and girls, lithe and fragile in their youth, and quite without any of that ferocity which distinguishes their elders. The impression is that we are beholding well brought up, ordinary mortals in disguise. The artists have strengthened that effect by showing more clearly than usual the line of demarcation between face and colored tufts, and distinguishing between the latter and real hair, which the ladies arrange in well-ordered braids. The erotic elements have increased and are now beginning to pervade the picture. There are love knots, a whole collection of them held on a wooden pole; a holly tree is being grafted in the hope that its magic will help the preservation of loyalty; and on one of the tapestries there is even "Frau Minne," the equivalent of Venus in the wild-man pageant for Orazio Bentivoglio. She is all clad in red tufts and seated on a lion, the symbol of constancy. Beside her there stands, rather fittingly, a fountain of youth.[71]

* Fig. 44.

The abundant inscriptions which extol the delights of the hunt and of love have in part been dealt with earlier in this chapter. Those on the above tapestry are closely allied with the occupations shown, with the exception of one which is a word play upon "wild:" *Lieber gesel*, says the wild woman, *sich umb dich gar. Un nim des gewiltz ebben war* — "Dear fellow, look around and see the wild game." Whereupon he answers, shifting to the time-honored sentiment and rhyme: *Hand kein sorg ir wiplich bild, ich will üch geben zams und wiltz* — "Do not worry, lady, I shall give you tame things and wild." The corresponding representations on this tapestry consist of the departure of the wild man to the hunt as his damsel sees him off, standing at the entrance of their bower, cooking ladle in hand; the grafting of a tree, symbol of fecundity; an amorous scene, and the sharing by the two of their hunting prey. There is a noticeable similarity between works of art such as this and the "Ballad of Hind Etin," which also refers to the happy unison of the couple living in the woods.

There is every reason to believe that the works of art discussed, although thoroughly escapist in mood, were meant to be taken seriously. Another tapestry,* Alsatian and from the end of the fourteenth century, breaks with that rule and does so in a manner so amusing as to make it quite certain that the artist had his tongue in his cheek when designing this take-off on the ideal of living away from it all.[72] The fifteen scenes show a variety of amusements, often shared by whole groups of wild men, some sentimental, some childish, and all of them so intermingled as to give the impression of utter lack of purpose. Everything is treated as a game or a joke. There are the habitual hunting scenes, distinguished only by the fact that in one of them a naïve and clumsy wild *hausfrau* lends a helping hand in the task of killing the boar. In addition we see a mock tournament fought with wooden forks by two wild men mounted on a lion and a doe, a storming of the castle of love with the roles exchanged, so that the men become the defenders and the women the attackers, and a number of similar scenes, all of them either parlor games or treated as if they were. One of these which can be identified is a variant on the quintain game, showing a wild man and wild woman, the latter sitting on a crouching male, and

* Fig. 42.

both trying to push each other off base with their naked feet. Not far from this scene a wild man, with childish pathos, offers a big flower to his mate and baby with a gesture which is grand as well as subtly ridiculous.[73] Perhaps funniest of all are the scenes of "camping out," which help to give to the whole series the air of a picnic arranged by a competent and resourceful camp counselor: the skinning of the deer, the turning of the roast on a stick over the fire, and finally the meal consumed by a wild man and woman with an air of clumsy contentment at a time when other wild men are still returning from the hunt, bringing a dead squirrel hanging from a pole and a fish on a platter.

An even stranger aberration from the usual clichés of wild-man iconography than this excursion into the field of humor is to be seen in a tapestry of the fifteenth century in Vienna,* where we find the wild men, usually so satisfied with the alternation of the hunt and amorous idleness, engaged in useful labor. Incredible as it would seem, they have turned agriculturists and appear expert enough in the arts of plowing with oxen, harrowing, and harvesting the fields, tying the sheaves into bundles, and hoisting them upon the harvest wagon. If there is anything, beside their pretty fancy dress, which can remind one of their wild brethren, it is the fact that, here as elsewhere, a picnic is being prepared, with a wild man cooking in a lean-to. In no other work known to me do the wild men and women come as close as they do here to being demons of fertility, for clearly their preoccupation with plowing and with the harvest indicates that the bounty of nature is regarded as their province.[74] But here, as elsewhere, escapist and erotic motives are mixed with mythological ones, and in the inscriptions conventional warnings against disloyalty and complaints about it are appended to the remarks germane to the work at hand. It would seem that the mythological context of the tapestry is to serve as a framework for the acting out of one of the idyllic pastorals then so much in vogue among those who could afford to treat agricultural labor as a game.

We come to the relatively most numerous group of wild-man tapestries which show the creatures in company of or riding on the back of various ferocious animals — that is, occupied in a manner

* Fig. 41.

which is thoroughly in keeping with their mythological character. It is somewhat surprising, therefore, to note that introducing the wild men in this way seems to have been an afterthought to which the artists were led by beholding earlier works of their own creation. In the first tapestries of the type fashionable ladies led the monsters on iron chains and leashes. Then it seems to have occurred to some to put wild men on the backs of the beasts, while still consigning steed and rider to the care and wardenship of their human captors. Finally, the fashionable damsels were omitted, and the wild men were either allowed to fight it out among themselves, mounted and with the escutcheons of their patrons in hand, or given the task, congenial to them, of leading the wild beasts. The erotic intention which we noted in other tapestries was not abandoned, however, and on one which shows wild men driving savage creatures with lashes, we see love knots interspersed with the luxuriant leafage surrounding them.[75]

The intention in showing beasts under the control of men and ladies had, of course, always been a symbolic and amorous one, and even before the wild men entered into the fray. There had been lions, emblems of loyalty and strength; unicorns, emblems of ferocity tamed and of feminine victory; elephants, emblems of chastity, and stags, which in this period were looked upon as living examples of faithfulness and honor. All these creatures could easily be taken to be the natural companions of the wild man, notably the stags, which had always been regarded as his steeds. We find, therefore, that the tapestries with which we are concerned show a rather successful fusion of love symbolism with wild-man lore. It must be owned that a few other creatures occurring on the tapestries, like the griffon, have no known amorous significance and that some have not been properly identified, since the artists took colossal liberties with them in order to enhance their appearance and to sharpen their ferocity. All that one can safely say, since many parts are distorted beyond recognition, is that the creatures are horned and shaggy. If a guess is to be attempted, they may be ibex or mountain goats, members of the native fauna, which modern folklore tells us serve as steeds for the wild man.[76]

We shall terminate this short catalogue of works of art by introducing the so-called "Feer tapestry," which in some ways remains the last word in amorous wild-man iconography.* It is a marriage tapestry, equipped with the typical joint family escutcheon, and by its heraldic testimony was made for a Lucerne family in the fifteenth century. Here we find the hunting scenes previously described, but see them subordinated to a formal design by the device of narrowing down the hunting motives to the inscriptions and to representations unobtrusively interspersed in the background foliage. By giving an inferior place to the narrative elements of the scene, the designer was able to assign due prominence and rhythmical equality to the images of the loving couples who face each other across the tendrils, one fully clothed member of either sex versus the corresponding wild man or woman. Once more there is a strong impression, stronger perhaps than on any other Swiss or Rhenish tapestry, of a masquerade, from the incongruity of showing some persons in contemporary costume beside others in shaggy fur. In addition, the artist, besides distinguishing between natural hair and tufts, characterizes the shaggy costume as fancy dress by showing one wild man with the kind of leather pouch which fully dressed people of the time were accustomed to wear over their jackets. Surely no explanation of the wild-man tapestries can be complete which omits their very obvious theatrical aspects.

As we glance once more at the tapestries described, it is strikingly apparent that their common denominator lies in the fusion, accomplished in various ways, of amorous and escapist motives. Most of the tapestries preach the doctrine that the finest consummation of love is reserved to those who abandon the safety of human habitation and have the courage to retire into the woods; and that only by thus cutting the ties that link us with common humanity can we hope to preserve those values of absolute loyalty and faithfulness which are in jeopardy whenever the pressure of the multitude prevails.

In maintaining such doctrines the designer of the tapestries exploited an experience which was shared by many in the Middle Ages. Life in the houses and hamlets was then largely communal, allowing little privacy for those whose feelings were too intimate

* Fig. 43.

to be exposed to the glance of their companions. Once made public, such feelings became a matter of ostentation and parade, culminating in gorgeous wedding feasts. The wedding tour, invention of a later more sensitive and more prudish age, was as yet unknown, and the young couple, sometimes after having their closest intimacies exposed to the glance of their friends at the wedding, settled immediately into a life of routine. Under such circumstances it is only natural that the woods, where for once one could be alone, should have been regarded as a lovers' paradise, and that the idea of settling there permanently should have been tempting to many. The more a marriage rose above the level of crudity, the more insistent must have been the desire to escape from continuous communal supervision into the freedom and intimacy of nature.[77]

In the romances such escape of the lovers into the woods is a constantly recurring theme, only that, since these literary works deal with the impediments to love rather than with its consummation, and, furthermore, usually with illegal relationships, the forests are here regarded as the trysting places for the unwedded. Famous is the description of such love-making, under great physical privation, in the romance of "Tristan et Iseult," the culmination poetically of the entire tale.[78] The lovers have fled into the woods of Morois and now are alone. "They wandered in the depth of the wild wood, restless and in haste, like beasts that are hunted, nor did they often return by night to the shelter of yesterday. They ate but the flesh of wild animals, and missed the taste of salt. Their faces sank and grew pale, their clothes ragged, for the trees tore them. They loved each other and did not know what they suffered." In a later passage: "The summer passed and the winter came; the two lovers lived, all hidden in the hollow of a rock, and on the frozen earth the cold crisped their couch with dead leaves. In the strength of their love neither felt these mortal things. But when the open skies came back with the springtime, they built a hut of green branches under the great trees." Sublimity such as this will hardly be found in other medieval romances; but the theme persists, and in the tale of "Aucassin and Nicolette," for instance, the maiden builds for her lover the same kind of hut, made of branches, which also occurs on the wild-man tapestries.[79]

It is instructive to see that even the disguise of the lovers, which appears to be the main motive of many tapestries, is not unknown in certain types of romances, and that the close association of the pair with the beasts is admitted as a secondary theme. In the romance of "Guillaume de Palerne" (Palermo), a French epic of the late twelfth century, these topics, taken from contemporary folklore, are the common threads which hold the story together.[80] Guillaume, we are told, son of the king of Sicily and Apulia, is brought up in the woods by a werewolf, so that he may not be poisoned by his plotting uncle. When grown up, he comes to the court of the emperor of Rome and there falls in love with his daughter, Melior, enjoying her embraces in secret as long as circumstances permit. Comes the day when the princess is to be wedded to the emperor of Greece. The two lovers, who have no other choice than to flee, have themselves sewed into white bearskins, and escape into the woods with all their clothes hidden under the pelts. The transformation is complete, for Alisaundre, the maid who has helped to bring it about, admires her mistress as a fierce and grizzly bear, and, after Guillaume has been laced in, the maid claims to be quite frightened at "so hideous a sight of your seemly face."

The lovers pass through the garden gate, walking on all fours, as they do from now on during the daytime, while at night they stand up. They are inefficient bears or wild men, however, and quite incapable of finding their own food, so that the friendly werewolf has to appear to provide them with bread, meat, and wine. Their preoccupation is with love, after all, and their fuzzy wrapping does not prevent them form kissing affectionately and sleeping sweetly together. Finally, after being almost caught in their capacity as bears, the lovers decide to change their masquerade, disguise themselves as hart and hind, and are led into Sicily by the friendly werewolf. There they find the dynastic situation favorable to their interests and, after shedding their own disguises and seeing to it that the werewolf is restored to his human form, they confirm their long attachment through marriage.

It is quite apparent, of course, that this delightful story, which is restful to read after the usual repetitious tales of adventure, has affinities with the wild-man tapestries, even though the lovers in disguise appear more completely hirsute and therefore far more bestial than conventional wild men. There is the same motive of happy escape which we found in the tapestries, the same sense of closeness to and sympathy with a sylvan environment, the same sentimental belief that loyalty and affection fare best when hidden under a bristly and unprepossessing exterior. There is even the mythical theme of friendship with an animal or with animals, although this last ingredient of the story is motivated in a manner not found in the tapestries.[81] Considering the distance both in space and in time which separates the epic from the corresponding works of art, we cannot but find it striking how closely they do agree not only in mythological theme, but also in mood and erotic attitude.

We do not believe, however that the connection between them can be a direct one, in spite of the close affinities which we found to exist between the mythology of bears and of wild men. The designers of tapestries could not have allowed themselves the liberty, so easily accorded to the practitioners of folklore, of transforming bears into wild men. Even if this unlikely operation could have been performed, the epic would have proved refractory to any attempt at projecting into it the usual wild-man mythology. In the tapestries wild men and women are depicted as sufficiently resourceful and self-reliant not to be overtaxed by the need of making a living in the forest: while the disguised lad and lass in "Guillaume de Palerne" are so weakened by civilized refinement or so hindered by their bulky pelts that they are unable to provide for themselves.[82] Even Guillaume's rugged upbringing by a werewolf, which should have made him familiar with elementary woodman's lore, seems of no help to him when he is confronted with the task of fending for himself in a sylvan environment. We cannot but conclude that he and his lady love, as depicted in the epic, are merely somewhat effete and probably remote relatives of that sturdy race of bestial wild men to which the tufted boys and girls in the tapestries trace their direct ancestry. If there is a historical connection between the epic and the tapestries, it is due to the effect upon both of a common substratum of folklore.[83]

It is to the chapters on popular beliefs and practices and particularly to that on the theatrical activities of the wild man that we must go in order to find the source from which the tapestry designers drew their inspiration. Our description of the ill-fated "Bal des Ardents," held at the French court to celebrate the marriage of a lady in waiting, will be recalled; and, together with this description of a charivari as actually performed, there were the literary accounts of imaginary events, such as the noisy serenade from the "Roman de Fauvel" and the devils' debauch in the "Lay de Luque la Maudite," both obstreperous contributions to wedding festivities.

As conceived in France and in those parts of Europe which followed the French lead, the charivari, with its violence and obscenity, was far from being an expression of respectful and friendly sentiment and so could not normally be used as the basis for a wedding gift. On the contrary, the French charivari was and still is a noisy sneer upon newlyweds, meant to humiliate them by upsetting the happiness of the wedding night, and hence to bring home to them the disapproval and censure of the group.[84] Charivaris are accorded to the marriages of unpopular persons and to unpopular marriages. It is quite in keeping with this rule that among the medieval French examples one charivari, that for the horse Fauvel, should have been held to disturb the wedding night of a companion out of favor, while the other, for Luque la Maudite, was a demoniac orgy organized to celebrate the wedding, at her deathbed, of a witch and poisoner to the devil himself. Even acts of revenge against the married couple fit into the framework of a charivari. According to the "Vita Merlini," apparently the earliest testimony to the custom extant, Merlin prepared what must be regarded as a charivari for his wife Gwendoloena, after having sanctioned her marriage to another man. Merlin the wild man appeared before the bride's house during the wedding night, accompanied by a great herd of deer which he had brought together in the woods. When the new husband incautiously put his head out of the window to see what was causing the fracas, Merlin, overwhelmed by sudden jealousy, wrenched off the antlers from the stag he was riding and threw them at his rival, killing him outright.[85]

Charivaris were organized also in order to discourage second marriages by widows, which, although approved by the church, ran counter to traditional notions of propriety. It appears that in this as in numerous other instances groups of masked young men belonging to secret societies took it upon themselves to enforce those traditional standards of behavior which were not expressly regulated by the church, and thus to play the part of a community police. To this type belonged the charivari at the French court known as the "Bal des Ardents," even though it seems to have been performed with friendly intentions and for the sake of the pleasure afforded by a masquerade. It is possible that the wild-man tapestry at Saumur, referred to in Chapter 3, may be the visual record of a similar festivity held on the occasion of a widow's second marriage, and that its uniqueness among French works of art reflects reluctance to surround a second wedding with the same pomp and circumstance which generally accompanied the first.

It would thus appear that actual wedding festivities could hardly have been in the mind of the Rhenish artists, when they made the designs for the large and fanciful group of tapestries described. But here a surprise is in store for us. For although charivaris are known in German-speaking countries, they are often without those censorious implications which may make of the French ceremony an evil omen for the ability of the newly married to maintain themselves at all as members of their respective communities.[86] Instead of being a mark of abuse, charivaris in the Tyrol and in Switzerland are a normal and necessary part of the traditional wedding festivities, the omission of which would be regarded as a dishonor and a misfortune.[87] No less noisy than the corresponding French festivities and a hard trial for sensitive nerves, such charivaris consist mainly of a great deal of shooting, clanging, and banging with whatever noise-producing agents are at hand, but without the demoniac disguises which give to the French performances their sinister reality. Their purpose is usually not so much that of embodying demons as of driving them away. One further step toward the neutralization of the pagan custom, and we arrive at the German institution of the Polterabend, the "bachelors' party" or "noisy eve," in which the demoniac visitation has degenerated into a mere boisterous and sentimental gathering of friends.

It will be argued here that, in spite of this tendency toward harmlessness and magical inefficacy, such pagan marriage customs in Germany come closer to the original intent of the event than do the French. We can maintain this opinion with all the greater confidence since the earliest western example of a charivari preserves unmistakable traces of its older, beneficial purpose: the ceremony offered by Merlin to Gwendoloena was originally meant to be congratulatory, with the bringing of wedding gifts.[88] It is only the ill-timed appearance of the bridegroom which transforms Merlin's friendly impulse into murderous rage and, by implication, symbolizes the change from propitious magic to malediction.

It is thus clear that, in some German-speaking countries, resorting to pagan marriage customs for the establishment of artistic iconography could not have been objected to on grounds of custom and propriety. Nor does there seem to have been a lack of native folklore on which artists could draw, even though in the historical sources available to us its original wealth has been compressed into a few tantalizingly short quotations. Beside the charivari proper, whose name points to its French associations or origin, German weddings, if celebrated with pristine pomp and circumstance, used to have their own demoniac visitations, which may be regarded as native pagan contributions to the wedding feast. In the Tyrol, for instance, where ancient customs were maintained longer than they were in most other parts of central Europe, no rural wedding banquet would have been complete without the appearance in mask and costume of disguised young men, who proceeded to take the groom to task, embarrassing him through satirical allusions to his past.[89] The friendly mockery which was exhibited at such times is not without kinship to the cynical abuse of the French charivari. In the Tyrol itself abusive marriage masquerades are not unknown: when a maiden has had the misfortune to be abandoned by her fiancé, the young men in the village take it upon themselves to heap insult upon injury by performing before her house a noisy mock wedding.[90]

The masks and costumes worn at wedding masquerades seem to have originally been those of the Wild Horde; in the Tyrol, these were the treasured possessions of individual families and were brought out whenever occasion demanded it. Among the demons expected to make their dreaded, uninvited appearance at the wedding feast was the "Schimmelreiter," the rider on the white horse, who is of course no other than the Wild Hunter himself.[91] The identity of other droll guests at the wedding may be conjectured when we hear North German writers refer to them synonymously as *incubi* or *satyri*, that is, demons of sex, or as *umbrae*, ghosts.[92] Apparently they are compounded of the same mixture of macabre unreality and sexual potency as the wild man. We may regard it as significant that they should make their appearance on an occasion sanctioning the emergence of new human life, encouraging and strengthening the fecundity of the newly wedded couple by calling up the disembodied forces of the racial past.

Persons got up as feminine demons added their magic to that of their masculine counterpart. We may get an inkling of the geographical distribution of this feature in the marriage masquerades, if we consider that female impersonations of "Feien," fairies, were part of the wedding celebrations in areas of the province of Brandenburg in Prussia, and that a similar story about the presence of three "wild women" at a rural wedding comes from Reichenhall in the southeast corner of Bavaria.[93]

Historical references to the marriage masquerades are, unfortunately, neither as frequent nor as specific as one would like, since the writers who dealt with them at all seem to have expected their audiences to fill in the particulars from their own experience. We are merely told, for instance, that there were *larvati* at a marriage in Rostock in 1536, or that in 1593, at a wedding in Unterlienz in the Inn valley, the lads from a neighboring village were in evidence all dressed up "as carnival fools." But we hear at least that the custom was sufficiently inveterate and obnoxious to be worth prohibiting, and that in 1508, in Venice, an enactment had to be passed against it. Most important for us, because of its locality and because of its great age, is the decision by the second Trullan Council of 692 in Constantinople to forbid the presence of clerics at the marriage masquerades so that they would not defile their office by witnessing indelicacies. Badly incomplete as is the existing documentation, it would seem likely that the wedding masquerades, like those at the time of the Carnival and Twelfth-night, may be a survival, perhaps in grossly barbaric form, of customs that go back to late antiquity.[94]

The demoniac impersonations at the time of an actual human marriage are not the only appearance of "wild" masks in contexts which one might vaguely designate as conjugal or amorous. Just as there are elements of the Carnival in the traditional wedding feasts, so the performance of a mock wedding or the presence of persons disguised as bridal couples is part of the traditional Carnival. The transition from one to the other is an almost imperceptible one, for in a part of Europe extending intermittently from the Tyrol and Switzerland to Sweden, the Carnival and Twelfth-night are periods set apart for human marriage, so that the real bridal couple may take the place of the couple in disguise.[95] There was, as often in traditional societies, a distinct effort to subsume even the nonperiodic festivities, such as weddings, under the yearly cycle. Therefore popular pressure was applied in order to enforce the timing, and cruel satirical ceremonies awaited those marriageable maidens who by the time of the Carnival had not yet submitted to the general clamor for fertility. In a large area stretching from Silesia to the west of France and from the southern Tyrol to Holland, the task of distributing the available maidens among the bachelors at hand was undertaken on the Sunday following upon the Carnival, with the understanding, of course, that the lads had a right either to influence the selection of their "brides" beforehand or to redeem themselves if it did not coincide with their own desire.[96] The custom goes back at least to the fifteenth century. In the town of Liestal near Basel, in the very neighborhood which produced the wild-man tapestries, the mayor was entitled by a city ordinance of 1411 to make pairs of the marriageable boys and girls who had not been betrothed by the time of the Carnival, that is, in the period during which, as the text asserts, "people usually marry."

The tradition of introducing into the Carnival the masks of newly-married couples, for whose sake the whole performance is presumably given, appears to be as old as the Carnival itself, and thus to go back to the closing centuries of classical antiquity. Originally, of course, the principals of the wedding were not ordinary mortals, who were eased into this position only at a late date, but divinities; the wedding, consequently, had all the appurtenances, although not the high seriousness and solemnity, of a *hieros gamos*, a holy mating of the gods. Probably the earliest example, if not the prototype, of such mock bridals, was the mating of Mars and the aged Anna Perenna, even though Ovid, who tells us about it, fails to say whether the occasion was celebrated through masquerade and pantomime. The image evoked by the combination of the hairy Mamurius and his old and wrinkled bride is so similar to that of innumerable later travesties that it is impossible not to sense a historical connection, even though the links by which we may trace it have long disappeared.

We must be satisfied with having for a second example one which is many centuries later and belongs to a somewhat different stream of mythology. It would seem that the dance of Orcus and Maia, or, as we interpreted it in Chapter 2, of the wild man and his spouse, which is castigated in a Spanish penitential of the ninth or tenth century, is best interpreted as a wedding feast, at least if we are to look upon it in the light of earlier and later festivities. The fact that the ceremony took the form of a dance, in which the participants leaped and bounded (*saltatio*), would at least not militate against such an interpretation, since the same fast and jerky movements are part of similar modern rituals. Assuming that it may be safe to argue from historically distant analogies, we suggest on the basis of modern parallels that Pela, the third in the pagan ritual, is the wild couple's child, ludicrous and unlikely as its presence at the wedding would be. This burlesque detail can be explained as a crudely obvious parade of the working and effect of fertility.

Since the facetious wedding of the hairy demon and his hideous spouse is thus very old, old enough in fact to have antedated the division of the Roman Empire into separate cultural spheres, we should not be surprised to find the ceremony alive today within almost the entire orbit of the former empire. It survives in Morocco, Asia Minor, the Balkans, and central Europe; and while the long period that has elapsed since the institution of such rituals has resulted in the growth of many local variants, the central feature is still everywhere the same: a "bridal couple" of usually hirsute or otherwise unattractive appearance enters upon the scene and is given licence to engage in rather indelicate horseplay, the very vulgarity of which seems to be looked upon as a guarantee for its magical efficacy.[97]

In the eastern Balkans, for instance, where the festivity is rather elaborate, the hairy man "Kuker" appears together with his mate or bride the "Baba" or "Kukeritza," who is of course a man in woman's clothes doing his best to play up to "her" companion's

indecorous advances. The fact that the Baba is a bride is no impediment to her coming upon the scene with her child, or even producing her offspring publicly right after conceiving it. A number
of other masks join in, among them those of human bridal couples,
often ten or more, who apparently profit from the fertility engen-
dered. Sometimes the entire pageant is conceived as the Kuker's
wedding feast. At other times, through a further extension of the
pageant, a king is charged with some of the Kuker's magical functions, and may be seen distributing grain among the onlookers or
pulling a ceremonial plow. Either the Kuker or the king may have
to seal the magical compact with the community by sacrificing their
lives, and may then be thrown into the water in order to transmit
their potency to the fertilizing element.[98]

The pageants here somewhat sketchily outlined are those performed in the European areas adjoining Constantinople. Similar
though less ambitious ceremonies are known in almost the entire
Balkan peninsula, from Bulgaria and the Aegean Islands to the
Dalmatian coast.

It is in central Europe and adjoining areas, however, that we
must seek the inspiration for the marital elements in the wild-man
tapestries. There the oldest document telling of the hairy mummers
and their brides is the one, referred to in Chapter 3, concerning
the Pentecost celebration of 1224 in the Flemish town of Huy —
provided, of course, that we are right in believing that the feminine
masks then worn were those of the "brides" of other Figures dressed
in fur. Similar ceremonies, now always connected with the Carnival,
have survived in many places. In the Mur region of lower Austria,
for instance, a "wedding" (which however, does not come off) is
the pretext of the entire masquerade, and all the various masks —
bears with their leaders, devils, fools, bridesmaids, and best men —
are conceived as members of the wedding party. In other places,
such as Telfs in the Inn valley, the masks are traditionally arranged
in couples, appearing in the procession as the peasant and his wife,
the herdsman, the innkeeper, the old man — all with the corresponding feminine impersonation. In the Grisons and in Lombardy
there are the couples of "Il Veglio" and "La Veglia," the old ones.
Finally, there is, in the Folgareit region in the southern Alps the
combination, as husband and wife, of the mask impersonating the

wild man, *igl um selvadi,* and *la donna brava Berta,* who, in spite of her innocent-sounding name, is no other than the Percht, the wild woman as leader of the Wild Horde. All these variants are closely related to each other, and it must be mentioned that here as elsewhere the female masks no less than the male have always been worn by men belonging to those secret societies which took upon themselves the execution of traditional pagan ceremonies.[99]

Distinct from rituals of this kind is the wedding of the wild man and his savage spouse performed, originally, not during the Carnival, but somewhat later in the year, since it was to serve as a substitute for human bridals that had not come off at the festive time. As arranged before the Austrian police saw fit to change such matters, the wedding — known as "the pulling of the log" — was held only in those years during which the Carnival had gone by without a real human match, and thus was regarded as a means of righting the balance of fertility which might otherwise have been impaired.[100] We notice with interest the implication of wild bridals and human weddings being interchangeable, on the assumption, apparently, that the human couple also has the mythological and magical functions ordinarily associated with its savage counterpart.

The ceremony, as performed in communities in the upper Inn valley, is a simple one: the wild man, his mate, and significantly, their child are caught somewhere in the woods; then a small pageant comes to order consisting of the wild family, which walks in front, a big log or tree pulled behind it on a carriage, and a fool and a witch who perform their antics on the wagon. A number of other masks may be in attendance. The whole noisy display moves slowly through the village and stops before the inns, where the wild couple is ceremoniously presented. As here described the ceremony is known only in this valley. There is reason to believe, however, that formerly the ritual was much more widespread than it is today, for it is mentioned in a Bavarian document of 1544, and is still performed in the Appenzell canton in Switzerland, where, however, the place of the wild couple in its archaic vestments is taken by a man and woman resplendent in the finery of the regional Sunday costume. It is most likely that before acquiring its modern trimmings the Swiss ritual was similar to the more primitive ceremony practiced in the central Alps.[101]

In France, as in the Tyrol, the wild man retained his hold over the pagan post-Carnival proceedings. At Gourdon, in the Quercy region of Aquitaine, the first Sunday in the Lenten season is popularly known as *lou dimenge dei salvagi*, because on that day, in spite of frequent ecclesiastic prohibitions in the past, young men were accustomed to appear all got up as satyrs. While in this French custom the connection with human marriage seems to have been lost, another ritual recorded in the northern part of the Vosges reflects this purpose all the more faithfully. There, in the neighborhood of Sarrebourg, the village shepherd is the master of ceremonies: he appears on the evening of the first Sunday in Lent, masked and dressed as a satyr or wild man, and proclaims with stentorian voice all the secret love affairs and engagements which are currently taking place in the community. Besides dispensing supernatural sanction for human passion, his action, like the ceremony of log-pulling in the Alps, serves the purpose of providing a substitute for human attachments which failed to ripen into marriage during the preceding Carnival season.[102]

We shall end this survey of mock bridals by introducing an example, this time a Carnival ceremony proper, from the very region and historic period that produced the wild-man tapestries. According to Bullinger's *Chronica Tigurina*, written in the sixteenth century, the butchers of Zurich had the privilege, granted to them as early as 1330, of holding a masquerade on Ash Wednesday.[103] Besides secondary figures such as the familiar "bear" on a chain, a lion, and numerous nondescript fools and other mummers, their pageant contained the masks of a bride and bridegroom, who engaged in the usual indelicate jests and ended their short career as popular buffoons by being thrown bodily into a fountain. These central figures in the Zurich pageant were of course demons of the same variety as the Kuker and Kukeritza in Bulgaria and the numerous other mythological couples we have met. It merely serves to confirm the obvious, when we hear from a later writer that some of the participants — among them presumably the bride and bridegroom — were equipped with garments of moss and greenery befitting their demoniac roles.

The artists who designed the Rhenish wild-man tapestries found themselves thus confronted with ritual material facilitating their task of presenting human love life in terms of the erotic behavior of the wild man. The mock weddings celebrated over a large part of Europe were predicated on the belief that in the act of procreation man grows temporarily beyond the limits of his personality and becomes identified with those general and mythical powers which maintain the growth of the community. Only on this basis could there be established and maintained a system of customs whereby human bridals and their demoniac counterfeits were treated as interchangeable, and mock ceremonies were allowed to be held in imitation of the corresponding human events or as magical substitutes for them if they failed to materialize.

It was this unity or equivalence of demoniac natural forces with the loving couples in which they were embodied that provided the artists or their patrons with their chance to recast human erotic sentiment in forms borrowed from the life of the wild man. Since this life was lived in an environment and under conditions other than those which determine ordinary human existence, this mythological equivalence afforded an easy passage from the world of social fact into that of dreams and unrealized desires, enabling artists to treat the sober business relationship of marriage as if it were a mere flight of fancy, a romantic escapade. A tender and sentimental interpretation of marriage thus became possible. It will be noted, however, that the expression of the new attitude became feasible only because the transition had been made easy through the intermediate ambiguities of folklore. As yet the realities of marital happiness had hardly begun to be looked upon as a worthy or even as a possible subject for art. The designers of our tapestries preferred therefore to rely upon the convenient fiction that the satisfactions and mythical identifications of the wedding feast could be extended into the permanent felicity of wild-man life in the woods. Instead of merely representing the pagan wedding custom, as the designer of the tapestry in Saumur had done, they concentrated upon the lasting aspects of the wild man's life. While depicting his pelt as fancy dress and thus deliberately disclosing the ritual aspect of their subject, they retained the ancient traditions about the good life of the uncivilized and thus united in their designs the customs of the day, the dreams to which they gave rise, and the hallowed, never forgotten ideals of the Golden Age."

6

His Heraldic
Role

It is ironical, after having been steeped in the ambiguities and shifts of meaning infusing the mythological, theatrical, and erotic phases of the wild man, that we should at long last find ourselves confronted with an aspect which seems to carry with it the very denial of all this. Heraldry is by its nature a collection of arbitrary conventions combined in various arbitrary ways. Any mythological creature made to yield to its proud formalities would therefore lose its blurred identity and be squeezed into the narrow confines of a type. The wild man as a heraldic figure is deprived of much of his aura of ambivalence and allowed free play only in the fields of semantic combination and artistic design. Since neither of these is in itself of interest to us here, we are compelled to give a rather cursory account of the wild man in heraldry, concentrating chiefly upon those works of art which retain some allusions to broader mythological possibilities. It will be the exception rather than the rule which will occupy us.

It is likely, although beyond the range of direct proof, that the frequent representations of the wild man in the coats of arms of families, houses, inns, and cities are often last and stereotyped remainders of pagan ceremonies with which these localities and groups were once associated. Many of the inns "Zum wilden Mann" or "du Sauvage," for instance, may have once offered their hospitality to scenes of pagan merrymaking in which the mask of a wild man took a prominent part. It may be in token of similar memories that the wild men appear so frequently painted on the whitewashed walls of ancient houses in the Grisons. Again, when cities like Lucerne and Winterthur in Switzerland or Hanover in Germany adopted the wild man as their heraldic device, the decision may have been prompted by pride in ancient local custom.[1]

In other cases the reasons for the adoption of the device may have been of a different kind: the Swedish province of Lapland, for instance, is likely to owe the presence of the wild man in its armorial shield to the existence within its borders of a primitive people whose appearance and mode of life must have seemed "wild" to their Germanic neighbors. What, finally, prompted the adoption by more than two hundred European families of the wild man as their heraldic emblem, it is impossible to tell; while some may have prided themselves on their traditional participation in pagan carnivals, others meant to display their sturdiness, strength, and fecundity. The occasional occurrence of the term "wild man" as a proper name is perhaps due as much to the disapproving commentary of neighbors on the brutal or dissolute manners and way of life of those thus designated as to their own interpretation of themselves. Names of this kind, such as "Uolricus miles dictus Wildeman" or "Heinricus der Wildeman ein ritter," have appeared in Germany since the twelfth century. An important minnesinger of the late Hohenstaufen age was known as "der wilde Mann."[2]

Even more frequent than the escutcheons with the wild man as a heraldic emblem are those maintained and guarded by members of the hairy race. Among them are the coats of arms of the kingdoms of Denmark and, formerly, of Prussia, and the former dukedoms of Pomerania, Brunswick-Wolfenbüttel, and Hanover-Brunswick, to mention just a few among the most highly placed principalities and sovereign families.[3] Below this heraldic level the number of families in Europe that used the wild man as shield-supporter is legion, and it would be worse than useless to try to enumerate them. The purpose of stationing the wild man as a retainer outside the shield rather than an emblem within it was probably a talismanic one, based upon the thought that a creature as overwhelmingly strong as the wild man could surely be trusted to protect and defend the escutcheon.[4] Therefore, in the majority of cases, no direct reference to the owner of the shield may have been intended and the wild man may have been regarded as his servant rather than his mythological substitute. If any allusions to ritual or theatrical activities were meant to be conveyed, they were probably connected rather with the wild man's occasional participation in tournaments than with a local festival of a humbly popular kind.[5] But even those pageants in which persons dressed as wild men carried armorial shields were so rare and came so late in the history of medieval heraldry that they could not have exerted more than an occasional influence upon our theme.[6] The rise of the artistic motive of the wild man as shield-bearer could not have been due to any such external influence, since the first representations of the motive in art antedate the recorded examples of its use at the jousts by more than fifty years.

So we must seek the origin of our motive in art within the history of heraldic conventions themselves. When wild men began to take their place beside the escutcheons of noble families, the creatures found themselves joining an already existing and rather motley company of other figures similarly employed. The task of holding and protecting a human coat of arms had been entrusted to guardian angels, patron saints, and the Archangel Michael, strong celestial powers whom it was natural to invoke for the preservation of the family and the group; then, almost simultaneously, to the knight and his lady themselves, who had the closest interest in the protection of their own coat of arms; finally, through a process of artistic extrapolation, to the unicorns, lions, griffons, and other savage beasts which had left their place within the heraldic shield to take up their station beside it. In this process of progressive secularization the wild men came almost last. Their appearance as shield-supporters had by then been so well prepared that to explain it one need only point to the heraldic requirement of having for every family an individually distinctive device. The choice of the wild man may have been variously suggested by his previous presence within the shield, by his obvious talismanic potentialities, and by his kinship to the beasts that preceded him.[7]

To my knowledge, the first examples of the wild man as shield-supporter occur in the last quarter of the fourteenth century, primarily on seals [8] and on the margins of manuscripts such as those written and illustrated for King Wenceslaus of Bohemia. It is characteristic of the caution with which iconographic changes were introduced in the Middle Ages that, in spite of this thorough preparation, the new motive was first tried on a miniature scale before the artists committed themselves to rendering it monumentally. But its power as talisman assured its popularity, and by the time the fifteenth century had come the theme of the wild man as shield-supporter had found its way into the most diverse media of art. An idea of its ubiquity can be given by mentioning that it occurs on English baptismal fonts as well as on Spanish tombs,[9] on Swiss glass windows as well as in the sculpture of a Spanish palace. The motive even crossed the Atlantic with Spanish workmen and on Spanish ships, and is seen on the sixteenth-century façade of the Casa del Montejo in Mérida, Mexico.[10]

The wild woman in her turn followed the wild man's lead. Her appearance in the heraldic context is an event of the well-advanced fifteenth century, and the pictures in the Hours of Etienne Chevalier by Jean Fouquet in which she holds up Etienne's coat of arms may well be among the earliest of their kind. The late fifteenth century also added the combination of the wild man and his wife holding the same armorial shield, a motive which has a strong erotic component and seems to have been derived from older representations of wild-man families and their happy life in the woods. This motive was especially popular as a printer's mark, and was used as such by some of the chief Parisian printers of the late fifteenth century, such as Philippe Pigouchet (active 1488–1512) * and Jean Poitevin (active 1498–1518), whose prominence induced other printers in Paris, Caen, Lyons, and Cologne to adopt it in their turn.[11] As employed by this group of tradesmen, the mark shows a coat of arms hanging from a fruit-bearing tree, while a wild man and a wild woman with wreaths in their hair and branches in their hands are engaged in guarding the heraldic device suspended between them. It is interesting to note that this international trademark seems to have come to the attention of Albrecht Dürer, who

* Fig. 48.

used the combination of a wild man and woman with an armorial shield in one of his designs for a book owned by his friend Willibald Pirckheimer.[12]

By the second half of the fifteenth century the representations of the wild folk as shield-supporters had become common coinage to such an extent that artists, bored by the excessive familiarity of the theme, began to experiment with deviations from it. It occurred to German engravers that they might try to meet an increasing demand for prototypes of heraldic designs by representing the wild man or woman with an empty shield, or one containing a merely decorative design, making it possible for other artists to avail themselves of these models by merely placing the proper emblems into the reserved space. There are engravings of this kind from the hand of the Master E.S. and Martin Schongauer;[*][13] even Dürer fell back upon the precedent established by his forerunners when he inscribed into the otherwise empty escutcheon of his "Coat of Arms of Death" the purely allegorical device of a human skull.[†]

While German artists concerned themselves thus with making heraldic designs more available, their Spanish contemporaries labored to increase their magical efficacy. It occurred to them that the best way to assure the wild man's ability to defend the heraldic shield was to relieve him of his burden and to place him merely in its vicinity as a bodyguard, the advantage being that the number of demoniac attendants could be multiplied, thus increasing their cumulative talismanic power. In the Salón de Salvajes for instance, in the Palacio del Infantado, Guadalajara, Spain, the armorial shield in a corner of the room is held by two huge griffons, while along the cornice wild men are shown in a variety of boisterous and aggressive attitudes.[14]

We owe to the same tendency toward heraldic amplification one of the most astounding documents of late medieval sculpture, which marks the high point of the expansion of wild-man iconography into areas originally reserved for other types of art. The façade of the church of San Gregorio in Valladolid,[‡] built between 1488 and 1496, during the reign of Ferdinand and Isabella, is distinguished by the unique and shocking device of placing the wild men on the jambs of the portal, that is, in that location on the

* Fig. 47.   † Fig. 50.   ‡ Fig. 49.

building which, since the beginning of Gothic architecture, had been reserved for the figures of the prophets and the saints.[15] The wild men appear on the jambs proper, on the frontal wall of the doorway, and even on its outer side, making a further appearance on the highest level of the façade. The intrusion of the pagan creatures in those parts of the church which had always been adorned with important sacred figures seems puzzling until it is realized that the whole church front, with the exception of the tympanum, is conceived as one large heraldic showpiece in honor of the king and queen and their relationship to the see of Toledo. The key to all that seems unusual lies therefore in the panel above the doorway containing the royal coat of arms and the tree and fountain of life in which it is rooted. Once it is understood that the rest of the façade is to be read as the heraldic accompaniment of this central triumphant theme, one will comprehend also why there should be heralds on the side, wild men in the doorways, and finally fleurs-de-lis in the coats of arms held by angels over the spandrels; for the fleur-de-lis, emblem of the virgin Mary and of her purity, was also the emblem of the see of Toledo, which thus proclaims its participation and interest in what, after all, is the decoration of a sacred building. In this combination of heraldic elements the wild men function as the outer guardians who are closest to the visitors of the church and furthest removed from the symbolic splendor of the royal shield. They are thus given the same humble position which they hold as festival police in many contemporary pageants, ecclesiastical and secular.[16] It is interesting to note, in the light of what has been said before, that, although deprived of their former task of upholding the royal coat of arms, the wild men all have their own shields, inscribed with masks and ornamental designs.

To the majority of medieval beholders the figure of the wild man as shield-supporter may have had no more mythological implications than did lions or griffons or unicorns. It was enough to know that these creatures all commanded extraordinary strength and that anything confided to their care could be trusted to be well kept and defended. It was inevitable, however, because of the widespread knowledge of wild-man mythology and because of its vitality and exuberance, that part of the large complex of legends, beliefs, and practices connected with this figure should have found its way into the tight precincts of heraldry. All heraldry is a symbol of and a monument to the idea of racial permanence. It was only fitting, therefore, that its restrictions should have been sometimes relaxed in order to give full play to the procreative magic of the wild man as harbinger of fertility. We will expect, therefore, that at times the wild man as shield-bearer would discover his identity with the wild man, the tempestuous lover, and begin to act as the alter ego of the bridegroom.

Allusions and innuendos of this kind occur almost from the beginnings of the history of our motive. In the manuscripts written for King Wenceslaus, for instance, the wild men are depicted as dividing their attention between their amorous preoccupations and the task, entrusted to them, of holding the royal helmet and coat of arms. It will be remembered that these manuscripts were to be monuments to Wenceslaus' love for his own wife, and that, when we see the wild man languishing in chains, we must regard him as the king himself, enchanted and tormented by her charms. It was only natural that this motive should have been supplemented by the other of the king, once more in his wild-man guise, upholding the royal coat of arms, triumphant, with his wishes fulfilled, and expectant of the royal offspring.

When Dürer combined the images of a wild man and woman in his coat of arms of Willibald Pirckheimer, he had similar allusions in mind. He gave to the wild man the heavy jowl and flat features of his friend, thus referring jestingly to his "wild" appearance that seems to have been a standing joke between the two. The wild woman, accordingly, is likely to be one of those "lady friends" whose presence and importance in Pirckheimer's life gave Dürer in his letters a pretext for some good-natured jocularity. Given the tone of banter under which the two friends hid their very real affection for each other, it was perhaps in the order of things that the dynastic implications of the theme should have given way to pointed allusions to less respectable, more debatable relationships.

Finally, on the façade of San Gregorio in Valladolid, where the wild men are unambiguously displayed as guardians, their environment gives to their presence a shading more than faintly progenitive. The royal coat of arms, as we have mentioned, is set in the powerful bifurcation of the tree of life which arises out of the fountain and in whose branches naked *putti* are playing. The vital force that wells forth and floods the royal lineage spills over into the remoter parts of the façade, drowning the outer string courses, the capitals, and the intrados of the cusped arch in an inundation of luxuriant tendrils and naked babies. Clearly the wild men who stand in the jambs immediately beneath could not be conceived as unaffected by or indifferent to such a burst of vital energy, and must themselves be regarded as involved in this elaborate display of and prayer for fertility.

Is is again Albrecht Dürer whose ability to synthesize vast ranges of thought in one concise image enabled him to present to the world the most succinct, powerful, and profound version of the theme. His engraving of the "Coat of Arms of Death" (1503) * is based upon the subject of the wild man as shield-supporter, showing him with the escutcheon, the helmet appurtenant thereto, and a magnificently designed set of tendrils and eagle's wings. But the wild man is not satisfied with his usual task of holding a heraldic device, but leans over to offer his not unwanted attentions to a coyly hesitant maiden in front of him. In stark contrast to this scene of courtship the coat of arms held by the wild man contains the frightening image of a human skull.

In spite of its macabre allusion to the then widely represented theme of death and the maiden, this engraving is in a sense a marriage print, and as such is intimately connected with the wedding feast and with the visitations expected to appear at the festive time. As we scan the print for details, we discover that the maiden wears over her elaborately braided hair a crown and so is appareled not only for a feast, as her dress betrays, but for one in which she will be the chief protagonist. The crown is a bridal crown of the kind which in Dürer's day was worn at most weddings and of which other representations have survived in Brueghel's picture of a peasant wedding and in Roger van der Weyden's marriage scene in his Altar of the Seven Sacraments. The reader will observe that the crown in Dürer's print is a broad, low, richly wrought ornament covering both the head and the braids. Allowing for the changes of taste in about sixty years, the crown in Roger's picture, although round and bejeweled, seems to belong to the same general

* Fig. 50.

type. The connection of Dürer's print with the wedding ceremony is further borne out by the fact that it was the basis for an Italian engraving of the sixteenth century in which Dürer's design is retained and only the skull is exchanged for a hopeful and congratulatory impresa, *Meliora lapsis* — "Better things than in the past." This print was made for the marriage of Isabella Gonzaga to the Marquis of Pescara and, since it is printed on precious ivory, probably served as a wedding gift.[17]

Behind the festively attired bride in Dürer's print the wild man leans to kiss her, presumably because the marriage ceremony gives him a right to press his attentions upon her. One might hesitate before deciding whether the creature thus preparing to take possession of the bride is the groom in his now legitimate wildness or whether it is a ghostly visitor from the other world, a revenant. The issue is decided by the presence of the armorial device of a human skull, which could not reasonably be regarded as the bridegroom's coat of arms. Only a macabre interpretation will tally with this reminder of man's mortality; and since the scene for the allegorical action is a human wedding feast, we must assume that one of the ghosts who so often frightened the guests by their unbidden appearance at the wedding is here revealing his true identity. We learn that his kiss is an icy embrace and its issue death.

Dürer's intention was thus to show that even and precisely when life is at its greatest height and amplitude, as it is on the wedding day, it may be cut short. It is a poignant refinement of this theme that death should be caused by one of those apparitions whose presence at the wedding is needed for the assurance of later progeny. The contrast between the fulfillment of love and the lurking shadow prepared to destroy it could not have been brought to greater sharpness and intensity.

It is clear, then, that Dürer occupies a unique rank among the commentators on wild-man mythology, as the only artist who rose above the usual one-sided pleasantries and became aware of the tragic and paradoxical potentialities in the figure of the wild man. Dürer must have distilled his image from many and at first conflicting memories; reminiscences of the creature's rage and fury as it raced through his native town as a member of the death-dealing Wild Horde; of its promise and erotic allusiveness as it intruded itself in the gaiety of the wedding feast; of its herculean strength as it braced itself to uphold a patrician coat of arms. In these divergent moods and activities Dürer recognized facets of one demoniac personality and resolved to assemble them into one allegorical image. It speaks for the depth and accuracy of his mythological insight that he should have used his knowledge to expand the conventional theme of the wild man as shield-supporter into an allegory of the eternal polarity of love and death, creation and destruction, being and nonbeing.

Notes

Notes

1. THE NATURAL HISTORY OF THE WILD MAN

1. A good description of the range of occurrence of wild men in medieval art is in F. von der Leyen and A. Spamer, *Die Altdeutschen Wandteppiche im Regensburger Rathaus* (Regensburg, 1910), pp. 16–18. See also R. van Marle, *Iconographie de l'Art Profane au Moyen Age et à la Renaissance* (The Hague, 1931–32), I, 183.

2. The episode is amusingly described by R. Boyer in the June 18, 1938, issue of the *New Yorker*. The nature man, Joe Knowles, entered the wilderness between King and Bartlett Lake in Maine. His later claims included the strangling of a deer, the killing of a bear with his own hands, and the catching of fish without fishing tackle. After his emergence from the wilderness on October 4, 1913, he passed through the towns of Maine and Massachusetts in uninterrupted triumph and received a rousing reception from great crowds lining the Boston streets. His claims were later exposed by the press, and it was proved that he had always relied upon the help of trappers.

3. It will be noted that the description here offered of a psychic force, although given without benefit of psychoanalytic language and subtlety, corresponds, on the whole, to Freud's concept of the "id."

4. W. Förster, *Kristian von Troyes' Yvain* (Halle, 1902), v. 330.

5. Heinrich von Hesler, "Die Apokalypse," ed. K. Helm, in *Deutsche Texte des Mittelalters*, Vol. VIII (Berlin, 1907), vv. 20065, 20066.

6. Richard de Fournival, *Bestiaire d'Amour*, ed. John Holmsberg (Uppsala, 1925). Other similar expressions of opinion are not rare. See for instance the Westphalian version of the story of the "Eisenhans," where the wild man is referred to as *dat dier*, the animal (Grimm's *Fairy Tales — Kinder- und Hausmärchen*, Berlin, 1812–1815 — no. 50).

7. About the earliest German card games see M. Geisberg, *Das Aelteste Deutsche Kartenspiel* (Strassburg, 1905); M. Lehrs, *Die Aeltesten Deutschen Spielkarten des kgl. Kupferstichkabinetts* (Dresden, 1885); M. Lehrs, *Geschichte und Kritischer Katalog des Deutschen, Niederländischen und Französischen Kupferstichs im XV jahrhundert* (Vienna, 1908–1934). Since the card game by the "Master of the Playing Cards" is not entirely preserved, the original cards must be supplemented by others, made in imitation of them by the "Master of 1462," now usually referred to as the "Master of the Power of Women." Of the two card games by the "Master E.S.," the successor of the "Master of the Playing Cards" as the leading Rhenish engraver, the so-called small card game is too incompletely preserved to permit any conclusion about the wild man's position in it. The large card game shows the wild man as a member of the human race. See M. Lehrs, *The Playing Cards by the Master E.S. of 1466* (London, 1892), and M. Geisberg, *Der Meister E.S.* (Leipzig, 1924). On the Bourdichon miniatures see Grete Ring, *A Century of French Painting, 1400–1500* (London, 1949), plates 151–154.

8. An instance of the tail is in Ms. 1561, Bibliothèque de la Ville, Arras, fol. 46 v., second part of thirteenth century. The wild man is here represented as a Sagittarius shooting a deer. See the description of such irregularities in von der Leyen and Spamer, p. 17, with particular reference to Codex 1857, Vienna Hofbibliothek. An extreme example of the same tendencies, which appear earlier in literature than they do in art, is in *Le Livre d'Artus* ed. H. O. Sommer (Washington, D. C., 1913), pp. 124–125. It seems that there was a literary tradition in the description of human ugliness and deformity, which reaches back through the Roman schools of rhetoric to Homer's Thersites. Part of this tradition was conveyed to the high Middle Ages through the Alexander romance and the description contained therein of human monstrosities dwelling in faraway lands.

9. "Wolfdietrich" (B), ed. O. Jänicke, in *Deutsches Heldenbuch* (Berlin, 1866–1873), vol. III, v. 311, p. 213. *Faërie Queene* (Everyman ed., 1931), bk. vi, canto iv.

10. This thesis had been proclaimed by Nizâmî al-'Arûdî (*c.* 1150–1160) in his *Chahâr maqâla*, Gibb Memorial Series, vol. XI, part 2 (1921), in connection with the so-called Nasnâs, a demon related in some way to the European wild man. About this creature he says the following (p. 9): "The highest animal is the Nasnâs, a creature inhabiting the plains of Turkestan, of erect carriage and vertical stature, with wide, flat nails. . . This, after mankind, is the highest of animals, in as much as in several respects it resembles man: first in its erect stature, secondly in the breadth of its nails, and third in the hair on its head." The importance of this quotation for the history of the theory of evolution was brought out by G. Sarton in his introduction to M. F. Ashley Montague, *Edward Tyson, M.D., F.R.S.* (Philadelphia, 1943), p. XVII. See also G. Sarton, *Introduction to the History of Science* (Baltimore, 1927–), II, 363. There were in the Middle Ages no translations of Nizâmî al-'Arûdî's works. Artistic representations of the Nasnâs do not occur prior to the fifteenth century, when one appears in an illustrated manuscript of Nizâmî, executed in the school of Herat. See A. Bay Sakisian, *La miniature Persane du 12. au 17th siecle* (Paris, 1929), pl. 36.

11. The development of this idea has been admirably explained by A. O.

Lovejoy in *The Great Chain of Being* (Cambridge, 1936), pp. 89 f. Among the proponents of a carefully limited gradualism were, according to Lovejoy, St. Thomas, Albertus Magnus, and Nicolaus Cusanus. The argument was chiefly used to justify the existence of angels, as of the chief "transitional" species. On the same grounds the existence of wild men could have been argued, had there been an inclination to do so.

12. For Sir Dodinel, see E. Brugger, "Bliocadran, the Father of Perceval," in *Medieval Studies in Memory of Gertrude Schoepperle Loomis* (New York, 1927), pp. 165 f. Dodinel, member of King Arthur's Round Table according to numerous romances, may have been the hero of an independent epic now lost. For the second title, see "Palmerin of England," 1, 31, ed. in *Antony Munday's Romances of Chivalry*, The Library, 4th series, vol. vi (1925). *Palmerin de Ingleterra*, ed. R. Tenreiro (Madrid, 1924).

13. Heinrich von Hesler, vv. 20052, 20070–75.

14. Heinrich von Hesler, vv. 20060, 20061.

15. *Faërie Queene*, vi, iv, 13.

16. *Gawain and the Green Knight*, translated into modern English by H. Banks (New York, 1929), v. 720.

17. A wild woman's hole near Sölden is mentioned by J. V. Zingerle, *Sagen, Märchen und Gebräuche aus Tyrol* (Innsbruck, 1859), p. 31. Another one was in the Oetztal. In Italy, for instance, there was one at the foot of the Paréi du Slet and another on the Paréi del Colomber. See F. Neri, "La Maschera del Selvaggio," in *Giornale Storico della Letteratura Italiana*, LIX (1912), 54, quoting A. Massara, "Leggende Popolari Sacre," Pitré's *Archivio*, XXII, 31–32, and G. I. Armandi, "Dal Santuario di San Giovanni alla Casa del'Huomo Selvatico," in *Nuova Antologia*, August 16, 1901. For instances in Germany, see V. Höttges, *Typenverzeichnis der Deutschen Riesen und Riesischen Teufelssagen* (Helsinki, 1937), p. 155. W. Mannhard, *Wald und Feldkulte* (Berlin, 1875), I, 88.

18. Von der Leyen and Spamer, p. 16.

19. Compare the description of such a battle in Altswert's "Der Kittel" (fifteenth century), ed. Holland and Kettler (Stuttgart, 1850), p. 15. See also the English epic of *Valentine and Orson*, tr. Henry Watson, ed. A. Dickson (Oxford, 1937), chap. vi, p. 38. Artistic representations of the scene are so frequent that it would be useless to try to enumerate them. We are reminded of the Biblical reference to Ishmael in Genesis 16:12: "And he will be a wild man; his hand will be against every man, and every man's hand against him. . ."

20. *Faërie Queene*, i, vi, 24.

21. Sir Thomas Malory, "Morte d'Arthur," *Works of Sir Thomas Malory*, ed. E. Vinaver (Oxford, 1947), pp. 409 and 602. The wild man's contentiousness was once made the subject of an entire Carnival play. See "Ein Spiel von Holzmennern," *Deutsche Fastnachtsspiele aus dem 15ten Jahrhundert*, ed. A. von Keller (Tübingen, 1853–1858). The famous engraving by Pollaiuolo, "The Battle of the Nudes," is probably not concerned with wild men.

22. Dickson (1937), page cited. Shakespeare, *Tempest*, Act. I, scene 2, lines 354–364.

23. *Faërie Queene*, vi, iv, 11 and 14.

24. Compare for this, for instance, Heinrich von Hesler, v. 20050: *die* [the wild people] *sin man wib und kint — die nach menschen sind gebildet — und aber also vorwildet — daz sie Gotes wort nie vornamen —*" They are men, women, and children formed like other men, but grown so wild that they have never heard God's word."

25. For a concise account of the little that is known on this subject see J. S. Tatlock, "Geoffrey of Monmouth's Vita Merlini," in *Speculum* (1943), p. 280.

26. "Morte d'Arthur," Vinaver ed., p. 498. It is likely that the use of the term is in part due to the similar sound of the word "wood" as a component of woodman or woodwose, and of "wode," the Anglo-Saxon term for "mad, insane." Wode was frequently written as "wood," "woode," even by Malory himself.

27. Grimm's *Wörterbuch* under "Wilder Mann."

28. For instance, Yates Thomson Catalogue, vol. VII, pl. 49, fol. 258v. of a Bible of 1432. The earliest example of this representation known to me is found in the Bible of Roda, Catalan, eleventh century. See W. Neuss, *Die Katalanische Bibelillustration um die Wende des Ersten Jahrtausends und die Altspanische Buchmalerei* (Leipzig, 1922), fig. 100.

29. See, for the literature on the Lailoken fragments, Tatlock, p. 268, n. 6; also J. D. Bruce, *The Evolution of Arthurian Romance from the Beginnings to the Year 1300* (Baltimore, 1923), I, 141.

30. Tatlock, p. 265. Text edition of the "Vita Merlini," by J. J. Parry, in University of Illinois Studies in Language and Literature (Urbana, 1925).

31. See the distinction in Giraldus Cambrensis, *Itinerarium Cambriae* (c. 1188–1191), 2, 8, in Th. Wright's modern English translation (London, 1913), p. 452. According to Tatlock, p. 272, the distinction began even earlier than this, being found in library catalogues of the middle of the twelfth century.

32. "Vita Merlini," vv. 72, 74, 80, 76 and 141, 83, 85–97f., 208.

33. *Yvain*, ed. Förster, v. 2827. Le *Livre de Lancelot du Lac*, ed. H. O. Sommer (Washington, D. C., 1910), III, 412–419; IV, 154–155; V, 380–381 and 393–401. Tatlock, p. 285. *Prose Romance of Tristan*, ed. E. Löseth (Paris, 1890), pp. 63–83. Later examples of the same motive in Straparola, *Le Piacevoli Notti*, (fifteenth century; most recent ed. Rome, 1945), 5, 2, and in recent folklore. The wild man whose "house" is shown under the Paréi du Slet (n. 17, above) is said to have chosen this strange abode because the girl he had loved had died.

34. That wild men and women were black seems to have been a widespread belief, particularly in Germany. See, for instance, the description of a wild woman in "Wigalois" by Wirnt von Gravensberg (thirteenth century), ed.

J. M. Kapteyn (Bonn, 1926), v. 6288: *Diu was in einer varwe gar swarz, ruch als ein beer* — "She was of a black color and as rough [hairy] as a bear." The same is said of the enchanted Wolf- dietrich in the epic of that name. Hartmann von Aue's Iwein also had the same trait in his temporary state of in- sanity: *unz daz der edel tore wart gelich einem mōre in allem sīnem lībe* — "the noble fool became like a negro in all his body," Hartmann von Aue, *Iwein, der Ritter mit dem Löwen,* ed. H. Naumann and H. Steinger (Leip- zig, 1933), v. 3237.

35. "Der Busant," ed. in F. H. von der Hagen, *Gesamtabenteuer* (Stuttgart, 1850), I, 331.

36. H. Michelant, "Renaus de Mont- aubon oder die Haimonskinder," *Alt- französisches Gedicht nach den Hand- schriften herausgegeben* (Stuttgart, 1862), p. 86, l. 10; p. 87, l. 10; p. 88, l. 31, and p. 93, l. 8. See also the analysis of the epic in J. Bédier, *Les Légendes Epiques,* vol. IV (Paris, 1921). The self-description is emphatically repeated by several of the brothers participating in the council. See also Jean Bodel, *Chanson des Saxons,* ed. F. Michel (Paris, 1839), p. xix: *Aprendre lui con- vient vie d'hom sauvage et gesir mainte nuit al vent et al orage* — "He adopted the life of a wild man lying many a night in the wind and storm." Related to the situation thus described is that of a wild woman in a Swiss tapestry of the fifteenth century (B. Kurth, *Die Deutschen Bildteppiche des Mittelalters,* Vienna, 1926, pl. 141) who, while seated in the forest beside a unicorn gives vent to the following moralizing complaint: *Min zit der welt gegeben, nuon muss ich hie im ellenden leben, o wee* — "I have given my time to the world, now I must live here in misery, oh."

37. See A. Dickson, *Valentine and Orson, a Study in Late Medieval Ro- mance* (New York, 1929), and the text edition (Oxford, 1937) cited above. "Valentine and Orson," as preserved in the English version of about 1510, and in the French text printed in Lyon in 1489, is based on an earlier epic of

Valentin und Namelos (nameless) pre- served in German, Swedish, and Dutch versions and dating back to the four- teenth century. In almost all editions of Grimm's Fairy Tales occurs the story of "Der Eisenhans," in which the wild man is caught by bailing out the pond in which he lives.

38. The legend, told not only of St. John Chrysostom but also of Juan Garin, hermit of Montserrat, has a long prehistory leading back into the early Christian period and further into the ancient Orient. We shall not deal with it here, since it has been handled ad- mirably in A. Williams' two essays, "Oriental Affinities of the Legend of the Hairy Anchorite" and "The Ger- man Legends of the Hairy Anchorite," in University of Illinois Studies in Lan- guage and Literature (Urbana, 1925– 1927 and 1935, respectively). An article on the artistic representations of the hairy anchorite by M. d'Ancona will soon appear in the *Gazette des Beaux Arts.* It may be added to Prof. Wil- liams' otherwise exhaustive documenta- tion that among the figures of the hairy and hoary hermits in the desert is that of the ancient saint visited by St. Bren- dan during his fabulous voyages in the Atlantic Ocean. For the Irish monks the ocean was the desert, and the islands in it were oases. See C. Plummer, *Lives of the Irish Saints* (Oxford, 1922), II, 67, 76, and 88; also Plummer, *Vitae Sanctorum Hiberniae* (Oxford, 1910), I, 131, 139, 148; II, 289. The story of St. Chrysostomus differs from all earlier related legends by the elements of his capture and removal to the king's castle, details obviously taken from European wild-man mythology. About the artistic history of the motive of the hairy Chrysostomus see E. Wind, "The Saint as Monster," *Journal of the Warburg Institute,* I (1938), 183.

39. The ill-treatment of the wild man by the ignorant occurs in the Lailoken fragments and is part of the legend of St. Chrysostomus. For the story of the wild man of Orford, who was caught and released again when efforts to make him speak proved fruitless, see Christina

Hole, *English Folklore* (New York, 1940), p. 113.
40. Dickson (1937), pp. 144, 74, 326.
41. On Munday's "knight," see note 12, above. Diego de San Pedro, *Carcel de Amor* (Seville, 1492; new ed. Barcelona, 1904), p. 6.
42. *Tristan de Nanteuil* is summarized in Dickson (1929), p. 110. For Sir Satyrane, see *Faërie Queene*, i, vi, 20, ff.
43. For the story of the bear-son see F. Panzer, *Beowulf* (Munich, 1910), and, more recently, Rhys Carpenter, *Folktale, Fiction and Saga in the Homeric Epics* (Berkeley, 1946), p. 136. See also Dickson (1929), p. 117.
44. "Perceval," v. 2167. Correspondingly, in the English "Perceval," v. 596: "He was a wilde manne." In Pseudo-Wauchier's "Perceval," ed. Potvin, *Perceval le Gallois, ou le Conte de Graal* (Mons, 1866–1871), v. 20604, an

hom sauvage is introduced who later becomes a knight. According to another reading this wild man is Perceval himself. See E. Brugger, "Bliocadran," p. 167.
45. *Le Chevalier au Cygne et Godefroid de Bouillon,* ed. de Reiffenberg (Brussels, 1846), 1, 1264, and p. 191.
46. An excellent discussion of the implications in medieval language of the terms "wild" and "tame" is in von der Leyen and Spamer, p. 18.
47. See, for instance, Johannes Tauler, *Das Väterbuch* (Berlin, 1918), v. 6712.
48. Rather unexpectedly to the nonphilologist, German *wild* is not related to German *Wald*. See F. Kluge, *Etymologisches Wörterbuch der Deutschen Sprache* (Strassburg, 1905), article "Wild."

2. HIS MYTHOLOGICAL PERSONALITY

1. Zingerle, pp. 66, 77, 79, 80, 81, 82, 83, 86. *Handwörterbuch des Deutschen Aberglaubens* (Berlin and Leipzig, 1927–1942), article "Wilder Mann"; Nisselburg in the Tyrol is supposed to have disappeared in this way. Mannhard, I, 113. *Handwörterbuch*, article "Fängge." This trait of exchanging children, like all the more violent characteristics, is reported more frequently of the wild woman than of the wild man. The exchange of demoniac offspring for human children played an important part in the theory of witchcraft. See J. Hansen, *Quellen und Untersuchungen zur Geschichte des Hexenwahns und der Hexenverfolgung im Mittelalter* (Bonn, 1901), p. 82.
2. *Handwörterbuch*, article "Wilder Mann." According to modern theories of folklore many of the characteristics of the wild man may have been invented to serve as pedagogical fictions. See reference to this habit in Lorenzo Lippi's "Malmantile Riacquistato" (seventeenth century) in Benedetto Croce, *Saggi sulla Letteratura Italiana del Seicento* (Bari, 1911), p. 75.
3. Mannhard, I, 87, 94, 98, 105, 111.

Zingerle, p. 82. F. Ranke, *Die Deutsche Volkssage* (Munich, 1918), p. 176.
4. Zingerle, p. 66. See also Schiller's ballad "Der Alpenjäger," where the mountain spirit reproaches the hunter: *Raum für alle hat die Erde, was verfolgst Du meine Herde?* — "There is space for all on earth, why do you persecute my herd?" Schiller, *Sämtliche Werke* (Säkularausgabe, 1908), I, 108. Mannhard, I, 95–97, Pitré's *Archivio*, VIII, 124. Zingerle, pp. 43–45, 82.
5. Mannhard, I, 93 and 111. Neri, p. 55. Zingerle, p. 46.
6. Mannhard, I, 97, 98, 112, 113. *Anabasis* 1, 2, 13. *De Situ Graeciae* 1, 45. *Metamorphoses*, 9, 90; *Fasti*, 3, 285 and 344. *Variae Historiae*, 3, 18. For comprehensive dsicussion see Mannhard, I, 141.
7. *Faërie Queene*, vi, iv, 12.
8. Lehrs, *The Master of the Amsterdam Cabinet* (London, 1893–94), Nos. 51 and 52. Heinrich Wittenweiler, *Der Ring*, ed. L. Bechstein (Stuttgart, 1851), p. 232.
9. F. Panzer, *Merlin und Seifried de Ardemont von Albrecht von Scharffenberg* (Tübingen, 1902), vv. 151–159.

10. Yvain, ed. Förster, vv. 278 f. These primeval bulls give way in Förster's manuscript F to bulls and leopards. In the Swedish and English translations there are lions, bears, and panthers. Hartmann von Aue's text has bisons and primeval bulls. The fact that all these wild creatures are conceived as interchangeable is characteristic of wild-man mythology. Förster surmises (p. xxxix) that the versions with several varieties of animals may preserve a more ancient form of the story than that contained in Chrétien's French story.

11. This is the opinion of Förster, and of L. A. Paton, in "The Story of Grisandoles," *Publications of the Modern Language Association*, XXII (1907), 269.

12. The wild man in *Yvain* would thus turn out to be one of the pagan demons associated with a spring, of which there are many examples from classical antiquity. The importance of the spring in the forest of Brocéliande as a center of pagan activities need not be emphasized, for rain-making has been going on there from ancient until very recent times. See J. Grimm, *Deutsche Mythologie* (4th ed. Berlin, 1870), I, 494, and J. Frazer, *The Golden Bough* (London, 1911-15), I, 306. If the suggestion that the wild man and Esclados are identical is correct, then the wild man is a relative of such figures beside a spring as the Silenus in the Ficoronian Cista. See O. Jahn, *Die ficoronische Cista* (Leipzig, 1852), pp. 24, 31.

13. Aucassin et Nicolette, ed. M. Roques (Paris, 1925), 24, 2. The description of the creature seems to be derived from Chrétien's of the wild herdsman. Guillaume de Lorris and Jean de Meun, *Roman de la Rose*, ed. E. Langlois (Paris, 1914-24), vv. 3155, 3755, 15304. The creature is described as powerful and ugly and as having a mace. *Le Livre d'Artus*, pp. 124-125. The description of Merlin is again patterned after that of the wild herdsman in *Yvain*. We are told that all around him deer and other animals are grazing, and that they dare eat and drink only

upon his command. They drink from the spring of Brocéliande which thus is conceived as quite close, much closer than in Chrétien's "Yvain." The situation postulated for the source of Chrétien's version is thus preserved here, and it may be permissible to use the later book in reconstructing the tradition from which Chrétien departed.

14. Chrétien de Troyes, *Perceval*, ed. A. Hilka (Halle, 1935), v. 9225. See also G. L. Kittredge, *A Study of Gawain and the Green Knight* (Cambridge, 1916), pp. 42, 87, 226, 256. Paien de Maisières, *La Mule sanz Frain*, ed. R. T. Hill (Baltimore, 1911), v. 286.

15. Von der Leyen and Spamer, p. 23. The demon in question is called the *diure karl*, the churl of the animals. "Dietrichs Drachenkämpfe," ed. in *Deutsches Heldenbuch* (1866-1873), vol. V, vv. 106-113.

16. Orendel, ed. H. Steinger (Halle, 1935), vv. 1253-1260.

17. R. S. Loomis, *Celtic Myth and Arthurian Romance* (New York, 1927), p. 118. Like his counterpart in the Alps the Fer Caille (man of the woods) has a huge, monstrously hideous spouse. The fact that he carries an iron pole connects him with giants in other areas of European folklore. The fact that his pole is forked may deserve a minor investigation of its own.

18. J. Loth, *Les Mabinogion* (Paris, 1884), II, 9.

19. W. Mulertt, "Der Wilde Mann in Frankreich," *Zeitschrift fuer Französische Sprache und Literatur*, LVI (1932), 72 f. Richard de Fournival, *Bestiaire d'Amour*, ed. J. Homsberg (Uppsala, 1925). The verses are quoted from Mulertt, pp. 73-74. The poem is said to be wrongly attributed to Conon de Bethune, and appears in the edition of his works (Helsingfors, 1891).

20. Neri, pp. 56 and 57, where further literature is cited. L. Boiardo, *Orlando Inamorato*, ed. F. Zoffano (Bologna 1906-7), I, 23.

21. While the wild man is recorded in the Tyrol, the Swiss Alps, the Böhmerwald, the Hartz mountains, Hesse, and Sweden, the wild woman occurs also in Styria, lower Austria, the Oberpfalz, lower Saxony, the Mark Brandenburg, and Flanders. See Mannhard, p. 122, and Höttges, pp. 154 and 156.

22. Handwörterbuch, article "Fängge." Mannhard, I, 89.

23. Mannhard, I, 74. Ranke, p. 169.

24. Mannhard, I, 90, 99, 108. In recent years the traditions about these creatures, which appear to be more closely akin to the fairies than other types of wild women, were limited to the Alps. In the late Middle Ages, however, the stories about *selige Frauwen, Holden*, or *wysse Frauwen* were told also in the area of the lower Rhine; W. Liungman, *Traditionswanderungen: Euphrat-Rhein. Studien zur Geschichte der Volksbräuche*, Folklore Fellowship Communications, nos. 118–119 (Helsinki, 1937–38), II, 627. Zingerle, pp. 24, 30, 32, 37, 38. Ranke, p. 172. *Handwörterbuch*, article "Fängge." Höttges, p. 156 (legends from the Havel region and from lower Saxony).

25. Compare the excellent treatment of this subject by W. H. Roscher in his "Ephialtes, Eine pathologisch-mythologische Abhandlung über Alpträume und Alpdämonen des klassischen Altertums," *Abhandlungen der sächsischen Akademie der Wissenschaften*, vol. XX (1900).

26. Mannhard, I, 93, 117, 133. The dragging breasts are reported not only from Switzerland, as noted before, but also, for instance, from Pomerania; see Höttges, p. 154. A Mediterranean example of the same tradition is in G. B. Basile's *Pentamerone*, ed. N. M. Penzer (London, 1932), fifth day, fourth tale.

27. Hansen, p. 618, quoting from G. Sievers and E. Steinmeier, *Die Althochdeutschen Glossen* (Berlin, 1879–1898). The Biblical quotation is from Isaiah 34:14, where the word *lamia* appears as Jerome's equivalent for Hebrew *lilith*, the name of the Jewish she-monster. It must be noted that these glosses are very largely dependent upon each other, and cannot all be regarded as firsthand evidence.

28. Gervasius of Tilbury, "De Lamiis et Nocturnis Larvis," in his *Otia Imperialia*, ed. F. Liebrecht (Hanover,

1856), p. 39. Guglielmus Alvernus, *Tractatus de Universo* (Paris, 1674), pp. 1004 and 1066. See also John of Salisbury, *Polycraticus*, 2, 17. For the development of the ideas involved see Grimm, *Deutsche Mythologie*, II, 884–886; Hansen, p. 650; G. L. Kittredge, *Witchcraft in Old and New England* (Cambridge, 1929), p. 224. Gervasius of Tilbury said: *Lamiae quae vulgo mascae out in Gallica lingua striae*. The implication is in Gervasius, as in the writings of antiquity, that *lamiae* have wings. See also Guglielmus Alvernus, p. 1004: *Malignis spiritis quas vulgus striges et lamias vocant*. In the writers of the fifteenth and sixteenth centuries this identification is a commonplace.

29. Creditisti, quod quidem credere solent, quod sint agrestes feminae, quas silvaticas vocant, quas dicunt esse corporeas, et quando voluerint, ostendant se suis amatoribus et cum eis dicunt se oblectasse et item quando voluerint abscondant se et evanescant (Grimm, *Deutsche Mythologie*, I, 359).

30. Codex Lat. Mon. 17736, folio 144r.

31. J. Hansen, *Zauberwahn, Inquisition und Hexenprozesse im Mittelalter und die Entstehung der Grossen Hexenverfolgung* (Munich, 1900), p. 188. It was claimed that the knights had made contact with *daemones in figura seu specie mulierum*. A similar accusation was made in 1318 by Pope John XXII against sorcerers.

32. Mannhard, I, 136.

33. Giraldus Cambrensis, I, 5, p. 374, in T. Wright's modern English translation: "Having on a certain night, namely that of Palm Sunday, met a damsel whom he had long loved, in a pleasant and convenient place, while he was indulging her embraces, suddenly instead of a beautiful girl he found in his arms a hairy, rough, and hideous creature, the sight of which deprived him of his reason, and he became mad."

34. Der Ritter von Stauffenberg, ed. E. Schröder in *Zwei altdeutsche Rittermären* (3d ed., Berlin, 1920).

35. "Wolfdietrich" (B), vv. 307–337.

36. "Ortnit," Codex Dresden, v. 277, quoted from von der Leyen and

Spamer, p. 17. F. J. Child, *The English and Scottish Popular Ballads* (Boston, 1882), no. 36, "Allison Gross."

37. *Kudrun*, ed. K. Bartsch (Leipzig, 1874), v. 2117, *Von einem wilden wibe is Wate arzet.* "Eckenliet," ed. J. Zupitza, in *Deutsches Heldenbuch* (Berlin, 1866–1873), v. 172.

38. *Wigalois*, ed. J. M. N. Kapteyn (Bonn, 1926), vv. 6283–6410. Panzer, *Merlin und Seifried de Ardemont*, vv. 202–215. Heinrich von dem Türlein, *Diu Crône*, ed. G. H. F. Scholl (Stuttgart, 1852), v. 9129. See also "Chevalier du Papegan," ed. F. Saran, in *Beiträge zur Geschichte der Deutschen Literatur*, XXI (1896), 400. *Seifried de Ardemont* (Panzer), v. 207; *Wigalois*, vv. 6379 and 6443.

39. *Wigalois*, v. 6284. "Wigamur," ed. von der Hagen und Büsching, in *Deutsche Gedichte des Mittelalters* (1808), vol. I, p. 112, v. 200–227.

40. W. Weisbach, *Religiöse Reform und Mittelalterliche Kunst* (Zürich, 1945), p. 81.

41. J. Adhémar, *Influence antiques dans l'art du moyen age français* (London, 1939), p. 197. E. Mâle, *L'Art religieux du XIIe Siècle en France* (Paris, 1924), p. 375. The representation of Luxuria developed in the thirteenth century into that of the "prince of the world," as on the cathedrals of Strassburg and Freiburg, presenting himself from the front as a courtly and attractive youth while his back crawls with snakes and toads. This convention, too, seems to have been adopted from native folklore, for it was said of the wild woman that while she may be most alluring when viewed from the front, her back may be hollow like a rotten tree trunk. See Mannhard, I, 120, 125, 128, 133. An example of the same idea is found in *Wigalois*, v. 6602, where the dwarf Karioz is introduced as the son of a wild woman, and it is asserted of him that his back is hollow. See also von der Leyen and Spamer, p. 24.

42. Hole, *English Folklore*, p. 113. The tradition in question seems to be a modern one.

43. Hansen, *Quellen und Untersuchungen*, p. 650. Mannhard, I, 124. The

wild woman in "Wigamur" is referred to as *merwîp*, p. 168, v. 338, and *merminne*, v. 350. Von der Leyen and Spamer, p. 20.

44. *Diu Crône*, vv. 9210–9555.

45. *Serena en mer hante — Cuntre tempeste chante — E plure en bel tens* ("The siren lives in the sea. She sings when it storms and cries when the weather is nice."). Philippe de Thaun, *Bestiaire*, ed. E. Walberg (Paris, 1900), quoted from Mulertt, p. 75.

46. "Les Chansons du Conte de Bretagne," *Mélange A. Jeanroy* (Paris, 1928), p. 474, quoted from W. Mulertt, page cited.

47. *A New English Dictionary on Historical Principles*, article "woodwose." The term "wild man" seems to have become popular in the thirteenth century. "Wodewasan" is an Anglo-Saxon term. "Wasa" is of uncertain etymology. *Handwörterbuch*, article "Schrat."

48. Neri, p. 53. Mannhard, I, 113.

49. The various forms, *holzmove, -mowa, -muowa, -muevo, -muhwa, -mûa, -muoia, -miua, -moa*, are all collected in Hansen, *Quellen und Untersuchungen*, pp. 618 and 649. They are related to German *Muhme*. The form *Maia* survives in the Carnival in the Vintschgau, the Tyrol, and is there applied to the mask of a man dressed as a woman who sprinkles water on the spectators. Liungman, II, 899. Whether there is any connection between the Roman goddess Maia and Maia the May Queen in recent modern festivities, I would not dare decide.

50. Von der Leyen and Spamer, p. 22.

51. Basile, *Il Pentamerone*, particularly the fifth and ninth tales of the first day where the *huorco* is described as living in the innermost recesses of the woods. The ogress in the *Pentamerone* corresponds also to the usual descriptions of extreme human monstrosities; see for instance the seventh tale of the second day.

52. Lorenzo Lippi, *Malmantile riacquistato*, 7, vv. 53f. Lippi's description is again derived from the astoundingly persistent canons of human ugliness.

53. W. H. Waschersleben, *Bussord-nungen der Abendländischen Kirche* (Halle, 1851), p. 533.

54. The leader of this school of thought is, of course, W. Mannhard, whose influence persisted into the first quarter of this century.

55. Sererhard, *Einfältige Delineation aller Gemeinden gemeiner dreyer Pündten* (Chur, 1742), p. 30, quoted from *Handwörterbuch*, article "Fängge": *Den Menschen an Gestalt gleich, doch etwas kuerzer und dicker, am ganzen Leib mit Haaren bewachsen.* See also Mannhard, I, 94.

56. Von der Leyen and Spamer, pp. 22–23; Mannhard, I, 111.

57. Caesarius of Heisterbach, *Dialogus Miraculorum*, tr. by H. von Scott and C. C. S. Bland (New York, 1929), chap. lv.

58. Von der Leyen and Spamer, p. 23.

59. *Der anglo-normännische Boeve de Haumtonne*, ed. A. Stimming (Halle, 1899), v. 572: *plus estoit velu ke nul porc or tusun. Mort Aymeri de Narbonne*, ed. J. Couraye du Parc (Paris, 1884), v. 647: *Toz fu veluz jusqu'as talons.* See also *La Prise de Cordres et de Sebille*, ed. O. Densusianu (Paris, 1896), v. 493; *Aliscans*, ed. E. Wienbeck, W. Hartnacke, and P. Basch (Halle, 1903), the figure of Brun le Velu, v. 7772; *Anséis de Cartage*, ed. J. Alton (Stuttgart, 1892), v. 6753. All this and further related material is collected in H. Wohlgemut, *Riesen und*

Zwerge in der Französischen Literatur des Mittelalters (Erlangen, 1906), p. 33.

60. *Don Quixote*, 2, 41.

61. *Laurin und der kleine Rosengarten*, ed. G. Holz (Halle, 1897), version D, vv. 175–183. "Wolfdietrich" (B), v. 461. See also, for a similar situation, *Tandareis und Flordibel*, ed. F. Khull (Graz, 1886), v. 9896. Albrecht von Kemenaten, "Goldemar," ed. E. Henrici, in *Deutsches Heldenbuch* (Berlin 1866–1873), V, 204. Also, "Wolfdietrich" (B), vv. 718f.; also vv. 795f., where the dwarf Billung is first introduced as a wild man.

62. G. C. Druce, "Some Abnormal and Composite Human Forms in English Church Architecture," *Archeological Journal*, LXX (1915), 159.

63. M. Geisberg, *Anfänge des Kupferstichs* (Leipzig, 1923), pl. 74, and Lehrs, *Geschichte und kritischer Katalog*, figs. 109 and 262–273. The derivation of the design from similar ornamental variants is quite clear, since in the corresponding prints of the same series the wild men are frequently replaced by human figures without "wild" characteristics. It is likely that the whole type of design is ultimately derived from ancient Roman ornament.

64. Compare with this print the tournament between apes and wild men painted on one page of the prayer book of Mary of Burgundy. O. Pächt, *The Master of Mary of Burgundy* (London, 1948), pl. 33.

3. HIS THEATRICAL EMBODIMENT

1. According to some well-informed opinion it is not a question of a cult, but of the rationalization of the superstitious belief that it would be bad luck to take the entire harvest away without leaving something. The so-called offerings to the wood damsels would then have to be regarded as causal fictions, meant to explain established custom. This may well be true. See C. W. von Sydow, "The Mannhardian Theories about the Last Sheaf and the Fertility Demons from a Modern Critical Point of View," *Folklore* (1934).

2. Mannhard, I, 77. Grimm, *Deutsche Mythologie*, I, 359. O. Erich, *Wörterbuch der Deutschen Volkskunde* (Leipzig, 1936), p. 83.

3. A. d'Ancona, *Origini del Teatro Italiano* (Turin, 1891), p. 89. J. Bächtold, *Geschichte der Deutschen Literatur in der Schweiz* (Frauenfeld, 1892), p. 219 n.

4. Grimm's *Wörterbuch*, article "wilder Mann": *Obschon wegen dem öffentlichen Ausstehen und Medizinverkaufen der Marktschreier und sogenannten Waldmänner bereits unter* dem 14. November 1783 die Inhibitions-verordnungen erlassen worden, so will doch vorkommen, dass dessen ungeachtet an einigen Orten selbe wiederum öffentlich ausstehn und Medizinen verkaufen (Bavarian order of April 1800). Another set of police orders, this time from Würzburg, is mentioned in von der Leyen and Spamer, p. 24.

5. R. Stumpfl, Kultspiele der Germanen als Ursprung des Mittelalterlichen Dramas (Berlin, 1936), p. 249.

6. O. Karpf, "Ueber Tiermasken," Wörter und Sachen, V (1913), 103. K. Meuli, Schweitzer Masken (Zürich, 1943), p. 41. A. Spamer, Handbuch der Deutschen Volkskunde (Leipzig, 1935), II, 100. K. Weinhold, "Der Wildemännletanz in Oberstdorf," Zeitschrift des Vereins für Volkskunde, VII (1897), 427.

7. Mannhard, I, 336. E. Hoffmann-Krayer, "Fastnachtsgebräuche in der Schweitz," in Schweitzerisches Archiv für Volkskunde, I (1897), 282. O. Höfler, "Vildiver," Wiener Prähistorische Zeitschrift (1932–33), p. 381. A. Dörrer, Das Schemenlaufen in Tirol und Verwandte Alpenländische Masken und Fastnachtsbräuche (Innsbruck, 1938), pp. 18, 41. L. Felicetti, "La Caccia del 'Salvanel' a Panchia e a Tesero in Fiemme," in Pro Cultura di Trento, II (1911), 97. Spamer, vol. II, fig. 82. G. Boccaccio, Il Decamerone, 4, 2.

8. Mannhard, I, 337.

9. O. Höfler; p. 381.

10. Mannhard, I, 336.

11. Mannhard, I, p. 333.

12. For the hunt of a snorting wild man in Littau, the Grisons, see Schweitzerisches Archiv für Volkskunde, XII (1909), 200. According to Professor Rhys Carpenter the equivalence of bear and wild man is a very ancient one, and the bear may possibly be the older figure. A trace of this connection is found, according to Professor Carpenter, in the original linguistic equivalence of orcus (wild man), and ursus (bear). For Czechoslovakia, Hesse, etc.: O. Höfler, quoting Egerer Jahrbuch (1910), p. 132; R. Wolfram, "Bärenjagen und Faschingslaufen im Murtal," Wiener Zeitschrift für Volks-

kunde (1932), pp. 68–70; Liungman, II, 1075; Handwörterbuch, article "bear."

13. V. Alford, "The Springtime Bear in the Pyrenees," Folklore, XX, 202. A. van Gennep, Manuel de folklore français contemporain (Paris, 1936–), vol. I, part 3, p. 908. The marriage of a girl to a bear is also a frequent motive in fairy tales such as "Snow White and Rose Red" in Grimm's Fairy Tales.

14. Migne, Patrologia Latina, CXXV, 776: "Ne turpia ioca cum urso vel tornatricibus ante se facere permittat nec larvas daemonum quas vulgo talamascas dicunt."

15. De Disciplinis Ecclesiasticis, 1, 213, ed. W. H. Waschersleben, I, 216. Regino's admonition is clearly a close variant of Hincmar's and dependent upon it.

16. Liungman, II, 967 and 1056. F. Schneider, "Ueber Calendae Januariae und Martiae im Mittelalter," Archiv für Religionswissenschaft, XX, 392.

17. Ghesellen die daer speelen mitten wilden manne. G. Kalff, Geschiedenis der Nederlandischen Letterkunde (Groningen, 1906–1910), II, 6.

18. Boccaccio, place cited: "Today we make a great rejoicing when one person is to bring a man clothed like a bear, another like the wild man, and so on, and in this manner people are to come under different disguises in St. Mark's Square as to a hunt."

19. Mannhard, I, 358, and see Christina Hole, English Customs and Usage (1946), on English mumming plays at Christmas. About the killing of the Carnival bear see Mannhard, I, 411, and Liungman, II, 1058. The burning of the wild man ends the Carnival festivities in the town of Grevenmacher in Luxembourg.

20. This point of view, first pronounced by H. Schurtz, Altersklassen und Männerbünde, Eine Darstellung der Grundformen der Gesellschaft (Berlin, 1902), has been given considerable emphasis by recent German scholars. See for instance: O. Höfler, Kultische Geheimbünde der Germanen, Vol. I (Frankfurt, 1934); L. Weiser, Altgermanische Jünglingsweihen und Männerbünde (Bühl, 1927); R. Stumpfl,

Kultspiele der Germanen als Ursprung des Mittelalterlichen Dramas (Berlin, 1936); R. Wolfram, Schwerttanz und Maennerbund (Kassel, 1935-). This entire literature, particularly Höfler's contribution, lies too close to the official Nazi party line not to be suspect. However, the merit of some of these books, particularly Höfler's, is such as to deserve our attention, even though we may be unable to accept their more extreme claims. For the hunt of the wild man see Schurtz, p. 116, and Stumpfl, p. 257.

21. See for instance the threat against any member of the Bavarian Haberfeldtreiben betraying the common cause, in Wolfram, p. 231.

22. Höfler, Kultische Geheimbünde, pp. 22, 28, 345f.

23. Ibid., p. 25, and L. Rütimeyer, "Ueber Masken und Maskengebräuche im Lötschental," Globus, I (1907), 202. See also Meuli, p. 13.

24. For the close correspondence of legend and ritual see L. Röhrich, "Sage und Brauch," Forschungen und Fortschritte (November 1949).

25. This is stressed and considerably exaggerated by Höfler, who seems to believe that the medieval guilds developed out of such associations. See also E. Hoffman-Krayer, "Knabenschaften und Volksjustiz in der Schweit," Schweitzerisches Archiv für Volkskunde, vol. VIII (1905). Switzerland is still the classical country for such associations.

26. On the English dance, see Thomas Hall's Chronicle (London, 1548, reëdited 1809), p. 580. On the Bal des Ardents, see below, n. 67. On Basel and Nuremberg, E. E. Knuchel, Die Umzüge der Kleinbaseler Ehrenzeichen (Basel, 1913); S. L. Sumberg, The Nürnberg Schembart Carnival (New York, 1941).

27. Sebastian Franck, Weltbuch, Spiegel und Bildnisz des ganzen Erdbodens (Tübingen, 1534), quoted from A. Spamer, Deutsche Fastnachtsbräuche (Jena, 1936), p. 11.

28. Pictures of this pageant are (or were) preserved in the Dresden Print Room. See A. Spamer, Deutsche Fastnachtsbräuche, p. 12.

29. J. Geiler von Kaysersberg, Die Emeis (Strassburg, 1509-1519). Geiler von Kaysersberg seems to have been the first to try to bring systematic order into the lore of the wild man. His five categories of wild men are: solitarii (the hermits, among whom he enumerates Aegidius, Onuphrius, Maria Magdalena, and Maria Aegyptica), sacchani (the wild men proper, here identified with satyrs), hyspani (the wild creatures from foreign lands as enumerated in the Merveilles du Monde), piginini (pygmies), and diaboli. See the comments on this system in von der Leyen and Spamer, p. 19.

30. As to Munich, it is particularly clear, in this instance, that the performance served as an initiation ritual, for the apprentices who performed it were subsequently received into the butchers' guild. A similar custom prevailed in Salzburg (Liungman, II, 961). In Merano the initiate had to dress in a costume with cow tails hanging from it, and then was carried through the town by his fellow butchers and thrown into the fountain. Dörrer, p. 19. For Basel, Knuchel, p. 28.

31. Sumberg, pp. 88, 100 (order of 1469), Hans Sachs, Collected Works, ed. A. v. Keller and E. Götze (Stuttgart, 1870-1908), IV, 200. Sumberg quotes the order of 1469 from J. Baader, Nürnberger Polizeiverordnungen aus dem 13. bis 15. Jahrhundert (Tübingen, 1861).

32. Sumberg, figs. 17, 18, 28, 19, 21-23.

33. For Nuremberg, see Sumberg, p. 86. For Chester, see Harleian Ms. 2155, fol. 356, quoted from R. Withington, English Pageants, a Historical Outline (Cambridge, 1918), I, 73.

34. For the Inn valley, Dörrer, p. 36; Liungman, II, 922. For Belgium, C. Leirens, Belgian Folklore (New York, 1948), p. 28. Another Belgian performance, in which the wild man appears conspicuously, although in a subordinate capacity, is the "Lumeçon" in Mons, a festival held on Trinity Sunday in June. See Leirens, p. 36. The story enacted is the slaying of a monster, the Dou-Dou, by a knight Gilles de Chin

(also called St. George) with the help of a group of wild men who appear dressed in green. For Barcelona, von der Leyen and Spamer, p. 26.

35. Don Quixote 2, 20 and 41.

36. See p. 178, below, for a refutation of this theory as a general explanation of the appearance of external shield-supporters in heraldry. The theory was first maintained by Viollet-le-Duc in the article "Armoire" in his *Dictionnaire de l'architecture,* vol. I.

37. M. Soder, "Fastnachtsbräuche im Oberaargau," *Schweitzerisches Archiv für Volkskunde* (1935), p. 110. Wolfram, *Schwerttanz und Männerbund* (Kassel, 1935-), pp. 245, 246, and fig. 37. W. Hein, "Das Huttlerlaufen," *Zeitschrift für Volkskunde,* IX (1899), 109. Instead of "Hudler" the name may be written "Huttler" or "Hutler"; the derivation is from *Hudeln,* rags. Since the etymology is not likely to have been suggested during the Nazi period, I would like to draw attention to the fact that "Hitler" seems to belong to the same group of words: the most demoniac of all political leaders had a a very fitting name.

38. Wolfram, *Schwerttanz,* pp. 247, 280. Liungman, II, 895. Hole, *English Customs and Usage,* pp. 22–24, figs. 19–21.

39. For the derivation and history of the term see O. Driesen, *Der Ursprung des Harlekin, ein Kulturgeschichtliches Problem* (Berlin, 1904), and the excellent essay by H. M. Flasdieck, "Harlekin, Germanischer Mythos in Romanischer Wandlung," *Anglia,* vol. LXI (1937).

40. Ordericus Vitalis, *Historiae Ecclesiasticae Libri XIII,* ed. Le Prévost (Paris, 1838–1855), III, 376. Driesen, p. 24. Höfler, *Kultische Geheimbünde,* p. 99.

41. Characteristic is the mask of the Herlequin Croquesots in Adam de la Halle's "Play of the Bower," Driesen, p. 57.

42.
. . . il firent en l moment
Tot le plus fort tornoiement
Qui jamès soit ne onques fust
Leur lances estoient de fust,

De tel fust con il le troverent:
Mout bien leur force i esproverent
Chascun l arbre enbracha
En lieu d'escu et l'esracha.
Lors firent leur tornoiement . . .
Mes li l d'eus si s'en fui
et les autres torjors après
Qui le suirent de si près
Torjors de muete et de randone
Si qu'en la forest de Brotonne
le chacerent torjorz batant.
Lors s'aresta celui estal;
So lors livra a touz estant
Lors veissiez grant batestal.
"Le Dit de Luque La Maudite," ed. G. Raynaud, *Romania,* vol. XII (1883). Driesen, p. 94.

43. *Roman de Fauvel,* ed. P. Aubry (Paris, 1907). Driesen, p. 104.

44. Driesen, p. 121.

45. J. Froissart, *Chronicles of England, France and Spain and the Adjoining Countries,* tr. J. Bourchier, Lord Berners (London, 1924), part II, par. 188, p. 419.

46. See pp. 171ff. on Balkan "wedding" pageants.

47. E. de Monstrelet, *Chronique,* ed. Donet-d-Arq (Paris, 1857–1862), V, 3. Van Gennep, I, 923; Withington, I, 75. From 1220 to 1556 it was the custom in Lille to elect the so-called "Roi de l'Epinette" on Mardi Gras, and then to proceed with the tournaments. Representatives from all over France used to come to the festivities. It was customary to have different disguises and colors every year. Carnival visits of the entire citizenry of one town to another were frequent events in the late Middle Ages. See Meulli, p. 78.

48. For Paris, see Michaut et Poujoulat, *Nouvelle Collection des memoires,* ser. 1, vol. IV, p. 250, quoted from J. von Schlosser, "Die Bilderhandschriften König Wenzel's," *Jahrbuch der Kunsthistorischen Sammlungen des Allerhöchsten Kaiserhauses,* XIV (1894), 214. For Brussels, see M. Hermann, *Forschungen zur Deutschen Theatergeschichte des Mittelalters und der Renaissance* (Berlin, 1914), p. 368. For Bruges, R. Dupuis, *La Triomphante et Solennele Entrée de Charles Quint en sa ville de Bruges* (Bruges, 1850), p. 13, quoted from Withington, I, 76.

49. A. Gattari, "Diario del Concilio di Basilea," in *Concilium Basiliense* (1896-), V, 402, 412, 413; and R. Burckhard, *Gewirkte Bildteppiche des 15. und 16. Jahrhunderts im Historischen Museum in Basel* (Leipzig, 1923).

50. Knuchel, pp. 6, 27.

51. J. M. de Azcárate, "El Tema iconográfico del salvaje," *Archivo Español de Arte*, no. 82 (1948), p. 98.

52. Don Quixote, 2, 20.

53. R. Brotanek, *Die Englischen Mysterienspiele* (Vienna, 1902), p. 3.

54. Withington, I, 73; II, 13. A. Nicoll, *Stuart Masques and the Renaissance Stage* (New York, 1938), p. 205.

55. Thomas Hall's Chronicle, p. 580. Withington, I, 79, 217. Plays based upon the story of Valentine and Orson occurred not only in England. A popular performance of such a play took place in 1833 in Kiefersfelden near Kufstein, Bavaria. Its title was "Valentinus und Ursinus, die zwey Zwillingsbrüder, oder das Diamantencreitz"; see *Bayrischer Heimatschutz*, XXIV (1928), 82. It is necessary to mention at this juncture the so-called satyrs' dance in Shakespeare's *Winter's Tale*, Act IV, scene 4. From their description (herdsmen "that have made themselves all men of hair. They call themselves Saltiers") it would seem likely that these "satyrs" are meant to be wild men. Webster's defines saltier as "a satyr — confused with *saulter*, leaper, dancer."

56. P. Lacroix, *Ballets et Mascarades de cour sous Henry IV et Louis XIII* (Geneva, 1868-1870).

57. Neri, p. 64. De Azcárate, p. 97.

58. See Neri, p. 65, where other appearances of wild men in dramatic performances of the Renaissance are mentioned, and J. Lieure, *Jacques Callot* (Paris, 1924), vol. I, pl. 179 and 183. As noted in Chapter 2, the representation of river gods as conventional wild men is not rare in the sixteenth and seventeenth centuries.

59.
Die wilden Maenner sinds genannt
Am Harzgebirge wohlbekannt
Natuerlich nackt in aller Kraft

Sie kommen alle riesenhaft.
Den Fichtenbaum in rechter Hand
Und um den Leib ein wulstig Band
Den derbsten Schurz von Zweig und Blatt
Leibwache wie der Papst nicht hat.
Goethe, *Faust*, tr. George M. Priest (New York: Covici-Friede, 1932), p. 176, ll. 5864-5871; by permission of the publishers. The entire plot of the first act of the second part of *Faust* is strongly influenced by Goethe's acquaintance with Froissart's account of the Bal des Ardents. From this source comes the motive of a fire breaking out during a masquerade in which the emperor himself participates.

60. See the detailed and exhaustive documentation in Liungman, II, 764f. (See n. 24 to Chapter 2, above.) Liungman offers descriptions of the Kuker in Kirk-Kilisse (p. 769), in Malko-Tirnovo near Adrianople (p. 777), in Madzura, Bulgaria (p. 778), and of the corresponding figure in Dubrovnik-Ragusa in Dalmatia (p. 807) and in Kruševa near Monastir (p. 815); there was also a Kuker in Kara-Buner on the Black Sea (p. 794 and fig. 113), a corresponding figure on the island of Skyros in the Aegean (fig. 99), a Startzi in Radomir, Bulgaria (p. 826), and a masculine mask in Srêdna-Gora, east of Sofia (p. 806), to mention a few examples. See also pp. 769f., 777, 790, 794, 807, 810, 811, 813f., 875, and fig. 132.

61. For Morocco, see Liungman, p. 853; for the Balkans, pp. 778-790. The most elaborate plays are given in Urumbegh and Hagios Georgios near Viza, about 110 miles from Constantinople.

62. Such detailed maps are shown in Liungman, pp. 767 and 886, and serve as a basis for the author's argument. It is hardly necessary to point out that such maps cannot offer conclusive evidence for the spread of historical movements, since traditions may not always spread from a locality to its immediate geographical neighbors.

63. E. K. Chambers: *The Medieval Stage* (Oxford, 1903), II, 290, 306. Liungman, pp. 730f. F. Schneider, "Ueber Calendae Januariae and Martiae im Mittelalter," *Archiv für Religions-*

wissenschaft, XX (1920), 379. M. Nilsson, "Studien zur Vorgeschichte des Weihnachtsfests," in the same journal, XIX (1916), 71f. The performances in question were usually held on January first.

64. Migne, *Patrologia Latina*, XXXIX, 2001, sermon "De Calendis Januariis"; LII, 609; LVII, 257.

65. On Eastern Church councils, see K. J. von Hefele, *Konziliengeschichte* (Freiburg, 1869–1890), III, 307. On Constantine Porphyrogenitus, see Liungman, p. 743. See also V. Cottas, *Le Theatre à Byzance* (Paris, 1931), and H. Reich, *Der Mimus*, Vol. I (Berlin, 1903). Canon 61 of the Council forbade "playing with the bear." A bear figures in the modern Carnival in Athens. See Liungman, p. 811. On the Tusla relief, see Liungman, p. 1054; date uncertain, but probably Middle Byzantine. A man in a bear mask, standing upright, has a leash attached to his neck. The foot of the "bear leader" is visible; the rest of the figure has broken off. Liungman derives Nordic representations of upright bears on leashes such as those on a helmet from Vendel, Sweden, from prototypes of this kind.

66. On the Byzantine butchers, Cottas, pp. 9, 14, 18. For the eastern Alps, see Wolfram, "Bärenjagen und Faschingslaufen im Murtal," p. 80.

67. Migne, LXXXVII, 524; CXL, 965. Pseudo-Theodore of Canterbury, 12, 19; see Nilsson, p. 76.

68. *Quidam eorum erant armati loricis et galeis fulgentibus, gladiosque nudos portantes in manibus suis pellifices habeant pellicea grisea et vulpina deforis pilos habentes et omnes alii prout poterant at modum mulierum erant adornati.* Quoted from R. Stumpfl, *Kultspiele der Germanen als Ursprung des Mittelalterlichen Dramas* (Berlin, 1936), p. 302. The calendar date of this performance, like that of the almost contemporary festivities in Padua, is exceptional and unexplained.

69. Flasdieck, "Harlekin," pp. 294f.

70. Some of the documents relating to Hecate (Diana) as a leader of souls have been collected in historical order by K. Meisen, *Die Sagen vom Wütenden Heer und Wilden Jäger* (Münster,

1935), p. 24. The earliest of them date from the fifth century B.C. For Herodias see Liungman, p. 587. The authenticity of the passage from the Council of Ancyra is disputed by G. D. Mansi (*Sacrorum Conciliorum Nova et Amplissima Collectio*, Florence 1759–1798, II, 535). It occurs only in the Latin accounts of the Council. On the *Vita Damasi Papae*, see Mansi, III, 1259. On Regino of Prüm, W. H. Waschersleben, II, 371. On Burchard of Worms, J Grimm, *Deutsche Mythologie*, III, 404.

71. Liungman, pp. 648–649, 651. V. Waschnitius, "Percht, Holda, und Verwandte Gestalten," *Sitzungsberichte der Akademie der Wissenschaften in Wien, Phil. Hist. Klasse*, vol. CLXXIV, part 2, (1914).

72. See *The Golden Bough* (abridged edition, New York, 1922), p. 577–578.

73. Ovid, *Fasti*, 3, 675. H. Usener, "Italische Mythen," *Kleine Schriften*, vol. IV (Leipzig, 1913). One would be tempted to believe that the Lupercalia, celebrated in Rome on February 15, were another such remote source of origin of the European Carnival, were it not that this very ancient festival was completely local and connected with the Lupercal, a grotto on the foot of the Palatine Hill. The Lupercalia were devoted to Faunus, god of herds and of the countryside. The chief ceremony consisted of a run around the Palatine Hill by young men dressed in the fur of rams sacrificed on the morning of the festive day.

74. Hartman von Aue, *Iwein*, v. 66.

75. *Thomas Hall's Chronicle*, p. 580, referring to the wild men dancing for Henry VIII at Greenwich. Neri, p. 65, referring to Castiglione's eclogue *Tirsi*, performed in 1506 in Urbino.

76. See for instance the illustrations from Froissart's Chronicles in M. Davenport, *The Book of Costume* (New York, 1948), I, 334.

77. Van Gennep, vol. I, part 3, p. 923.

78. *Ibid.*

79. Driesen, p. 143; Froissart, page cited.

80. Driesen, p. 184.

4. THE LEARNED ASPECT

1. Herodotus, 4, 191.

2. Ctesias, "Indica," ed. J. W. Mc-Crindle in *Ancient India as Described in Classical Literature* (London, 1901).

3. The standard work on fantastic lore about India is: R. Wittkower, "Marvels of the East," *Journal of the Warburg and Courtauld Institutes* (London, 1942), pp. 159, 163; also W. Reese, *Die griechischen Nachrichten über Indien* (Leipzig, 1914); J. W. McCrindle, *Ancient India as Described by Megasthenes and Arrian* (Calcutta, 1877).

4. Megasthenes, "Indica" in Strabo, *Geography*, 15, 1, 57 (ed. L. Jones, London, 1930, VII, 95).

5. Pliny, *Historia Naturalis*, 7, 2, 24; see also Solinus, *Collectanea rerum memorabilium*, ed. T. Mommsen (1895), 52, 32; Arrianus, *Indica*, 6, 23, 3; Quintus Curtius Rufus, *De rebus gestis Alexandri Magni*, ed. J. Rolfe (Cambridge, 1946), 9, 10, 9; Diodorus Siculus, *Historiae*, ed. C. H. Oldfather (London 1933–1947), 17, 105.3.

6. W. C. McDermott, *The Ape in Antiquity* (Baltimore, 1938), p. 77.

7. Pomponius Mela, *De Situ Orbis*, 3, 93, ed. G. Parthey (Berlin, 1867): *Feminas esse narrant toto corpore hirsutas et sine coitu marium sua sponde fecundas, adeo asperis efferisque moribus, ut quaedam contineri ne reluctentur vix vinculis possint.* Hanno's report is in K. Müller, *Geographi Graeci Minores* (Paris, 1855), p. xviii. Pliny, 6, 200. Agatharchides, "De Mari Eritreo," par. 51, in pp. 142–143; see McDermott, p. 69.

8. Quintus Curtius Rufus and Arrianus, pages cited. See also Agatharchides, par. 49, in Müller, p. 140. The Ichthyophagi may also be rather paradoxically relegated to the high mountains; see Brunetto Latini, *Li Livres dou Trésor*, ed. P. Chabaille (Paris, 1863), 1, 4, 123.

9. A. Ausfeld, *Der Griechische Alexanderroman* (Leipzig, 1907), II, 32, 33, 37. See also, for the original version of the romance, W. Kroll, *Pseudo-Kallisthenes* (Berlin, 1926). For reminiscences of earlier Oriental literature, B. Meiss-ner, *Alexander und Gilgamesch* (Leipzig, 1894).

10. L. Olschki, *Storia della Scoperta Geographica* (Florence, 1937). G. Chinard, *L'Exotism Américain dans la Litérature Française du 16ième siecle* (Paris, 1911).

11. F. Pfister, *Der Alexanderroman des Archipresbyter Leo* (Heidelberg, 1913). *Historia de Proeliis*, ed. F. Pfister, 3, 6 and 7.

12. In Rudolf von Ems's Alexander, for instance, the monstrous human beings possessing only one foot are called "wild." *Rudolf von Ems: Alexander, ein höfischer Versroman des 13. Jahrhunderts*, ed. V. Junk (Leipzig, 1928), v. 1620.

13. "Historia de Proeliis," recension J2, A. Hilka, *Der Altfranzösische Prosa-Alexanderroman* (Halle, 1920), p. 95.

14. H. Omont, "Lettre à l'Empéreur Adrian sur les Merveilles de l'Asie," *Bibliothèque de l'Ecole des Chartes*, LXXIV (1913), 507.

15. "Historia de Proeliis," ed. A. Hilka, 3, 6.

16. Pliny, 7, 2. Solinus, page cited. Martianus Capella, *De Nuptiis Mercurii cum Philologia*, ed. A. Dick (Leipzig, 1925), sixth book. Isidore of Seville, "Etymologiae," in Migne, vol. LXXXII; Hrabanus Maurus, "De Universo," 7, 7, in Migne, vol. CXI; Honorius Augustodinensis(?), *Imago Mundi*, 1, 11–13.

17. Montecassino, Codex 132, fol. 166. See A. M. Amelli, *Miniature Sacre e Profane del'Anno 1023 Illustranti l'Enciclopedia Medievale di Rabano Mauro* (Montecassino, 1896).

18. M. R. James, *Marvels of the East* (Oxford, 1929).

19. Tiberius BV fol. 80a, 81b; Bodleian 614 fol. 38b, 40b.

20. Dated between 989 and 1029 and thus one of the earliest of all Romanesque sculptures. It looks almost like an illustration of Chrétien's description of the wild herdsman with his beasts. This may not be due to chance, for in the eleventh century the influence of Celtic Brittany and the refugees from the British Isles who had settled there had expanded along the rivers into the interior of France. See Henri Focillon, *Moyen Age: Survivances et Reveils* (New York, 1943), pp. 71f.

21. A representation of a naked man with inscription, *Ethiop*[ian] occurs in the church of St. Sauveur, Nevers; A. Kingsley Porter, *Romanesque Sculpture of the Pilgrimage Roads* (Boston, 1923), pl. 129. It may be possible to identify tentatively on the basis of this example a number of other Romanesque wild men: The nude man riding on a basilisk at Vezelay, R. Hamann, "Das Tier in der Romanischen Plastik Frankreichs," *Medieval Studies in Memory of A. Kingsley Porter* (Cambridge, 1939), fig. 23; the nude man riding on a griffon at Autun, V. Terret, *La Sculpture Bourgignonne* (Autun, 1925), vol. I, pl. 30; the man in Autun fighting an oversize bird, Terret, vol. II, pl. 25; and the naked man similarly employed in Perrecey-les-Forges, A. Gardner, *Medieval Sculpture in France* (New York, 1931), pl. 89. Of particular interest is the creature seen on a capital in Cunault (Maine-et-Loire), P. Deschamps, *French Sculpture of the Romanesque Period* (New York, 1930), p. 67, for here an attempt seems to have been made to show the proverbial ugliness of the Arthurian wild man, with hair standing on end, long teeth, a nose sticking out like a carrot, and hairy legs(?). We can be sure that this is not a devil, for a knight, with his horse behind him, is fighting the creature, which is defending itself, spear in hand. The situation is thus the one familiar from the romances.

22. M.F. 2810. H. Omont, *Le Livre des Merveilles* (Paris, 1907), pl. 182, 189. See also Morgan Library ms. 461, fol. 41v.

23. See, for instance, M. R. James, *The Romance of Alexander* (Oxford, 1933), facsimile reproduction of a manuscript of 1338–1344, Bodl. 264, fol. 36v. The chapter heading is: *Comment Alexander combata avec ieaundis* (giants). The corresponding illustration shows Alexander and two knights, one shooting arrows against two enor-

mous wild men. See also fol. 66v and 67r. Similar is the illustration in Harleian ms. 4979 (*c.* 1300) of the text of a chapter entitled: *Coment Alexander trova un home sauvage et le fist ardoir pour ce que il navoit point dentendement mais estoit ausi come une beste.* See Druce, "*Some Abnormal and Composite Human Forms,*" p. 164.

24. Wittkower, p. 181. F. Zarncke, "Der Priester Johannes," *Abhandlungen der phil. hist. Klasse der kgl. Sächsischen Gesellschaft der Wissenschaften,* vols. VII, VIII (1876–1879), esp. VIII, 81. L. Olschki, "Der Brief des Presbyters Johannes," *Historische Zeitschrift,* CXLIV (1931), 1.

25. Roger Bacon, *Opus Maius,* ed. J. H. Bridges (Oxford, 1897), p. 372. The account comes immediately after a historically correct report on Chinese paper money. The creature cannot bend its knees and therefore must jump. It is totally hairy and does not speak. It is possible that we have here a faraway reflection of the Mohammedan Nasnâs whom Nizâmî al-'Arûdî located in Turkestan. See n. 10, Chapter 1, above.

26. *The Rare and Most Wonderful Things Which Edward Webbe an Englishman Borne Hath Seene and Passed in His Troublesome Travailes* (2nd ed., London, 1590).

27. De Azcárate, p. 97, n. 3.

28. According to Rhys Carpenter (oral communication) Silvanus is identical with Silenus historically and the two names have the same derivation. Mannhard, II, 123f. W. H. Roscher, *Mythologisches Lexikon,* articles "satyrus," "faunus."

29. Archaic Greek frieze in Xanthos, H. Brunn and F. Bruckmann, *Denkmäler Griechischer und Römischer Skulptur* (Munich, 1900), pl. 104.

30. S. Reinach: *Repertoire de la Statuaire Grecque et Romaine* (Paris, 1897–1924), vol. III, p. 19, no. 4; vol. IV, p. 32, no. 1–3; vol. V, p. 57, nos. 8, 9; vol. II, p. 53, no. 6, and p. 59, no. 6; vol. I, p. 425, no. 6.

31. "Phyllis and Flora," *Carmina Burana,* ed. J. A. Schmeller (4th ed., Breslau, 1904), no. 65, vv. 69, 70; translated, somewhat too freely, by John Addington Symonds as:

Fauns and Nymphs and Satyrs here
Flowery alleys haunted,
And before the Face of Love
Played and leaped and chaunted.
In their hands they carry thyme,
Crowns of fragrant roses;
Bacchus leads the choir divine,
And the dance composes;
Nymphs and fauns with feet in tune
Interchange their posies,
But Silenus trips and reels
When the chorus closes.

Symonds, *Wine, Women and Song, Medieval Latin Student Songs* (London, 1899).

32. Helen Waddell, *The Wandering Scholars* (London, 1926).

33. For the first capital, see Hamann, fig. 35. The satyr is stalking a female demon. See also the capital in St. Sernin, Toulouse, J. Baum, *Romanesque Architecture in France* (London, 1912), p. 74. For the second capital, see Porter, pl. 91. The representation is connected with the meeting of St. Anthony and St. Paul. As for thirteenth-century manuscripts, this is the case, for instance, in the drolleries in the Psalter of Yolande (French) in the Morgan Library. Another tradition which had a long history is that of putting the satyr's mask on the outside of a shield, for instance *Queen Mary's Psalter*, ed. Sir G. Warner (Oxford, 1912), pl. 88.

34. Isaias 13:21 (Douay): "and the hairy ones shall dance there." Isaiah 13:21 (King James): "and satyrs shall dance there."

35. Isaiah 34:14: *Et occurent daemonia onocentauri, et pilosus clamabit alter at alterum; ibi cubabit Lamia et invenit sibi requiem* (Douay: "And demons and monsters shall meet, and the hairy ones shall cry out one to another. There hath the lamia lain down and found rest for herself." King James: "The wild beasts of the desert shall also meet with the wild beasts of the island, and the satyr shall cry to his fellow; the screech owl also shall rest there, and find for herself a place of rest"). Lamia, here mentioned for the only time in the Bible, is the Hebrew Lilith.

36. Leviticus 17:7; translated in both versions as "devils." A similar creature is occasionally represented in Phoenician works of art and in Proto-Attic vases made in imitation of them (oral communication from Professor Mary Swindler).

37. Quodque sequitur pilosi saltabunt ibi, vel incubones vel satyros vel silvestres quosdam homines quos nonnulli fatuos ficarios vocant aut daemonum genera intelligunt.

38. See Roscher, "Ephialtes." St. Augustine, *Civitas Dei*, 15, 23.

39. Isidore of Seville, 8, 11, 104. From one of the three medieval collections known as the Mythographi Vaticani: "Mythographus Secundus," chap. xlix, ed. G. H. Bode in *Scriptorum Rerum Mythicarum Latini Tres Romae Nuper Reperti* (Celle, 1834). See also Eucherius Lugdunensis on Isaiah, quoted in article "pilosi" in C. Ducange, *Glossarium Mediae et Infimae Latinitatis* (Paris, 1937-38).

40. Qui fauni fatui dicti sunt, a quibusdam creduntur esse homines silvestres. Bartholomaeus Anglicus, *De Proprietatibus Rerum* (first printed in Basel, c. 1470; in England, 1495). *Dicuntur quidam et silvestres homines, quos nonnulli faunos ficarios vocant.* Isidore of Seville, 11, 3, 22.

41. Alio modo dicunt ut fatui ficarii fauni et satiri, qui inter agrestes ficus et alios arbores morant, quales sunt pilosi onocentaures et alia animalia monstruosa. A similar identification of *se'irim* with *Onocentauroi* in Hesychius, see Roscher, "Ephialtes," p. 64.

42. Grimm, *Deutsche Mythologie*, I, 67, on St. Eustace legend; I, 398, on Burchard of Worms.

43. Wace, *Roman de Rou*, ed. H. Andresen (Heilbronn, 1877-1879), vv. 6395-6420. Wace speaks of fairies which can be seen there (also mentioned in other medieval literature) and of animals.

44. C. V. L. Langlois, *La Connaissance de la nature et du monde d'après des écrits français à l'usage des laics* (Paris, 1927), p. 177.

45. *L'Estoire de Merlin*, ed. H. O. Sommer (Washington, 1908), p. 286. J. D. Bruce, *The Evolution of Arthurian Romance from the Beginnings Down to the Year 1300*, I, 134f, 144.

46. Philostratus, *Vita Apollonii*, ed. F. C. Conybeare (London, 1912), 6, 27.

47. *Faërie Queene*, i, vi, 22ff.

48. See for instance, the identification of Silvanus with Faunus and incubus in Gervasius of Tilbury, *Otia Imperialia*, 3, 86, p. 39; Vincentius of Beauvais: *Quem autem vulgo incubonem vocant, Romani faunum ficarium vocant*; Guglielmus Alvernus: *Tractatus de Universo*, pp. 1008–1011. Finally the glosses: *Incuba (incobus) satirus vel trut*, in a fourteenth-century glossary in Vienna; *faunus, alp vel scratiu, waldscrazze*, in a glossary of the twelfth century, the latter implying the identity of faun, incubus, and wild man. See Hansen, *Quellen und Untersuchungen*, p. 629. Most of this, with minor modifications, was repeated far into the fifteenth and sixteenth century. Kittredge, *Witchcraft in Old and New England*, p. 118.

49. Hansen, *Zauberwahn, Inquisition und Hexenprozesse*, pp. 188f. and 316f. Kittredge, p. 246.

50. Hansen, *Zauberwahn*, p. 186.

51. Bibliothèque de l'Arsenal, MS. 3516, quoted from Druce, p. 160.

52. Hermann, *Forschungen*, fig. 17, taken from Codex Vaticanus Lat. Urb. 355, fourteenth century.

53. This identification had a history; see E. Curtius, *Heracles der Satyr und Dreifussräuber* (Berlin, 1852).

54. A. Lovejoy and G. Boas, *Primitivism and Related Ideas in Antiquity* (Baltimore, 1935).

55. Virgil, *Aeneid*, 8, 314. Juvenal, *Satirae*, 6, 5; Lovejoy and Boas, p. 72. Empedocles, fragments 128 and 130, see Lovejoy and Boas, p. 33.

56. Virgil, passage cited. Ovid, *Fasti*, 2, 290–294.

57.
Gensque virum truncis et duro robore nata
Quis neque mos neque cultus erat
Rami atque asper victu venatus alebat

Virgil passage cited. See, for the effect of these lines on wild-man mythology, Castiglione's eclogue *Tirsi*, performed in Urbino in 1506. Castiglione asserts of the wild men: *Né dei né fauni son, ma per miracolo d'arbor son nati* — "They are neither gods nor fauns, but are miraculously born from trees." The lines from Juvenal (*Satirae*, 6, 7):
Aliter tunc . . .
Vivebant homines, qui rupto robore nati
Compositive luto nullos habere parentes
And, from the "Anonymus de monstris": *Fauni nascentur de vermibus natis inter lignum et corticem et post remo procedunt ad terram . . . et efficiuntur homines silvestres.* Grimm, *Deutsche Mythologie*, IV, 905. These wild men, however, have wings, in order to enable the author to carry out his comparison with caterpillars and butterflies. The anonymous author is, of course, in his turn dependent on Virgil. Servius said: *Hoc figmentum ortum est ex antiqua hominum habitatione qui ante factos domos aut in cavis arboribus aut in speluncis manebant; qui cum exinde egrederentur aut suam eccederent sobolem dicti sunt inde procreati* (*Commentarii in Virgilium*, ed. A. Lion, Göttingen, 1826, commentary on the *Aeneid*, 8, 315).

58. Ovid, *Ars Amatoria*, 2, 475; see Lovejoy and Boas, p. 373. Ovid, *Amores*, 3, 7:
. . . nec hirsuti torrebant farra coloni,
Nec notum terris area nomen erat:
Sed glandem quercus, oracula prima, ferebant;
Haec erat, et teneri caespitis herba, cibus.
See also Lovejoy and Boas, page cited. Juvenal, *Satirae*, 6, 7:
Silvestrem montana torum cum sterneret uxor
Frondibus et culmo vicinarumque ferarum
Pellibus . . .
Haut similis tibi, Cynthia, nec tibi, cuius
Turbavit nitidos extinctus passer ocellos
Sed potanda ferens infantibus ubera magnis
Et saepe horridior glandem ructante marito.

59. Lovejoy and Boas, pp. 192f. See also Erwin Panofsky, *Studies in Iconology* (New York, 1939), p. 39.

60. Isidore of Seville, 15, 2, 5: *Nam prius homines tamquam nudi et inermes nec contra beluas praesidia habebant, nec receptacula frigoris et caloris, nec ipsi inter se homines ab hominibus satis erant tuti. Tandem naturali sollertia speluncis silvestribus tegumentis tuguria sibi et casas virgultis arundinibus contexerunt, quo esset vita tutior.* There follows an account of further gradual progress.

61. Prudentius, *Contra Symmachum*, 2, 277-297. See G. Boas: *Essays on Primitivism in the Middle Ages* (Baltimore, 1948), p. 185.

62. A. Lovejoy and G. Boas, pp. 315-344, 348-349, 362-366.

63. Fasti, 2, 290-294.

64. A. Lovejoy and G. Boas, p. 348.

65. Müller, pp. 102-457. Dionysius "Periegetes" was a Greek author of *c.* 300 A.D.

66. Petrarch, *De Vita Solitaria*, ed. A. Altamura (Naples, 1943), p. 132. Pierre d'Ailly: *Imago Mundi*, ed. E. Buron, Paris 1930, quoted from Chinard, *L'Exotism Américain*, p. xii.

67. Brunetto Latini, 1, 4, 123. Chinard, p. 19.

68. Strabo, *Geography*, ed. L. Jones (London, 1930), 15, 1, 60; 15, 1, 69; 15, 1, 64.

69. On Palladius, F. Pfister, *Kleine Texte zum Alexanderroman* (Heidelberg, 1850). On the pseudo-Ambrose, J. Bernardi, *Analecta in Geographos Graecos Minores* (Halle, 1850).

70. Roger Bacon, p. 353. Petrarch, p. 121.

71. For the development of this literature see, F. P. Magoun, *The Gestes of Alexander of Macedon* (Cambridge, 1929) and G. Boas, p. 46. The text of the letter of Dindymus has been excellently translated into English by Boas, p. 148. The whole correspondence is preserved in recension J2 of the "*Historia de Proeliis*," in Hilka: *Der Altfranzösische Prosa-Alexanderroman*, p. 188. See also J. Makowski, *De Collatione Alexandri Magni et Dindimi*, Breslau Dissertation, 1919; F. Pfister,

"Die Brahmanen in der Alexandersage," *Berliner Philologische Wochenschrift*, XLI (1921), 569.

72. Strabo, 15, 164; Quintus Curtius Rufus, *De Gestis Alexandri Magni*, 7, 34-35. See also Lovejoy and Boas, p. 337.

73. On Vincent of Beauvais, see p. 147. Thomas de Cantimpré, "Natura Rerum," ed. A. Hilka, *Eine Moralisierende Bearbeitung des Liber de Monstruosis Hominibus Orientis aus Thomas von Cantimprés Natura Rerum*, Abhandlungen der Gesellschaft der Wissenschaften in Göttingen (Berlin, 1933). *Mandeville's Travels*, tr. from the French of Jean d'Outremeuse by P. Hamelius (London, 1919-1923), p. 197.

74. Magoun, pl. 2.

75. Omont, *Le Livre des Merveilles*, pls. 187, 188. See also Hartlieb's *Alexanderlied* (printed in Augsburg, 1473), fol. 104 and 114r, in A. Schramm, *Der Bilderschmuck der Früh drucke* (Leipzig, 1921-), vol. II, figs. 45, 46.

76. Petrarch, pp. 122, 123, from which the following quotations are taken.

77. Non placet incuriositas belluina somni cibique ne dum extremum curiosae vitae fugimus, in contrarium relabamur. . . Totum vero sub divo tempus agere non tam hominum quam ursorum judico, quamvis se coelum pro tecto terram totam pro lecto habere glorientur.

78. Illud importunae superbiae est quod se peccatum non habere confirmant seducentes se et mendacem facientes Spiritum Sanctum qui per os Sancti Johannis Apostoli insolentiam hanc retundit ad confessionem et poenitentiam nos invitans.

79. Placet ille contemptus mundi, qui iusto maior esse non potest, placet solitudo, placet libertas qua nulli gentium tanta est; placet silentium, placet otium, placet quies, placet intenta cogitatio, placet integritas atque securitas, modo temeritas absit; placet animorum aequalitas, unaque semper frons et nulli rei timor out cupiditas, placet sylvestris habitatio fontisque vicinitas, quem ut in eo libro scriptum est, quasi uber

terrae matris incorruptum atque inte-grum in os suum mulgere consueverant.
80. *Ruodlieb*, ed. F. Seiler (Halle, 1882), 17, 18.
81. Spenser, *Faërie Queene*, bk. vi, cantos iv, v, vii.
82. *Faërie Queene*, vi, v, 29.
83. Hans Sachs, *Werke*, ed. H. von Keller and E. Goetze (Tübingen, 1870–1908), III, 561–564: "Klag der Wilden Holzleut über die Ungetrewe Welt," vv. 85f.
84. M. Geisberg, *Der Deutsche Ein-blattholzschnitt in der Ersten Hälfte des 16. Jahrhunderts* (Munich, 1923–1929), pl. 1106.
85.
Seyt nun die welt ist so vertrogn
Mit untrew, list ganz ueberzogn
So seyen wir gangen darauss
Halten im wilden walde hauss
Mit unseren unerzogen kinden
Dass uns die falsch welt nit moeg finden.
Da wir der wilden fruecht uns nehrn
Von den wuertzlein der erden zehrn
Und trincken ein lautern brunnen.
Uns thut erwermen die liecht sunnen.
Miess laub und grass ist unser gwandt.
Davon wir auch bett und deck hand.
Eine steyne hoel ist unser hauss.
Da treybet keins das ander auss.
Unser gesellschafft und jubiliern
Ist im holz mit den wilden thiern
So wir den selben nichts nit than
Lassens uns auch mit frieden gan,
Also wir inn der wuesten sind
Geberen kind und kindeskind.
Eynig und bruederlich wir lebn.
Kein zanck ist sich bey uns begebn.
Ein jedes thut, als es dann wolt
Als ihm von jhem geschehen solt.
Um kein zeytliches thun wir sorgen,
Unser speiss finden wir alle morgen,
nemb wir zur notturft und nicht mehr
Und sagen Got drumb lob und ehr.
Fellt uns zu krankheyt oder todt,
Wiss wir das es uns kumbt von Got,
Der alle ding am besten thut.
Also inn einfeltigem muth
Vertreyben wir hie unser zeyt,
Bis ein enderung sich begeyt
Inn weyter welt umb und umb
Das yederman wird trew und frumb
Das stat hat armut und einfalt
Dann woell wir wider auss dem walt

Und wonen bey der menschen schar.
86. See pp. 156ff., below, for descriptions of these works of art.
87. Panofsky, *Albrecht Dürer* (Princeton, 1943), figs. 122, 123. The sketch for this print shows the same woman with a centaur. Apparently the wood demons were still interchangeable as they had been in the Middle Ages. On Altdorfer's painting of 1507 in Berlin, L. von Baldass, *Albrecht Altdorfer* (Zürich, 1941), p. 229, and on his drawing in Vienna, Baldass, p. 60, the latter showing wild men. E. Major and E. Gradmann, *Urs Graf* (Basel, undated), pl. 125.
88. B. Kurth, *Die Deutschen Bild-teppiche des Mittelalters* (Vienna, 1926), pl. 57.
89. J. Huizinga, *The Waning of the Middle Ages* (London, 1924), p. 22.
90. G. Vasari, *Le Vite de' piu eccelenti pittori, scultori ed architetti*, ed. Milanesi (Florence, 1878–1885), IV, 133. The classic discussion of Piero di Cosimo's pagan beliefs and output is Panofsky, *Studies in Iconology*, p. 52, upon which I am relying here.
91. The optimistic interpretation of the early stages of man's history must have been familiar to all Florentines of Piero di Cosimo's time, for it had been the theme of the sculptural decoration of Giotto's Campanile, which had only recently been finished by Luca della Robbia.
92. *De Architectura Libri Decem*, 2.1.
93. Panofsky, *Studies in Iconology*, fig. 28.
94. A Florentine sculpture of a wild man as shield supporter by Piero di Cosimo's older contemporary Bertoldo is in the Frick Collection in New York.
95. Formerly in the Kaiser Friedrich Museum in Berlin.
96. M. J. Friedländer and Jakob Rosenberg, *Die Gemälde von Lucas Cranach* (Berlin, 1932), pp. 213, 214). Compare with Cranach's pictures of the Age of Silver the interpretation given to the life of the wild man or satyr by Cranach's contemporaries, Altdorfer (Baldass, p. 60) and Urs Graf (Major and Gradmann, pl. 69), where the

forest man is shown with his mate and with the dead body of his rival he has slain. There is a relation between such representations and the Nuremberg Carnival play mentioned in no. 21, Chapter 1, above.

97. J. M. Manly, *Specimens of Pre-Shakesperian Drama* (Boston and London, 1897), p. 215.
98. Withington, II, 160.
99. For instance, G. Luck, *Räthische Alpensagen* (Davos, 1902), p. 131.

5. THE EROTIC CONNOTATIONS

1. R. S. Loomis, "A Phantom Tale of Feminine Ingratitude." *Modern Philology* (1917), p. 751. See also Loomis, *Arthurian Legends in Medieval Art* (New York, 1938). The rescue of a lady attacked by a wild man is represented in an oval ceiling fresco of the early fifteenth century in the Alhambra Granada, in de Azcárate, pl. 3, fig. 1. A similar theme occurs on a capital in the cloisters of the cathedral of Toledo, de Azcárate, pl. 3, fig. 5.
2. R. Koechlin, *Les Ivoires Gothiques Français* (Paris, 1924), p. 1290.
3. Ms. 10 E 4 Royal, British Museum, see J. P. Gilson, *Catalogue of Western Manuscripts in the Old Royal and Kings Collection* (London, 1921), I, 334. See also Loomis, "A Phantom Tale," page cited.
4. H. Yates Thomson Collection, now British Museum, fol. 61v–106v.
5. For instance, Kittredge, *A Study of Gawain and the Green Knight*, p. 236.
6. "Gismirante," ed. E. Levi in *Fiori di Leggende, Cantari Antichi* (Bari, 1914), series 1, p. 171.
7. *Handwörterbuch*, article "Zwerge."
8. *Laurin und der kleine Rosengarten*, ed. G. Holz (Halle, 1897), v. 720. Albrecht von Kemenaten, "Goldemar," ed. E. Henrici, V, xxix. See, for similar situations, "Wolfdietrich" (B), ed. O. Jänicke, vol. III, v. 795; "Ortnit," ed. O. Jänicke, vol. III, vv. 168–173, and *Orendel*, ed. H. Steinger, v. 2429. For a comprehensive catalogue of such subject matter see A. Lütjens, *Der Zwerg in der Deutschen Heldendichtung des Mittelalters* (Breslau, 1911).
9. In F. J. Child, *The English and Scottish Popular Ballads* (Boston, 1882), no. 41, all known versions are presented and discussed. It is in Version C in

Child's compendium that the kidnapper is a "forester." The family aspect of the story is best preserved in Norwegian and Swedish versions. In another group of Scandinavian and North German ballads the story is told of a merman obtaining a human maiden in marriage; see W. Entwistle, *European Balladry* (Oxford, 1939), p. 83, based upon S. Grundtvig, *Danmarks gamle Folkeviser* (Kopenhagen, 1853–1904), no. 39.
10. H. Kohlhausen, *Minnekästchen im Mittelalter* (Berlin, 1928), catalogue no. 162 and fig. 11. It is striking that in the various pictures of satyr families by Dürer, Altdorfer, and Urs Graf mentioned in Chapter 4, above, the man is always strongly characterized as a satyr or faun, while the woman and child seem to be entirely human. We should perhaps assume that the artist meant to portray the married life of a demon and his human mate.
11. Mannhard, I, 112, 120, 122, 123, 137–138. For central Germany see F. Ranke, *Die Deutschen Volkssagen* (Munich, 1910), p. 173. See also O. Höfler, *Kultische Geheimbünde*, pp. 71, 276. On the wild man as wild hunter, in England as in the Tyrol, see Liungman, II, 648.
12. Caesarius of Heisterbach, *Dialogus Miraculorum*, tr. by H. von Scott and C. C. Swinton Bland (New York, 1929), 12, 20; Vincent of Beauvais, *Speculum Historiale*, lib. 29, 20.
13. Albrecht von Kemenaten, "Eckenliet," ed. J. Zupitza, vv. 161–201.
14. "Der Wunderer" quoted from H. Schneider, *Germanische Heldensage* (Berlin, 1928), I, 266. "Virginal," ed. J. Zupitza in *Deutsches Heldenbuch*, vol. V, vv. 82–85, 451. On Orcus, see Chapter 2, above. Owing to a typical con-

fusion of motives this demon of death appears in "Virginal" as a Saracen and even speaks a few words of garbled Arabic.

15. The first group is led by W. Mannhard. The chief representative of the second group is O. Höfler.

16. Liungman, II, 618. F. S. Krauss, *Slavische Volksforschungen* (Leipzig, 1908), p. 82.

17. M. P. Nilsson, *Griechische Feste von religiöser Bedeutung* (Leipzig, 1906), p. 226.

18. It is, of course, possible that the motive in question originated in the East Adriatic area and was exported from there to Greece. We cannot here concern ourselves with the almost insoluble problems of remote preclassical origins.

19. Liungman, II, 673, 694. In the eastern Alps Herodias is identified with the Percht, and in Italy with Befana (Epiphania), the winter witch. Krauss, page cited.

20. Berchorius (Pierre Bersuire, a fourteenth-century Benedictine), in T. Walleys, *Metamorphosis Ovidiana moraliter . . . explanata* (Paris, 1515), fol. 50.

21. "Sir Orfeo," ed. O. Zielke (Breslau, 1880). For a translation into modern English see J. L. Weston, *Chief Middle-English Poets* (Boston, 1914), p. 133. The little epic is probably based upon a lost Breton lai. See also F. Delattre, *English Fairy Poetry* (London, 1912), p. 49. Compare also Chaucer's "Marchantes Tale," 983–985: "Pluto that is the king of fayerie — and many a lady in his companye — following his wyfe, the quene Proserpyne."

22. Panofsky, *Albrecht Dürer*, catalogue no. 898. F. Winkler, *Die Zeichnungen Albrecht Dürers* (Berlin, 1936–1940), no. 669. The fact that, in the drawing, the horseman rides over the bodies of several persons serves to confirm the proposed identification with the wild hunter.

23. "Sir Orfeo," vv. 144, 164. The wild man, too, may ride on a horse. Demoniac creatures often ride on horses or unicorns. One example,

among many, is to be found in the epic *Die Möhrin* by Hermann von Sachsenheim, ed. E. Martin (Tübingen, 1878), v. 704: *Da rait dort hear die moerin scwarz uff ainem gezoemten ainhorn.* "The negress comes riding on a tamed unicorn."

24. Kohlhausen, pl. 38. Lehrs, *The Master of the Amsterdam Cabinet,* nos. 51 and 52. Professor Panofsky draws my attention to the fact that in medieval art there are two kinds of unicorns, one the creature with the winding narwhal tooth, familiar from Christian scenes of the symbolic hunt, the other the other the straight-horned type here under discussion representative of and connected with night and demoniac powers.

25. The fresco is now destroyed. K. Escher, *Untersuchungen zur Geschichte der Wand- und Dechenmalerei in der Schweitz* (Strassburg, 1906), p. 44. For the dagger, see Kohlhausen, fig. 19. For the casket, see Kohlhausen, pl. 54.

26. Wolfram, "Bärenjagen und Faschingslaufen," p. 73, where examples of similar customs in various parts of Sweden are discussed. For a general treatment of bear rituals see A. J. Hallowell, "Bear Ceremonialism in the Northern Hemisphere," in *American Anthropologist,* vol. XXVIII (1926), and Rhys Carpenter, *Folktale, Fiction and Saga in the Homeric Epics* (Berkeley, 1946).

27. O. Shepard, *The Lore of the Unicorn* (New York, 1930). One of the most complete sequences of such secular representations is the series of tapestries, of the end of the fifteenth century, in the Cloisters in New York.

28. One of the first to use the term in the sense here discussed and perhaps the originator of its meaning in medieval poetry was St. Augustine: *Et silvescere ausus sum variis et umbrosis amoribus* — "And I dared to grow wild with various and shadowy love affairs" (*Confessions* 2, 2).

29. *Ich waz wilde, swie viel ich doch gesanc / ir schoeniu ougen daz wâren die ruote / dâ mite si mich von érste betwanc.* K. Lachmann and M. Haupt, *Des Minnesangs Frühling* (4th ed., Leipzig, 1923), p. 89.

30. Lachmann and Haupt, p. 36.

31. Von aller schone ein uebermaz / Wunschlichen zart, gebildet fin, / ach, hort, mich micht entgelten laz / Daz ich so gar verwildet bin / Zart frowe, gen dir, und weiz nit wie. H. Naumann and G. Weydt, *Herbst des Minnesangs* (Berlin, 1936), p. 68.

32. Suesser Puesse du solt mich zamen / Ich pin gewessen wilde. . . / Ich pin wilde gar gebesen / Und han von gebet nicht viel gelesen. Heinrich von Burgus, "Der Seele Rat," ed. H. F. Rosenfeld, *Deutsche Texte des Mittelalters* (Berlin, 1932), vv. 1920, 2935.

33. *Le Rime di Cino da Pistoia,* ed. G. Zaccagnini (Geneva, 1925), no. 7, p. 37. (The name of Cino da Pistoia's lady seems to have been Selvaggia.) Naumann and Weydt, p. 56.

34. *Carmina Burana,* 50, 17. Compare also, for instance, Hartwig von Rute, in Lachmann and Haupt, p. 134. Petrarche, Sonnet no. 227, and Chaucer, *Canterbury Tales,* v. 2993.

35. *Vaderlandsch Museum voor Nederduitsche Letterkunde, Oudheiden Geschiedenis,* II (Ghent, 1858), 96.

36.
Ic was wilt, ic ben ghevaen
ende bracht in mintliken bande;
dat heeft ene maghet ghedaen;
Ic was wilt, ic ben ghevaen;
al mochtig, in woude haer niet outgaen
des settic mine trouwe te pande.
Ich was wilt, ic ben ghevaen
ende bracht in mintliken bande.

37. Von der Leyen and Spamer, p. 25. Kohlhausen, pls. 48, 54.

38. Kohlhausen, p. 59.

39. Paton, "The Story of Grisandoles," p. 234. Bruce, I, 149.

40. G. F. Straparola, *Le Piacevoli Notti* (Rome, 1945).

41. "L'Estoire de Merlin," ed. H. O. Sommer, in *The Vulgate Versions of the Arthurian Romances* (Washington, D. C., 1910), II, 283f, 289. The demand that the lady who captures the wild man should be a virgin is not, to my knowledge, originally a part of wildman mythology. It is most likely that this detail was taken from the related tale about the capture of the unicorn.

42. Huizinga, *The Waning of the Middle Ages* (London, 1924).

43. Huizinga, p. 115.

44. Kurth, *Die Deutschen Bildteppiche,* pls. 66, 171.

45. Loomis, "The Allegorical Siege in the Art of the Middle Ages," *American Journal of Archaeology* (1919), p. 255.

46. R. C. Baskerville, "Early Romantic Plays in England," *Modern Philology,* XIV (1916–17), 89. Also from the early sixteenth century we have the description of the Carnival in Belluno (1507) during which "satyrs, fauns, and other selvaggi" attacked a castle held by nymphs (Neri, p. 64).

47. Kurth, pls. 108, 114–119.

48. Huizinga, p. 103.

49. Diego de San Pedro, *Carcel de Amor,* pp. 7, 8.

50. Hermann von Sachsenheim, *Die Möhrin,* v. 632.

51. Diego de San Pedro, pp. 8f.

52. J. von Schlosser, "Die Bilderhandschriften König Wenzels," *Jahrbuch der Kunsthistorischen Sammlungen des Allerhöchsten Kaiserhauses,* XIV (1893), 214. See also A. Stange, *Deutsche Malerei der Gothik* (Berlin, 1934–1938), vol. II, pls. 47, 50, 51.

53. Von Schlosser, p. 274. Usually, however, the king himself is represented in this attitude. The close relation between the representations of the king and of the wild man is demonstrated by an inscription on folio 27 of the second volume of the Wenceslaus Bible, where the king is shown in fetters and the accompanying inscription reads: *Ich pyn wilde unde czam — den guten gut, den posen gram —* "I am wild and tame, good to the good and hostile to the wicked."

54. A. Martin, *Deutsches Badewesen in vergangenen Tagen* (Jena, 1906). R. van Marle, *Iconographie de l'art profane au moyen-âge et à la renaissance* (The Hague, 1931–32), vol. I, figs. 478–517. See particularly fig. 507 representing a man in his bath assisted by three ladies, from the Manesse manuscript, German, c. 1300.

55. Von Schlosser, p. 284. Wenceslaus Bible, vol. I, fol. 150.

56. Von Schlosser, p. 298.
57. For instance, on the Altstädter Brückenturm and on the chapel in the Altstädter Rathaus, von Schlosser, pp. 276–278.
58. Von Schlosser, p. 272, and Wenceslaus Bible, vol. II, fol. 74.
59. Von Schlosser, p. 297.
60. See C. S. Lewis, *The Allegory of Love* (Oxford, 1936). See also the brilliant but controversial book by D. de Rougemont, *L'Amour et l'Occident* (Paris, 1939). About medieval marriage see, among many others, W. Goodsell, *A History of Marriage and of the Family* (New York, 1934), and G. C. Crum, *The Legacy of the Middle Ages* (Oxford, 1943).
61. Andreas Capellanus, *The Art of Courtly Love*, ed. and tr. J. J. Parry (New York, 1941). See also Lewis, pp. 36, 41.
62. On German attitudes, see H. Naumann, *Deutsche Kultur im Zeitalter des Rittertums* (Potsdam, 1938), p. 149. A good example of the tendency to romanticize marriage is the story of "Der Busant," summarized in Chapter 1, above. On satirizing of the courtly ideal, see R. L. Kilgour, *The Decline of Chivalry As Shown in the French Literature of the Late Middle Ages* (Cambridge, 1937), p. 108–143. On Chaucer, see Kittredge, "Chaucer's Discussion of Marriage," *Modern Philology* (1912), p. 435, and *Chaucer and His Poetry* (Cambridge, 1915), pp. 185–211.
63. Van Marle, vol. I. P. Schubring, *Cassoni, Truhen und Truhenbilder der Italienischen Frürenaissance* (Leipzig, 1915). Characteristic of the sensual trend are the frescoes in the Palazzo del Podestà in San Gimignano, from the school of Bartolo di Fredi, van Marle, vol. I, figs. 483, 512.
64. Such escutcheons appear upon the following wild-man tapestries: Kurth, pls. 55b, 56, 81, 82, 108, 109, 110–112.
65. Geiler von Kaysersberg, *Die Emeis*, introduction to the sermon delivered on Saturday after Reminiscere Sunday.

66. *Burlington Magazine*, vol. LX (1932), pl. opp. p. 86.
67. It is not likely that any allusion to sacred subject matter was intended, but rather that the artist, while searching for prototypes, made use of the readily available ecclesiastic iconography. This was frequently done in the early days of medieval secular illustration.
68. Kohlhausen, pl. 63. The prototype of this representation is to be found in a print by the "Master der Bandrollen," Lehrs, *Geschichte und kritischer Katalog*, vol. IV, pl. 335. Related to the scenes described is the subject of a Tournai tapestry of the early sixteenth century, included in our illustrations, showing wild men and women disturbed by a sea monster which abducts one of the women. The wild men and women are here equal in number.
69. For the second print cited, Lehrs, *Geschichte und kritischer Katalog*, vol. VIII, pl. 542. See also pl. 543, showing a wild woman with baby, seated among rocks, while on the other side of the rock and half hidden by it, there lurks an enormous ugly dragon. For a design showing a wild woman, riding on a unicorn, baby in arm, see Lehrs, *The Master of the Amsterdam Cabinet*, no. 51. For the Cranach, Friedländer and Rosenberg, *Die Gemälde von Lucas Cranach*, pl. 218. See also the other satyrs' families mentioned in n. 96, Chapter 4, above.
70. On the Romanesque sculpture, Adhémar, *Influences antiques*, pl. 14, figs. 46, 47. On the siren foster mother, Dickson, *Valentine and Orson* (1929), p. 110. The task of nurturing the wild man is later taken over by a hind, so that Tristan grows up among the beasts of the forest, as the mythological tradition demands.
71. Kurth, pl. 57.
72. A detailed discussion of this tapestry is in von der Leyen and Spamer, p. 31. See also for some details Kurth, pl. 123.
73. This is a frequent representation in pictures devoted to courtly love and occurs, for instance, on the well-known

bridal box by Domenico di Bartolo, formerly in the Figdor Collection, van Marle, vol. I, fig. 449; in the frescoes in the castle in Trent, van Marle, vol. I, fig. 470; and in a French *fleurette* tapestry of about 1500, van Marle, vol. I, fig. 457.

74. Compare the description of the occupation of such demons in Mannhard, I, 200–203.

75. Kurth, pls. 27, 28, 30, 31, 41, 42, 43, 44–46, 49a, b, 55b, 83a, b, and Kohlhausen, pl. 53.

76. On the lion, see for contemporary evidence Konrad von Megenberg, *Das Buch der Natur*, ed. F. Pfeifer (Stuttgart, 1861), p. 142: *Daz tier hat niht untrew noch valscher list an im* — "The creature is incapable of disloyalty and falsehood." Therefore, in Kurth, pl. 41, the lady says: *Ich will die welt lassen und mich zu den lewen halten* — "I shall flee the world and stay with the lions." In a fresco of the early fifteenth century in the Alhambra (de Azcárate, pl. 3, fig. 1) the wild man is shown attacking a young damsel who holds a lion, symbol of steadfastness, on a leash. In the "Bestiaire d'Amour" the lion symbolizes the power of love to spare those who acknowledge it and to annihilate those who resist it. On the stag, see Kohlhausen, p. 49, quoting the late-medieval poet Suchensinn (*Suchensinn und seine Dichtungen*, ed. E. Pflug, Breslau, 1908, p. 88): *Dem hirsz glichet ein junges wip — die spricht, sie trage eynen steden lip — er lebet nit der myn ere vertrib — ich will myn triuwe behalden* — "A young woman is like a stag, she says: My love is steady, there is no man who could take my honor away, I intend to stay faithful." The wild man Merlin rides on a stag, in the *Vita Merlini*, v. 453. Other examples of wild men riding on stags: Heinrich Wittenweiler, *Der Ring*, vv. 211, 231; Grimm, *Deutsche Mythologie*, I, 385; an artistic example, Kohlhausen, pls. 46, 47. For the symbolism of the griffon K. Rathe, "Der Richter auf dem Fabeltier," *Festschrift für Julius von Schlosser* (Vienna, 1927). On the mountain goat, *Handwörterbuch*, article "Zwerge." Representations of mountain goats were frequent in the region of the upper Rhine, especially on love caskets, and are easy to recognize. Kohlhausen, pls. 21, 22, and his catalogue no. 24.

77. This communal social condition is well described in Lewis Mumford, *The Culture of Cities* (New York, 1938), pp. 35ff. About the customs at weddings see Huizinga, p. 97.

78. *The Romance of Tristan and Iseult*, translated into English by H. Belloc (New York, 1945).

79. *Aucassin et Nicolette*, ed. M. Rocques (Paris, 1925), 19, 12, and 24, 70. Similar foliage huts have been built during the spring festivals all over central Europe down into recent times. Mannhard, I, 187.

80. *Guillaume de Palerne*, ed. H. Michelant, Publication de la Société d'Anciens Francais (Paris, 1876). See also K. F. Smith, "A Historical Study of the Werwolf in Literature," *Publications of the Modern Language Association of America*, vol. IX (1894).

81. For the friendship of a wild man with a wolf see the speech by Merlin in the *Vita Merlini*, vv. 102–112, beginning with *Tu, lupe, care comes*.

82. Compare, however, vv. 3321–3328 in *Guillaume de Palerne*, where it is said that, although their furry covering extends over their hands, the two lovers are able to use them at will.

83. The closest relatives of the story are probably those in which the love of a bear for a human maiden or the love of two bears is described. The motive has been dealt with by W. Panzer, *Beowulf* (Munich, 1910), A. Wesselski, *Märchen des Mittelalters* (Berlin, 1925), and Rhys Carpenter, *Folklore, Fiction, and Saga in the Homeric Epics* (Berkeley, 1946).

84. Van Gennep, *Manuel de Folklore*, II, 614ff. Driesen, p. 107. I have not been able to use G. Phillips, *Ueber den Ursprung der Katzenmusiken* (Freiburg, 1849).

85. *Vita Merlini*, v. 441f. Paton, p. 249. The word "charivari" does not occur in this literature, although the meaning of the performance is unmistakable.

86. G. Buschan, *Altgermanische Ueberlieferungen in Kultur und Brauchtum der Deutschen* (Munich, 1936), p. 223. Examples of the censorious use of charivaris in German-speaking countries are given also by Wolfram, *Schwerttanz und Männerbund*, pp. 251, 253. According to the Lübeck laws of 1462, for instance, regulating clothes, marriage, baptism, and funerals, it was forbidden to mock widows during their wedding night or to make a noise before their doors. It seems that, on the whole, these customs were most common in the area of the lower Rhine.

87. F. F. Kohl, *Die Tiroler Bauernhochzeit, Sitten Bräuche, Sprüche, Lieder und Tänze mit Singweisen* (Vienna, 1908), p. 207. Hoffmann-Krayer, "Knabenschaften und Volksjustiz in der Schweitz," p. 172.

88. *Vita Merlini,* v. 450.

89. Dörrer, *Das Schemenlaufen in Tyrol,* p. 5. The social purpose of such masquerades is the dismissal of the groom from the secret society, to which only unmarried men belong. The same social purpose underlies the institution of the bachelor's party.

90. Kohl, p. 207.

91. *Handwörterbuch,* article "Hochzeit," where the literature is given.

92. K. Weinhold, *Die Deutschen Frauen in dem Mittelalter* (3d ed., Vienna, 1897), p. 353.

93. On the Brandenburg custom, see Weinhold, and Mannhard, I, 442. On the Bavarian custom, Panzer, *Bayerische Sagen und Gebräuche* (Munich, 1848), I, 11. As one would expect, the "bear" — usually called the "pea bear" (*Erbsenbär*) from the manner of his clothing — is also a regular visitor at marriages. Mannhard, I, 442. Wolfram, "Bärenjagen und Faschingslaufen," pp. 73f.

94. On Rostock, Weinhold, page cited. On Unterlienz, "Maschgen und Faschingsnarren," Dörrer, p. 5. On Venice, Liungman, II, 753. On Trullan Council, H. Reich, *Der Mimus* (Berlin, 1903), I, 132, 151. *Larvati* is a Latin word for both "ghosts" and "masks."

95. Liungman, II, 919, 979. Kohl, p. 221.

96. Mannhard, I, 455.

97. For instance, Liungman, II, 778, 789. The entire documentation given in notes 60–61 to Chapter 3 applies also to this phase of the Carnival.

98. Liungman, II, 769, 780–790, 794, 804, 813, 817, 818. The human couples may in their turn be converted into as many Kukers and Babas (p. 813). It will be noted that the presence of the king at the ceremonial killing of the Kuker relates these performances to the similar one depicted by Pieter Brueghel in his Carnival painting in Vienna.

99. On Mur region, Wolfram, "Bärenjagen und Faschingslaufen," p. 63. On Telfs, Dörrer, p. 36. On "Il Veglio" and "Berta," Liungman, II, 1007. Compare also the division of the maskers into "girls" and "boys" in Imst, in the neighborhood of Garmisch, and in Switzerland, Wolfram, p. 285. The "bulavitra" and his "signura" in the upper Engadine valley are discussed by Meulli in *Schweitzer Masken,* p. 21. The division in the Tyrol of the masks and costumes worn into "ugly" and "beautiful" ones (*schöne und schiache Perchten*) seems to be again a related phenomenon.

100. Dörrer, p. 41.

101. On Inn valley, F. P. Priger, "Faschingsgebräuche in Prutz im Oberinntal," *Zeitschrift des Vereins für Volkskunde* (1900), p. 81. P. Sartori, *Sitte und Brauch* (Leipzig, 1914), II, 103. Sartori claims, without giving his evidence, that the custom occurs in Tyrol, Styria, and even Hungary. On Bavarian document, Spamer, *Deutsche Fastnachtsbräuche,* p. 40. On Switzerland, Hoffmann Krayer, "Die Fastnachtsgebräuche in der Schweitz," p. 270. The festival was held, however, on February 17, that is, during the Carnival season.

102. On Gourdon custom, van Gennep, vol. I, part 3, p. 922. Prohibitions against this custom date back at least to 1681. On Vosges ceremony, Mannhard, I, 456.

103. Mannhard, I, 433.

6. *HIS HERALDIC ROLE*

1. Von der Leyen and Spamer, pp. 16, 17. It must be noted, however, that in the Middle Ages individual house signs took the place of street numbers, which were unknown.

2. J. Siebmacher: *Das Grosse und Allgemeine Wappenbuch* (Nuremberg, 1850-), vol. I, pl. 101. T. de Renesse, *Dictionnaire des figures heraldiques*, II, 191-197, quoted from W. Mulertt, *Der Wilde Mann in Frankreich Zeitschrift für Französische Sprache und Literatur*, LVI (1932), 79f., 82. De Renesse enumerates 263 families which have the wild man in their coats of arms. Only about thirty of them have names related to the wild man.

3. Siebmacher, vol. I, part 1, figs. 10, 11, 18, pls. 13, 46, 52; part 3, figs. 45-51.

4. For the same reason giants were stationed at the entrance of important buildings, as for instance the church of Stift Wilten near Innsbruck. The so-called Rolands in medieval towns of northern Germany may have served a similar purpose.

5. This is the theory of Viollet-le-Duc; see n. 36, Chapter 3, above.

6. I know of no earlier example of the custom than the disguise of the heralds in the masquerade undertaken in 1438 by the citizens of Valenciennes for the benefit of their hosts, the good citizens of Lille (Chapter 3, above). In a similar category was the wild-man disguise in Basel, for the mummer was a living duplicate of the design in the coat of arms of the civic society in question. In the Nuremberg Carnival of 1588 two wild men served as shield-supporters, running beside the horses of maskers garbed as knights. See S. L. Sumberg, p. 106, n. 57.

7. Compare the excellent discussion of this subject of shield-supporters by E. Gevaert, *L'Heraldique, son esprit, son language et ses applications* (Brussels, 1924), p. 331. About the function of the guardian angel in the late Middle Ages, see Huizinga, p. 158. On St. Michael, Gevaert, figs. 465-466. A very early example of a coat of arms held by women is found in the seal of Heinrich von Scharfeneck, dated 1292, see G. Seyler, *Geschichte der Heraldik* (Nuremberg, 1885-1889), p. 464.

8. An example is the seal of 1374 of Bergen op Zoom, in *Oudheidkundig Jaarboek*, vol. IV (1924), p. 50, fig. 8, with three wild men surrounding the coat of arms.

9. De Azcárate, pl. 4, fig. 3, and pl. 3, figs. 2, 3.

10. J. Rubio Mañe, *La Casa de Montejo en Mérida de Jucatan* (México, 1941). See also the wild men supporting the arms of Charles V at Tlaxcala in E. W. Weismann, *Mexico in Sculpture* (Cambridge, 1950), fig. 19.

11. W. J. Meyer, *Die franzoesischen Drucker- und Verlegerzeichen des 15. Jahrhunderts* (Munich, 1926), pp. 22, 46, 123, 134, 143. E. Weil, *Die Deutschen Druckerzeichen des 15. Jahrhunderts* (Munich, 1924), p. 26. See also the wild family with a coat of arms in the printer's mark of Johann von Winterburg, *fl.* Vienna, 1492-1500, in Weil, p., 104, and the single wild man in the printer's marks of Guenther Zainer, *fl.* Ulm, 1468-1477, in Weil, p. 31, and of Matthias van der Goes, *fl.* Antwerp, 1481-1491, in R. Juchhoff, *Drucker- una Verlegerzeichen des 15. Jahrhunderts in den Niederlanden, England, Spanien, Boehmen, Maehren und Polen* (Munich, 1927), p. 2.

12. Philip Hofer, "A Newly Discovered Book with Painted Decoration from Willibald Pirckheimer's Library," *Harvard Library Bulletin* (1947), p. 66.

13. Geisberg, *Der Meister E.S.* pl. 38. Schongauer introduced into his series of ten heraldic prints three escutcheons held by wild men, one held by a wild woman. J. Baum, *Martin Schongauer* (Vienna, 1948), figs. 102 (wild woman with child), 105, 106, and 107 (wild men). The other shield-supporters are a peasant, a Turk, four maidens, and an angel.

14. De Azcárate, pl. 7, fig. 2.

15. A. C. Calvert, *Valladolid, Oviedo, Segovia, Zamora* (London, 1908). A. L. Mayer, *Gothik in Spanien* (Leipzig, 1928), fig. 45, p. 145. M. de Lozoya, *Historia del Arte Hispanico*, vol. II (Barcelona, 1934), pl. 39.

16. Compare the position of the wild man in contemporary Spanish Corpus Christi processions (Chapter 3, above).

17. Hofer, p. 70, pls. 1 and 5. In Dürer's own *oeuvre* the death-and-the-maiden theme appears in two prints: "Young Woman Attacked by Death," Panofsky, *Dürer*, catalogue no. 199 and fig. 93, and "Der Spaziergang," catalogue no. 201 and fig. 99. For the origin of the motive see H. Janson, "A Memento Mori among Early Italian Prints," *Journal of the Warburg Institute*, III (1939), 243. The Brueghel detail is given in G. Jedlicka, *Pieter Brueghel* (Zurich, 1938), pl. 99. The van der Weyden altarpiece is in the Musée Royale, Antwerp. L. van Puyvelde, *The Flemish Primitives* (Brussels, 1948), pl. 39. The Italian print is in the possession of Professor Samuel Chew, Bryn Mawr, who established the identity of the impresa. The impresa is reproduced in B. Pittoni, *Imprese di Diversi Principi, Duchi, Signori e d'Altri Personaggi ed Huomini Letterati ed Illustri* (Venice, 1568), bk. II, no. 47, and there expressly related to Isabella Gonzaga. Ieronimo Ruscelli, *Le Imprese Illustri con Esposizioni e Discorsi* (Venice, 1572), fol. 158v, assigns the same impresa to Isabella Gonzaga, commenting that after various misfortunes she had boarded the ship of hope when she married the Marchese di Pescara.

Index of Names

Authors, artists, and historical, imaginary, and mythological personalities

Index of Places